DO NOT BE AFRAID

NATHAN BROWN

Pacific Press®
Publishing Association
Nampa, Idaho | www.pacificpress.com

Cover design: Daniel Añez
Cover design resources: GettyImages.com
Interior design: Aaron Troia

To order additional copies of this book, call toll-free 1-800-765-6955
or visit AdventistBookCenter.com.

Library of Congress Cataloging-in-Publication Data

Names: Brown, Nathan, 1974- author.
Title: Do not be afraid / Nathan Brown.
Description: Nampa, Idaho : Pacific Press Publishing Association, 2024. |
Summary: "A collection of 365 daily devotional readings on what the Bible says about fear"— Provided by publisher.
Identifiers: LCCN 2024003781 (print) | LCCN 2024003782 (ebook) |
ISBN 9780816370153 | ISBN 9780816370160 (ebook)
Subjects: LCSH: Fear—Religious aspects—Christianity. | Fear—Prayers and devotions.
Classification: LCC BV4908.5 .B748 2024 (print) | LCC BV4908.5 (ebook) |
DDC 242/.4—dc23/eng/20240226
LC record available at https://lccn.loc.gov/2024003781
LC ebook record available at https://lccn.loc.gov/2024003782

March 2024

DEDICATION

For Angela
"Courage, dear heart."

CONTENTS

ACKNOWLEDGMENTS

This book began with an in-depth study of the Gospel of Luke as part of a graduate study program in 2017. After working our way through the Gospel chapter by chapter over a semester, our final paper was to explore a theme in the study that had caught our attention. I wrote on the "Do not be afraids" in the life and teaching of Jesus—and their implications for our faith and lives. My study became the basis for speaking about this theme and beginning to trace it out into other parts of the Bible as one of its recurring themes. I appreciate the contributions of the lecturers and fellow students at what was Kilns College in Bend, Oregon, at that time.

More immediately, writing this book was intertwined with my wife, Angela's, diagnosis of breast cancer and subsequent rounds of treatment. I have dedicated this book to her as it represents something of the time in which we, together and individually, confronted the fears and uncertainties of those experiences. It is also a resource for our ongoing challenges. Thank you to our family and friends who have supported us during this time.

I am grateful to my colleagues at Signs Publishing Company, who supported us during that year and understood my distraction while I was focused on writing this book in addition to my regular work. Particular thanks to Andrew Irvine and Lauren Webb.

Thanks to the leadership and staff at the Fiji Mission, where I was able to share some of these key ideas and road-test them in the midst of the writing process. Their kindness and responsiveness to the "Do not be afraid" messages encouraged me along the way. And the time away from writing, including a few days on a picture-perfect tropical island, was a valuable breathing space amid an intense season of writing.

Thank you also to the team at Pacific Press, who accepted my proposal for this book, trusted me to write it on a tight deadline—and allowed me to stretch that deadline a little—and then did the work to make it into a book and launch it out into the world.

"Do not be afraid" is a message we all need to hear from time to time, and it needs to be amplified in our world today. Thank you to those who have been agents of this message to me at different times—and to those readers who will grow as agents of courage and hope by spending time with this book. May our churches and communities become less afraid, and may we increasingly become people of courageous action in goodness for others, in the name of Jesus.

"DO NOT BE AFRAID"

Fear has become the currency of our lives. It is not only an acute condition, an immediate response to frightening things happening around us; it has also become chronic. There are so many things to be afraid of, and the multiplicity of our media feeds present these to us in a relentless stream of global consciousness. And, of course, there are many who hope to profit by using fear to grab our attention and motivate us to action—or passivity.

Fear is a regular ingredient in so much of our information and entertainment. Fear is a common stimulus employed in advertising, where a problem is created, and then someone is eager to sell us the solution to a fear we were not aware of fifteen seconds earlier. Fear is a political tactic, motivating us to vote in a particular way or otherwise lend our support to the next urgent issue or cause. Fear is also used too often in church contexts as a way of thinking about theology, a prod to greater holiness, a tool of evangelism, and a motivation for donations to whichever ministry can make the most sensationalist claims.

Given that so many people and organizations benefit from stoking and exploiting our fears, it is hardly surprising that a recent survey found that 69 percent of Protestant pastors in the United States said they "believe there is a growing sense of fear within their congregations about the future of the nation and world." The same survey found almost as much fear about the future of Christianity. "A large majority of pastors see their congregations moving toward fear rather than away from it," commented one of the authors of the research.*

But our fear is not only focused on the world around us; it is also deeply personal. We live with fear within ourselves and who we are. While we might manage it in different ways, we live with the awareness of our own mortality and all the big questions of meaning and purpose that awareness inevitably raises. Then there are our general fatigue, busyness, worries, and anxieties, as well as the concerns we always have for those we love and for

* Lifeway Research, "Fear Prevalent in Pews, According to Protestant Pastors," August 8, 2023, https://research.lifeway.com/2023/08/08/fear-prevalent-in-pews-according-to-protestant-pastors/.

their well-being. Anxiety and depression are serious and growing medical conditions—and should be treated by qualified medical professionals—but it seems we all live with some underlying sense of uncertainty and fear that is part of what it means to be human.

Amid these realities of our lives and our world, "Do not be afraid" is the most repeated command in the Bible. In its various forms and in different translations—*Do not fear, Be not afraid, Fear not, Don't panic, Don't be alarmed, Do not let your hearts be troubled, Take heart, Be courageous, Stand strong, Encourage one another, Do not worry*, and more—God speaks through the Bible in response to all our fears. This does not mean that we will not feel fear or that we should feel guilty when we inevitably do. In the Bible's story, we observe that "Do not be afraid" is necessary precisely because this is part of who we are. But "Do not be afraid" is also vital for restoring our relationships with God and with each other. As we are guided by and grow in this biblical command, fear will not be dominant in our lives, in our responses to other people and the world around us, or in our choices and faith. "Do not be afraid" is essential to living and loving well.

Of course, I am no expert or master of this topic. I hear these Bible verses so keenly because I am well aware of my own propensity to fear amid the circumstances of life that challenge faith, hope, and love. I took on this project and began writing this book amid treatments and operations that my wife was enduring following a diagnosis of breast cancer. I did not write the readings strictly in order but came to writing about the promises of a world without pain and death on the day a friend came to the end of her eighteen-month journey with cancer (see December 28). I wrote the last of these readings on the sixth anniversary of my father's death, which came in the week after I had first preached on the "Do not be afraids" in the book of Luke. On those days in particular, this repeated reminder was important.

I do not know the times, circumstances, and events—personally or in the world around us—in which you might read this book. But I expect that on at least some of those days, you will need to hear "Do not be afraid" again.

That's why God said it again and again to His people, His disciples, and those He encountered in their lives: "Do not be afraid."

That's why He says it again to us today and every day: "Do not be afraid."

January 1

JESUS SAID

"Do not be afraid."

—Luke 12:32

It begins with Jesus. In His life, His death, His resurrection, His teachings, and promises, we find a guide to living well, meaningfully, with purpose and hope in an uncertain, unjust, and troubled world by Someone who did it, experienced it, felt it, but who also overcame it and transcended it. So when He commanded His disciples—as well as His followers almost 2,000 years later—to "not be afraid," we ought to take notice. And when we find it echoed throughout the Gospels—in His story and His teaching and then throughout the Bible—it must grab our attention, challenge our assumptions, and shape our lives.

Too often, the power of Jesus' teachings has been diminished by a superficial reading that tends to minimize or trivialize them as "nice" sayings, spiritual-sounding slogans, or perhaps even naïve idealism. While familiarity is good, the fact that many of us have heard these sayings numerous times can cause us to risk taking them for granted. There is a place for hearing Jesus' teachings as words of comfort, but there must also be times when we hear them as words of challenge and command. Undoubtedly, there is comfort here, but we must also hear the command that transcends our circumstances and states of mind.

As such, Jesus' "Do not be afraid" commands—and various similar teachings—are more about our focus than they are about our feelings. As human beings in a difficult and dangerous world, we will feel afraid at times, but fear is not to dominate or direct our lives. Instead, we repeatedly choose to live by different assumptions and values. This command is founded in this same Jesus and the larger realities of His kingdom. It is the present reality and future hope of this kingdom in which we are invited—but also commanded—to live courageously, humbly, generously, and without fear. That is what Jesus calls us to.

January 2

TO THE LITTLE FLOCK

"Do not be afraid, little flock, for your Father has been pleased to give you the kingdom."

—Luke 12:32

As a recurring biblical theme, "Do not be afraid" has a ring of truth because the various commands recognize in themselves and in the circumstances in which they are given that fear is part of what it means to be human. Asking us to not be afraid or anxious includes an acknowledgment that there are many things in life that lead us to fear, aspects of life to which "anxiety is a natural response."* We don't usually say, "Don't be afraid," unless there is some apparent or threatened reality that might make us fearful.

Jesus takes this further in one of His most direct and explicit commands, calling His disciples a "little flock" after commanding them, "Do not be afraid" (Luke 12:32), thus implying and recognizing the apparent fragility of our human lives.† A "little flock" might remind us of a few sheep on the sparse hills of Judea, tended by a small boy on behalf of his family. The little flock might be threatened by a meager diet and the need to find water; it might be the target of thieves or predators. Its life and well-being seem tenuous—but for the care of a committed shepherd.

The Bible's many "Do not be afraids" are not distanced from the reality of our experiences; they were given within and amid those realities and acknowledge the pervasiveness of our fears, large and small. "Do not be afraid" is not some nice saying, glib slogan, or marketing campaign. Many of our causes for fear are real, and God knows and has experienced these in Jesus. But this is why such statements are so significant for what it means to live with faith in an often fearful and fear-filled world.

---

* Darrell L. Bock, *Luke 9:51—24:53*, Baker Exegetical Commentary on the New Testament (Grand Rapids, MI: Baker Books, 1996), 1165.

† Bock, 1165.

January 3

HOW THINGS OUGHT TO BE

God saw all that he had made, and it was very good.
—Genesis 1:31

It can be hard to imagine a world without fear. Fear is such a part of our world and our human experience that it seeps into even our best imagination. But a world of goodness without fear is the reality of our world as God made it. As God paused at the end of each act of creation, He saw that it was "good" (Genesis 1:3, 9, 12, 18, 21, 25). And near the end of that work, He saw that His completed world was "very good" (Genesis 1:31).

It is worth pausing here with this God's-eye view. God had made something very good. Nothing in the whole of creation would cause harm or fear. Instead, everything worked together for mutual flourishing and, it seems, particularly for human flourishing.

Within this new world, the first people were given the role of stewards. The first human responsibility was that of gardeners who were "to work" and "take care of" the garden (Genesis 2:15) and the good world God had made. They were to work in harmony with, and even to grow, God's intention for goodness, mutuality, and peace in the world.

If we give this description enough of our imagination, it should prompt feelings of regret, perhaps a kind of homesickness for a world without pain, grief, and fear. But it should also alert us to the glimpses and echoes of this original design that we can still see in our world today. Acts of kindness and moments of peace, glimpses of beauty, and examples of creativity are all reminders of how God intended our world to be. As seemingly insubstantial as a flower or a tiny bird or as difficult an act of service or sacrifice as we can imagine, as ordinary as a simple meal or as grand as a mountain range or ocean sunset—they point us back to their Creator and insist that a world without fear is not only possible but is intended and not beyond the reach of our imagination.

January 4

THE CREATION OF REST

God blessed the seventh day and made it holy, because on it he rested from all the work of creating that he had done.

—Genesis 2:3

God's final act of the creation story was the creation of rest. And while all the work of the other days was "good," this seventh day was designated "holy." This unlikely conclusion to the creation story emphasized the nature of the world God had made, His intention for human life, and God's nature as Creator. God demonstrated the absence of fear and anxiety by this practice of rest, and He declared such an attitude and posture holy.

When we launch a new project or operation, our instinct is to check on its progress and ensure its continuity. Sometimes, this is necessary; often, it says more about our state of mind. In contrast, when the work of creation was done, God rested.

"God did not show up to do more. God absented God's self from the office. God did not come back to check on creation in anxiety to be sure it was all working. . . . The world is an anxiety-free one because the creator is anxiety-free and publicly exhibits that freedom from anxiety by not checking things out. . . . God rests, confident, serene, at peace. God's rest, moreover, bestows [restfulness] on creatureliness."*

If it was not already there in the essential goodness of creation itself, God instilled an anxiety-free, stress-reducing, fear-rejecting rhythm into the nature of our world. This would be the rationale for the Sabbath commandment given to humanity at Mt. Sinai (see Exodus 20:8–11). At that time, it offered the recently enslaved Hebrews a different rhythm to their lives than the perpetual work of survival that had been forced upon them in Egypt. And it still invites us to live in the harmonies and relationships that God intended for our lives and our world.

---

* Walter Brueggemann, *Sabbath as Resistance: Saying No to the Culture of Now* (Louisville, KY: Westminster John Knox Press, 2014), 29, 30.

January 5

THE FIRST FEAR

The LORD God called to the man, "Where are you?"
He answered, "I heard you in the garden,
and I was afraid because I was naked; so I hid."
—Genesis 3:9, 10

The Bible story gives us limited insights into the initial relationship God had with Adam and Eve. The details of the processes by which they were each created portray God as intimately involved with them as creatures and then in conversation with them about their roles in this new world and the provisions He had made for their well-being. From the story in Genesis 3, it also seems that it was not unusual for God to come looking for them, to spend time walking and talking together with them "in the cool of the day" (Genesis 3:8).

But on that particular day, they hid from God. Something had changed. The story explains that they had listened to the God-questioning alternative offered by the serpent. It was not so much that they had questioned God but that they had questioned God apart from God. So, when they heard God looking for them, they felt afraid. God had not changed from the good creator they had previously known, but they had been changed by their distrust of God that the serpent's lies had prompted. As the story describes it, their shame and their fear in response to God's approach was "their first bitter taste of accepting the serpent's view of God."*

This is a wound that has been perpetuated and repeated in humanity ever since. "Biblically, anthropologically, and existentially *fear* is the most succinct description of the human condition."† Because of the broken relationship between us and our Creator, the God who is the source of all the goodness of our world and life itself is also an inevitable cause of fear in us. But the Bible insists that God is still good and has been working to overcome and undo our fear.

---

* Sigve K. Tonstad, *The Lost Meaning of the Seventh Day* (Berrien Springs, MI: Andrews University Press, 2009), 244, 245.

† Tonstad, 244.

January 6

BROKEN RELATIONSHIPS

The man said, "The woman you put here with me—
she gave me some fruit from the tree, and I ate it."
—Genesis 3:12

When we understand God as our creator and the source of life, the world, and all its goodness, it is hardly a surprise that breaking that relationship will damage all other aspects of our lives and relationships. The story in Genesis 3 details each of these broken relationships in turn.

First, we suffer from a broken relationship with ourselves, reflected in the sense of shame described in Genesis 3:7 (compare to Genesis 2:25). Our relationships with other people are also broken and strained. Without much prompting, Adam and Eve were quick to blame someone else for what had gone wrong (see Genesis 3:12, 13). Their marred human relationship to the earth itself and to the rest of creation was, as described by God, the consequence of their broken relationship (see Genesis 3:16–24).

These broken relationships are the origin of our many experiences of fear, ultimately all pointing us back to this "abiding human plight." "We fear that our lives have no story, because we have fled from the story God has given us. Our deep fears point us back to the deep story in which our flight from God leaves us fearful of a world that was meant to be received as a gift."* Every aspect of human life and experience was distorted by sin, and fear was the most obvious, immediate, and enduring result.

But even in describing these broken relationships and their consequences, God offered a promise (see Genesis 3:15). Somehow, within this broken and fearful human story, there would be One who would defeat the source of lies and fear, even if at great cost to Himself. In restoring these broken relationships, God would bring an end to fear and ultimately re-create the world as it was intended to be. At this tragic moment of sudden fear and shame, God gave hope.

---

* Scott Bader-Saye, *Following Jesus In a Culture of Fear* (Grand Rapids, MI: Brazos Press, 2007), 159.

January 7

A DECEPTIVE ENEMY

"And I will put enmity
between you and the woman,
and between your offspring and hers;
he will crush your head,
and you will strike his heel."

—Genesis 3:15

The fall of humanity and our world from what it was created to be is not only a story of existential angst and relational rupture. In the serpent of the Eden story, we are introduced to an enemy who actively works to sow lies, deception, and fear in God's otherwise good creation. From glimpses we see throughout the Bible story—made most plain in Revelation 12—this enemy's primary target is God. But one of the easiest ways for a less powerful but evil enemy to hurt God is to attack the people and creation He loves. As fearsome as they can be, these attacks are the devil taking cheap shots because his ability to fight against God is so limited (see Revelation 12:12).

So those things that we rightly fear, including death, disaster, disease, and despair, are not "acts of God" as some insurance policies, pop culture, and other poor theologies might describe them. Instead, we insist that "an enemy did this," as the farmer in Jesus' story explained (Matthew 13:28). We should not give too much of our time and attention to the tricks and plans of the enemy, although it is a reality of the Bible's big story.

This enemy is not only always the lesser power; he is now also a defeated power. In the Bible's telling, the enemy was sentenced to defeat at the time of his first victory. Yes, the devil has made many strikes throughout history and in each of our lives. All of us are bruised and wounded by these attacks. But it was he who was crushed by the self-sacrificing love of God in Jesus' death and resurrection. This defeated enemy continues to rage against God's people and creation, bringing fear and terror to our lives and our world "*because* he knows that his time is short" (Revelation 12:12, emphasis added). His fury is an admission of his defeat.

January 8

STEPPING INTO THE UNKNOWN

By faith Abraham, when called to go to a place he would later receive as his inheritance, obeyed and went, even though he did not know where he was going.

—Hebrews 11:8

One of the sacred starting points—or restarting points—in the story of God's relationship with the people He had made is the story of the call of Abraham, the beginning of a special history that is much of the story of the Bible. If we have an overall familiarity with how the story goes from this point, it can be easy for us to skip ahead to the highlights, direction, and momentum that seem inevitable in hindsight. We may just assume the stories of Abraham's descendants, the Exodus, the Israelite nation, the Psalms and prophets, the coming of Jesus, the new movements of God in the early church, and Jesus' promises to return and make all things new.

But this story begins with a much smaller focus—a single family and a specific day on which Abram and his household left their home and set out for somewhere God had called them, but they did not know where they were going. Imagine the uncertainty, the anxieties, and the fears this day brought. Imagine the last-minute packing without knowing what they might need and the sadness of saying goodbye to friends and everything that was familiar, all of which they would likely not see again. Then there were the dangers of travel, concerns about food and water and where they would find more, and fears about strangers they would encounter who might not be friendly to a traveling community of foreigners.

No wonder this starting-out (he "obeyed and went") was remembered centuries later as a demonstration of faith. All that came after resulted from this particular day, overcoming the fear and uncertainty of not knowing where they were going and choosing to follow the call and go.

January 9

THE LONG VIEW

After this, the word of the Lord came to Abram in a vision:

"Do not be afraid, Abram.
I am your shield,
your very great reward."

—Genesis 15:1

The story of Abram, whose name was changed by God to Abraham, plays out over a dozen or so chapters in the midst of the book of Genesis. From his initial call and blessing to his death and the descendants who came after, we see his victories and his losses, his courage and his failures. We read about the times when he followed and talked directly with God and even when he argued with God. We also see the times when he lost patience with God, tried to fulfill God's promises in his own way, and lied to protect himself, even at the risk of his wife, Sarah. It is not a straight line of faithfulness but a meandering journey with many highs and lows.

Consider this moment when God came to Abram. It was some time after the military victory he had won, rescuing his nephew Lot and demonstrating humility in response to this victory by returning tithe on the spoils and seeking nothing for himself. But Abram was troubled by the burning absence of a son to carry on his name and to whom the promises of God were to be fulfilled. Abram was keenly aware that it would take more than a single generation for God's promises to be fulfilled, and he was considering what other options might be available.

In response, God spoke with him again, urging him not to allow his fears to become greater than the promises God had already made, which He then renewed. Abram's response? "Abram believed the Lord, and he credited it to him as righteousness" (Genesis 15:6). There were still many ups and downs and twists in the story, but God's promises would be worked out on a larger scale than Abram could have imagined.

LYING TO LAUGHING

Sarah was afraid, so she lied and said, "I did not laugh."
But he said, "Yes, you did laugh."

—Genesis 18:15

The story of God's direct interaction with Bible characters might well seem strange to us, but it also seemed strange to the people themselves in the stories. Three men appeared on the road near Abraham's tent. God had changed Abram's name by then, again promising that he would be "the father of many nations" (Genesis 17:5) despite the obvious lack of the promised son and the advancing age of both Abraham and Sarah. Abraham noticed these strangers and invited them to eat with him.

As a meal was being prepared, these visitors dropped into the conversation an assurance that the long-promised son would arrive within a year. Listening through the tent walls, Sarah responded with an ironic laugh. *"As if this is going to happen,"* she chuckled to herself, *"after so long, now that we are too old."*

But her sarcasm was pulled up short. The Visitor had heard this quiet moment of resigned disappointment in Sarah's heart, and He queried Abraham about it. Hearing this response, Sarah was afraid, and her fear prompted her to lie to God and perhaps to herself. Fear causes us to respond in strange ways.

It was all very human and very strange at the same time. It seemed that this was the end of this conversation. But this story has an unlikely second part. A year later, "at the very time God had promised" (Genesis 21:2), Sarah gave birth to Isaac, whose name means "*laughter.*" She named this promised son for her laughter, a reminder of her disappointment, her fear, and the lie she had told. But the name was also a celebration of God fulfilling a long-standing promise. "Sarah said, 'God has brought me laughter, and everyone who hears about this will laugh with me' " (Genesis 21:6).

THE GOD WHO SEES

She gave this name to the LORD who spoke to her: "You are the God who sees me," for she said, "I have now seen the One who sees me."
—Genesis 16:13

One of the intriguing and troubling subplots amid the stories of Abraham is the story of Hagar. It seems that she doesn't belong and is incorporated into the story only as a direct result of Abraham's and Sarah's mutual failure of faith and courage. And when the alternative plan they concocted seemed to be working for them, we find Hagar at her lowest point.

Hagar was a foreigner—an Egyptian—in the household of Abraham, a female slave who could not make her own decisions, simultaneously abused by Abraham and Sarah and reliant on them for support and protection. When she became pregnant, Hagar was then the subject of Sarah's further jealous mistreatment. So she ran away, and an angel found her alone in the desert. From Hagar's perspective, the predicament in which she found herself seemed less of a problem than the circumstances from which she was escaping.

So, an angel brought her a message of encouragement. He asked her to tell her story and, in response, gave her a promise of her own. In the name the angel gave to her son was the promise that God hears (see Genesis 16:11).

Remarkably, Hagar then gave a name to God, who had sent this messenger. This foreign, abused, fugitive, and enslaved woman was the first person in the story of the Bible to name God—an act of great significance in those ancient cultures. For Hagar, the God whose messenger had found her in the desert, near the well that would also be named by this encounter, was the God who saw and knew her suffering.

And for all who are excluded, abused, oppressed, and afraid, God is the God who sees and knows your suffering, your loneliness, and your despair. A God who sees is a God who cares—and has been recognized and named as such by so many people in such situations throughout history.

January 12

HEARING A MOTHER'S HEART

God heard the boy crying, and the angel of God called to Hagar from heaven and said to her, "What is the matter, Hagar? Do not be afraid; God has heard the boy crying as he lies there. Lift the boy up and take him by the hand, for I will make him into a great nation."
—Genesis 21:17, 18

Despite the angel's reassurance during her pregnancy, the glimpse we are given of Hagar's experience of motherhood is troubled. Tension in Abraham's household led to him sending Hagar and Ishmael away from the safety and support of the community. Again, Hagar was alone in the desert, but this time with the added responsibility and heartbreak of seeing her child's suffering and anticipating that Ishmael would soon die. But "God heard the boy crying," and this time, God Himself spoke directly to Hagar.

On this occasion, God demonstrated that He is the "God who sees." He saw and heard Ishmael's suffering. But He also saw the fear and suffering of the boy's mother. God might have seemed harsh in instructing Abraham to send Hagar and Ishmael away (see Genesis 21:12), but God was responding to the distress in that household and had a bigger plan in mind. And we can hear the tenderness in His voice as He spoke to Hagar, and gave her an insight into His care for Ishmael and clear sight to see the well that was nearby (see verse 19).

We know little more of the story of this mother and son, but just as God was with Hagar in the times of her greatest distress, "God was with the boy as he grew up" (verse 20). It is likely that one of the ways in which Ishmael would have recognized God's presence would have been through his mother retelling the stories of her experiences with the God who sees and hears even the cries and fears of those who might be considered outsiders to the story and people of God.

A NEW GENERATION

That night the LORD appeared to him and said, "I am the God of your father Abraham. Do not be afraid, for I am with you; I will bless you and will increase the number of your descendants for the sake of my servant Abraham."

—Genesis 26:24

Isaac would have grown up with the stories of God's relationship with his father, Abraham, and God's promises to his parents, of which he was part of the fulfillment. Now, as Isaac found his own way in the world, God introduced Himself to him as his father's God and urged him to live with courage and expectation. To Isaac, He made the same promises He had made to Abraham. This would have been an important moment for Isaac. The relationship that had guided his father's life would now be part of his life. The God of Abraham was now the God of Isaac.

But there is another element of this generational dynamic that is pointed out in Hebrews 11. Yes, Abraham had a dynamic and growing relationship with God. Yes, he had received the miracle of the birth of a promised son much later in life than he expected. But the ultimate promises remained unfulfilled in Abraham's lifetime. Abraham, along with many others of the patriarchs, "did not receive the things promised; they only saw them and welcomed them from a distance. And they admitted that they were aliens and strangers on earth." Abraham was "still living by faith when . . . [he] died" (Hebrews 11:13).

Now Isaac was being invited into this same unfulfilled promise, with the recognition that this might not be completed in his lifetime either. He might have wondered whether this was the wisest choice to organize his life around. But to accept God's promises as his own was also to enter into a relationship with this same God and to live by this same faith. So God said to Isaac, as He had said to Abraham, "Do not be afraid, for I am with you."

January 14

IN THE HOUSE OF GOD

He was afraid and said, "How awesome is this place!
This is none other than the house of God; this is the gate of heaven."
—Genesis 28:17

Sometimes, we appreciate the significance and the daunting nature of an experience only in hindsight. Busyness, weariness, or other preoccupations can distract us from understanding the reality of the situation. As an occasional journalist, I have interviewed individuals, only to learn later the real significance of their story, work, or achievement, and then I had a longer list of questions that I wished I had asked, and I regretted the missed opportunity. Or sometimes, I have visited a historical location, only later to read more about its significance and what I should have been looking for.

Jacob had arrived at this place tired, alone, and afraid. He was running away from a deceived, disappointed father and a dangerously angry brother—setting off on his own journey into the unknown. He slumped on the ground, trying to get some rest, so tired that a stone was enough to serve as a pillow. It was only after Jacob experienced God's presence in this place and the offer of the promises God had given to his father and grandfather that Jacob awoke with a realization of the significance of what had taken place.

Perhaps he awoke to the first graying of the light amid the cool of the early morning, stiff from a day of hurried travel followed by sleeping on the hard ground. But he also awakened to a new relationship with God, a new vision for himself and his people, and new promises that would guide his life. Jacob trembled with the realization of God's presence in Bethel, yet this was a "Do not be afraid" moment. The God of Abraham and Isaac was now also the God of Jacob. And that uncomfortable pillow was now a memorial stone to the promises and presence of God (see Genesis 28:18, 19).

January 15

WRESTLING WITH GOD

So Jacob called the place Peniel, saying, "It is because I saw God face to face, and yet my life was spared."
—Genesis 32:30

It seems that Jacob had a pattern of encountering God but not realizing the importance of his encounter until the next morning. This time, he was at another transition point in his life, returning to the land where he had been born and preparing to meet his estranged brother. He had been a runaway; now, he was returning with a growing family and flocks of animals that marked him as a wealthy man. This was one of those moments in life when we reflect on how far we have come and, simultaneously, how little we have changed or achieved. Despite his seeming success, Jacob was uncertain, afraid, and alone.

To make a dark night darker, he was attacked by an unknown assailant in the night and began wrestling for his life—or so he thought. Throughout those hours, Jacob desperately fought until he had expended all his strength. Then his attacker, who seemed anxious to leave but also to have the upper hand, simply touched him in a way that put an end to Jacob's struggles, revealing Himself as a stronger but different kind of opponent, and Jacob immediately asked for a blessing.

In Jacob's story, he had sought blessings in a variety of ways—tricking his brother, lying to his father, outworking and outwitting his father-in-law. But this was a different kind of blessing. "Not a blessing that he can have now by the strength of his cunning or the force of his will, but a blessing he can have only as a gift."* Marking Jacob as one who had wrestled with God but whose life had been spared (see Genesis 32:26–31), God gave him the new and more noble name of Israel. And the new morning dawned around him, and Jacob was both truly beaten and truly blessed.

---

* Frederick Buechner, *The Magnificent Defeat* (New York: HarperCollins, 1985), 18.

January 16

FOR HIS FINAL JOURNEY

"I am God, the God of your father," he said. "Do not be afraid to go down to Egypt, for I will make you into a great nation there. I will go down to Egypt with you, and I will surely bring you back again. And Joseph's own hand will close your eyes."

—Genesis 46:3, 4

The Tomb of the Patriarchs, also known as the Ibrahimi Mosque, is claimed to be the oldest building in the world still used for its original purpose. In the center of Hebron, the largest city in the West Bank of the Palestinian Territories today, it was built by Herod the Great's builders over the Cave of Machpelah. This was the field that Abraham purchased from the Hittites about 3,800 years ago to bury his wife Sarah (see Genesis 23:16–20), the field where he was then buried, as were Isaac and Rebekah, and Leah and Jacob. Today, it is a holy site for both Jews and Muslims. The synagogue is entered from one side of the building, the mosque from the other, with the common shrines viewed through windows on each side of the religious divide.

Jacob's burial at this site was the fulfillment of God's promise to him as he set out on the last major journey of his wandering life. Again, it seemed that the promise of a land of his own was unfulfilled, that the journey to Egypt was a backward step, but God reassured Jacob of His plan. It had not worked out in the ways that Abraham, Isaac, or Jacob expected or hoped. But God would still be at work in the succeeding generations. First, Jacob would be reunited with his lost son, Joseph. Then a cavalcade of his sons, as well as all the senior officials of Egypt, would bring back Jacob's body to be buried in this sacred family site (see Genesis 50:1–13), still celebrated by the Jewish people as the first portion of the land of Canaan acquired by the father of their nation.

January 17

A FORGIVENESS "PRANK"

"It's all right," he said. "Don't be afraid. Your God, the God of your father, has given you treasure in your sacks; I received your silver."
—Genesis 43:23

Although it ended well, Joseph's life was filled with many difficult experiences, most of which could be traced back to the jealousy and betrayal of his brothers. He had been sold as a slave in a distant country and, without God's intervention, would likely have spent the rest of his life enslaved. So when his brothers came to Egypt seeking food for their families, Joseph had a profound choice to make. He was now in a position of power. His family included both people who had loved him and people who had caused him great harm. He could help them, or he could hurt them. He could seek revenge, or he could restore the relationship with his family.

Instead of approaching this situation directly, it seems Joseph chose to play a prank on his brothers, perhaps partly as a test of the character of his older brothers—whether they had changed or grown—but also to see how they would respond to an unexpected kindness. On their second visit to Egypt, necessitated by the ongoing famine, the brothers were acutely aware of the dangerous position they would be in if they were accused of stealing from this powerful foreign official. So Joseph had his manager rebuff their concerns and lay the ground for him to reveal his identity to his brothers.

Human relationships are often complex. Fear is often a component of relationships. We fear being alone, but connecting with others requires vulnerability, meaning fear of rejection and betrayal. Joseph needed a way to reconnect with his brothers. While he was testing his brothers, he was doing so with kindness, but finding out if it was safe for him to identify himself to them.

January 18

DISARMING REVENGE

Joseph said to them, "Don't be afraid. Am I in the place of God? You intended to harm me, but God intended it for good to accomplish what is now being done, the saving of many lives. So then, don't be afraid. I will provide for you and your children."

—Genesis 50:19–21

Celebrating being reunited with his father and extended family, Joseph might have thought he had made peace with his brothers. But after the death of Jacob, it became obvious that his brothers did not fully trust Joseph's claims of forgiveness. They were afraid he might still seek revenge for how they had treated him decades earlier.

To forgive is to say, "Don't be afraid." At times, we may need to be careful to stop people who might abuse or exploit us or others from being able to do it again. But we can choose to disarm ourselves, to make it clear that we will not be the ones to cause further hurt. Relationships are healed, as far as it is possible with us, by surrendering our "right" to revenge. For the good of ourselves and the good of others, we can choose not to use the weapons of fear and not be people who cause, create, or exploit fear.

Our faith gives us a special perspective on this. Like Joseph, we can trust that judgment is God's role. He can determine whether another person's apology is real or simply driven by fear of our revenge. We can trust that He also has an overview of our lives and can work amid, and sometimes despite, the circumstances that we find most difficult. With these perspectives in mind, we can see how it might be possible for us to disarm the weapons of revenge, bitterness, and fear that we are tempted to employ. Instead, we can respond with kindness and generosity, overcoming evil with good (see Romans 12:21).

THE TOOL OF TYRANNY

"Look," he said to his people, "the Israelites have become much too numerous for us. Come, we must deal shrewdly with them or they will become even more numerous and, if war breaks out, will join our enemies, fight against us and leave the country."
—Exodus 1:9, 10

As we are discovering, fear can infect all our relationships, but the largest scale of this is how fear has been used throughout history by nations and their rulers to oppress others, particularly those who are different in some way. This was the situation that began the story of Exodus. A new king "to whom Joseph meant nothing, came to power in Egypt" (Exodus 1:8). Ignorant of the history behind the presence of these "foreigners" in the land and likely as a way to consolidate his power, this new ruler's shrewd dealing included creating an imagined scenario in which these "foreigners" might be a threat. This political ploy would unite the "real Egyptians" against this perceived threat and justify the enslavement and exploitation of the other group, with the added boost to the Egyptian economy of a new and plentiful source of free labor.

The operating mechanism of this scenario was fear. "Tyrant kings and kingdoms are accustomed to controlling people through fear, especially through the threat of violence."* Tragically, this is a political tactic still much used today in varying degrees. The irony is that such "shrewdness" tends to create the dynamic it imagines. Those who are marginalized and oppressed in this way tend to become more willing to fight against the nation that enslaves them. In this case, the suffering of the enslaved people prompted God to intervene, bringing about the destruction of Egypt and the departure of the Israelites in search of a country in which they could be free.

* Brian Zahnd, *Postcards From Babylon: The Church in American Exile* (Spello Press, 2019), 74.

January 20

RESISTING FEAR

The midwives, however, feared God and did not do what the king of Egypt had told them to do; they let the boys live.

—Exodus 1:17

It was the kind of cruel, inhumane decree that fear can drive us to and that only fear can attempt to justify: "When you are helping the Hebrew women during childbirth on the delivery stool, if you see that the baby is a boy, kill him; but if it is a girl, let her live" (Exodus 1:16). But the two Hebrew midwives—remarkably, we know their names: Shiphrah and Puah—chose to reject the Egyptians' fear and the risk to themselves. They could do that because they had a larger motivation that directed their lives and actions.

By the time these humble Hebrew midwives were assisting with the birth of Moses, the people of Israel had been enslaved for many decades. They would have been tempted to assume that their enslavement was the natural order of things, and all the messages, methods, and mythology of Egyptian society would have reinforced this belief. But Shiphrah's and Puah's courageous acts and attitude of resistance offered an alternative way of thinking, a different theology to that insisted on by the powerful people of Egypt.

And their insistence that their fear of God was stronger than their fear of Egypt laid the groundwork for Israel's freedom, both by midwifing the birth of the boy who would lead their people out of Egypt and by maintaining an attitude that made faithfulness and freedom possible. "That genuine alternative, entrusted to us that bear that calling, is rooted not in social theory or in righteous indignation or in altruism but in the genuine alternative that Yahweh is. Yahweh makes possible and requires an alternative theology and an alternative sociology."* As the Hebrew midwives demonstrated, this is a different way of thinking and a different way of living.

---

* Walter Brueggemann, *The Prophetic Imagination,* 2nd ed. (Minneapolis: Fortress Press, 2001), 9.

January 21

REINTRODUCING THE GOD WHO SEES

The Lord said, "I have indeed seen the misery of my people in Egypt. I have heard them crying out because of their slave drivers, and I am concerned about their suffering."
—Exodus 3:7

However we measure it, the Israelites were in slavery for a long time. It sees the passing of enough generations that only the most important stories of a people's history are still remembered; even a national ruler like Joseph can be all but forgotten. Although we see a few examples of faith maintained among the Israelite people, it is also a long time for God to seem silent, perhaps unconcerned with the suffering of the people. In the telling of the story, it is suggested that even God might have forgotten His people in some sense: "The Israelites groaned in their slavery and cried out, and their cry for help because of their slavery went up to God. God heard their groaning and he remembered his covenant with Abraham, with Isaac and with Jacob. So God looked on the Israelites and was concerned about them" (Exodus 2:23–25).

God had to reintroduce Himself to the people of Israel. He did this in a way that was both distant and dramatic, meeting the fugitive Moses at a burning bush in the wilderness. To Moses—and through him, to the people—God reintroduced Himself as "the God who sees." Yes, He was the God of Abraham, Isaac, and Jacob, but He was also the God of Hagar, adopting the name she had given Him when He saw her distress. The Israelites were reminded of the old stories and the promises God had made to their ancestors, but the more important message was that God had seen, that He cared, and that He would intervene. "When they heard that the Lord was concerned about them and had seen their misery, they bowed down and worshiped" (Exodus 4:31).

January 22

THE DOUBTS OF A LEADER

Moses answered, "What if they do not believe me or listen to me and say, 'The Lord did not appear to you'?"

—Exodus 4:1

Many of us assume that we would have stronger faith and be able to live well and lead with greater purpose if only God would appear to us, talk to us more directly, and make our task plain. After a false start or two, this was the experience of Moses. God found him in the desert, appearing in an attention-grabbing burning bush and speaking directly to him, giving Moses the task of returning to the land of his birth to lead his people out of slavery. It was a daunting task to confront the most powerful ruler of the most powerful nation in the world at that time, but God could not have made it more plain.

So what was the problem? Perhaps Moses was afraid of the wrong things. Note his objection: "What if they do not believe *me* or listen to *me*?" Moses should have known better. His previous attempt to rescue his people had not gone well (see Exodus 2:11–15), but it seems his main concern was still focused on himself. And so his argument continues through most of this chapter. Despite God's appearance to him, despite the voice of God speaking directly to him, despite the miracles God gave Moses to convince the people, and despite God's assurance that He would be with him, Moses continued to protest. Finally, he said it bluntly: "Pardon your servant, Lord. Please send someone else" (Exodus 4:13).

Yes, it feels like it would be helpful at times to have a clear voice guiding our lives, our work, and our service to God and others. But what is often lacking is a focus on what is most important—our decision to trust God in doing it, even when it feels daunting and perhaps impossible. It is not about *me.*

GOD CAN TAKE IT

Moses returned to the LORD and said, "O Lord, why have you brought trouble upon this people? Is this why you sent me? Ever since I went to Pharaoh to speak in your name, he has brought trouble on this people, and you have not rescued your people at all."

—Exodus 5:22, 23

We all have days like this. We feel like we were trying to do the right thing, even what God has called us to do. We have mustered our courage and put in our best effort. And nothing changes. Or we feel as if all we have done is make the situation worse.

After their initial enthusiasm, the people were now turning on Moses, and Moses was directing his anger, fear, and disappointment toward God. Some might argue that Moses and the people should have simply continued praising God nonetheless, ignoring their worsening circumstances and the demands to make more bricks with fewer resources. But Moses vented his frustrations to God in blunt terms, accusing God of only making their situation worse.

Remarkably, God did not rebuke Moses or the people. He was big enough to take their criticism and absorb their anger. It seems He understood the frustration and fears of these people who had been enslaved for generations, who had begun to hope but were now feeling the brunt of the Egyptians' power and cruelty.

Instead, God assured Moses that He had only just begun to work on their behalf. After Moses' initial attempts to bring change, "the LORD said to Moses, 'Now you will see what I will do' " (Exodus 6:1). He reminded Moses that He had been the God of Abraham, Isaac, and Jacob, but that the Israelite people would now see and know more of God than their ancestors had. "Then you will know," God promised, "that I am the LORD your God, who brought you out from under the yoke of the Egyptians" (Exodus 6:7), introducing a description that He would later use to remind them of what He had done throughout their history.

January 24

AT THE EDGE OF THE SEA

Moses answered the people, "Do not be afraid. Stand firm and you will see the deliverance the LORD will bring you today. The Egyptians you see today you will never see again. The LORD will fight for you; you need only to be still."

—Exodus 14:13, 14

It had been quite a time for the people of Israel. After generations of slavery, they had received the hope of liberation. Then, their situation became worse as a series of plagues progressively devastated the Egyptian nation. Seeing the Israelites as the source of their problems, the Egyptians ordered them to leave, as God had predicted they would, and they began their journey into the wilderness. They would have had mixed emotions. While slavery was harsh, Egypt was the only home any of them had known, and their destination seemed vague and likely to involve conflict with other peoples along the way. Then, there was the rapid departure and the challenge of crossing the desert. But this was also an opportunity for freedom and the land that God had promised to their ancestors.

When they arrived at the shore of the Red Sea, someone raised the alarm that what was left of the Egyptian army was coming after them. It seemed that all the disturbance, hopes, and fears of the past weeks, months, years, and generations had led to this final showdown. It was partly a "liberty or death" moment, but once again, it was also a time of recriminations against Moses, who had dared to raise their hopes of freedom, only for their hopes to die with them in the wilderness. Or so it seemed.

Instead, this was to be the last stand of Egyptian oppression. Moses urged the people not to give in to their fears. This was a time to stand up, to march again as they had left Egypt "with fists raised in defiance" (Exodus 14:8, NLT). And again, it was God who would make a way for them through the sea and who would see them celebrating victory and freedom (see Exodus 15:1–21).

AT THE MOUNTAIN OF GOD

On the morning of the third day there was thunder and lightning, with a thick cloud over the mountain, and a very loud trumpet blast. Everyone in the camp trembled.

—Exodus 19:16

Only two months removed from Egyptian slavery, the people of Israel returned to the place at which God had broken His generational silence, appearing to Moses with the assurance that He had seen their suffering and He would intervene. Now, the people of Israel were confronted by a mountain-sized "burning bush" experience. Making camp in the wilderness, the people were confronted by thunder, lightning, and a cloud dominating their view of the mountain and shaking the ground beneath their feet. And shaking the people to their core.

Moses ordered the people not to go too close to the mountain, to sound the trumpets as loudly as possible, and to purify themselves in preparation to encounter God. Like Moses some months earlier, they were standing on holy ground and were rightly afraid of the Power and Presence before them.

But then God introduced Himself to the people: "I am the LORD your God, who brought you out of Egypt, out of the land of slavery" (Exodus 20:2). The God who was shaking the mountain in front of them and the ground beneath them was on their side. The God who had caused the ruin of Egypt and destroyed their armies and chariots was *their* God. And, although they were afraid, they were afraid in the best possible way.

God had changed their history, and now He was inviting them to share the future together with Him, establishing a new kind of nation that would honor God and be a light to the surrounding nations. His presence among them and the laws He would give were important steps in restoring the relationship that God had created and intended for humanity. Rejecting oppression and fear, their nation would be shaped by the fear of God in the best possible ways.

January 26

THE SUFFICIENCY OF SABBATH

"Remember the Sabbath day by keeping it holy. Six days you shall labor and do all your work, but the seventh day is a sabbath to the Lord *your God. On it you shall not do any work, neither you, nor your son or daughter, nor your male or female servant, nor your animals, nor any foreigner residing in your towns."*

—Exodus 20:8–10

Surviving amid slavery and oppression tends to harden people. They are forced to compete for limited resources and struggle to provide for the basic needs of themselves and their families. After generations of slavery, this was the mindset of the Israelites. They were measured by the number of bricks they produced and conditioned to self-preservation.

God wanted them to grow beyond this. He did this first by the provision of manna. Every morning, food was provided to them, with smelly object lessons for those who collected more than they needed. This was an everyday practice of an economy of sufficiency, training them out of the habits of scarcity. "Each morning everyone gathered as much as he needed, and when the sun grew hot, it melted away" (Exodus 16:21).

But there was a weekly interruption to this daily miracle food. On the sixth day of the week, God provided double the usual portion, each person or family collecting just as much as they needed for two days and not needing to compete with each other to survive. God would make it explicit in the fourth commandment, but He was already training them in Sabbath keeping as a practice of the economics of grace. It was a day when nobody could be made to work.

For these newly freed people, Sabbath became a "sanctuary in time . . . a truce in all conflicts, personal and social, peace between man and man, man and nature, peace within man."* Rightly understood and celebrated, the Sabbath was—and is—a practice of spiritual and practical equality, an economics of grace and sufficiency.

---

* Abraham Joshua Heschel, *The Sabbath* (New York: Farrar, Straus and Giroux, 1951), 29.

January 27

A LAW WITHOUT FEAR

Moses said to the people, "Do not be afraid. God has come to test you, so that the fear of God will be with you to keep you from sinning."
—Exodus 20:20

The thunder and lightning, the cloud and the earthquake were daunting, but the commandments that God gave to the people when He appeared to them at the mountain were both daunting and comforting. The God who had rescued them from slavery in Egypt also wanted the best for them as a new nation. If they remembered their trembling at the appearance of God, if they remembered their redemption and lived by the laws He had given them, they would live in a society that had no use for fear.

Their relationship with God would be different from that of the surrounding nations and their gods. These gods competed with each other and demanded elaborate idols, and their religious festivals, feasts, and rest days were often only for the powerful and wealthy. Taking a step back toward God's original intention for His relationship with humanity, this was not to be a relationship in which the Israelite people would be perpetually afraid of their God.

Similarly, their relationships with each other would also be restored and recalibrated every Sabbath with a new reminder of the equality and sufficiency of what God provided. This would mean that they did not need to lie and steal and kill to survive. They would have no need to envy their neighbors' well-being, and their most intimate relationships would be respected and protected—as God had intended.

It was a seemingly simple pattern for living without fear. As Jesus would later summarize it: " 'Love the Lord your God with all your heart and with all your soul and with all your mind.' This is the first and greatest commandment. And the second is like it: 'Love your neighbor as yourself.' All the Law and the Prophets hang on these two commandments" (Matthew 22:37–40).

January 28

A PLACE FOR GOD TO DWELL

"Then have them make a sanctuary for me, and I will dwell among them."

—Exodus 25:8

One of the key directions of the Bible's story is of God returning to humanity. After humanity's relationship with God was broken in the Garden of Eden, His promise was that He would work to renew that relationship that had become a source of fear. Of course, we see this promise fulfilled in the incarnation of Jesus, who "became flesh and made his dwelling among us" (John 1:14). We also anticipate it in Jesus' promises to return and in Revelation's final proclamation that "God's dwelling place is now among the people, and he will dwell with them" (Revelation 21:3).

The sanctuary in the wilderness was an earlier and important step in this biblical momentum. First introduced as the Israelites set out on their journey out of Egypt, the pillar of cloud and fire was a day-and-night visual reminder of God's leading, comforting, and protecting presence among them (see Exodus 13:21, 22). Now, that Presence would have a tent among their tents, with the promise that God would be with them all the way to their destination. But God's tent would be a special tent, rich with symbols and stories that would teach the people about Him. It would be a place of beauty to which all the people would contribute, and it would be made using the work of their finest artisans.

The people were not to forget God's power demonstrated in His judgments against Egypt or in the thunder and lightning of Mount Sinai, but God would also be an everyday Presence among them, not only to be worshiped but also to be trusted. If He was a foe, He was one to be feared, but He was also a traveling companion and guide with whom to be fearless. He would order when and where they would go, but He would also go with them.

January 29

GLOWING WITH GOD

When Aaron and all the Israelites saw Moses, his face was radiant, and they were afraid to come near him.
—Exodus 34:30

Throughout the story of the Exodus, we find two different portrayals of God. God repeatedly introduced Himself as the God who sees, the God who rescues, the God who comforts and heals, and the God who wants to dwell with the people. But God was also the God who was great, who defeated the Egyptians and their gods, the God whose appearance on the mountain was accompanied by thunder and lightning, the God whose presence would cause Moses to glow in such a way that the people were afraid of Him.

And both portrayals were true. Both are true. Intimate and transcendent, God is good, and God is great. God is our defender and comforter, whose presence with us calms our fears. But God is also overwhelmingly great, a terrifying Other who shakes the earth and all our assumptions and certitudes.

Bible students often talk about the contrast between the thundering God portrayed in the Old Testament and the seemingly friendlier face of God that we see in Jesus as described in the Gospels. But both these realities were present in Jesus. He could be transcendent—healing diseases, calming storms, transfiguration, and resurrection are some examples. But His transcendence was often veiled by His humanity. As Jesus said, "Anyone who has seen me has seen the Father" (John 14:9).

And it seems both these realities were also present in the God who heard the cries of the oppressed, brought plagues on the Egyptians, led as a pillar of fire, and thundered from the mountaintop, but who also fed the people with the dew each morning, wrote the commandments with His own finger, and spent time personally with Moses. So close was God's connection with Moses that he was even physically transformed—alarmingly so.

God is always both near and great, loving and awesome, with us and so far beyond us, today and eternally.

January 30

A PEOPLE CHANGED

"I am the Lord *your God, who brought you out of Egypt so that you would no longer be slaves to the Egyptians; I broke the bars of your yoke and enabled you to walk with heads held high."*

—Leviticus 26:13

An encounter with God changes people. I am sure you have met and heard the stories of such people. It is likely you have a story of encountering God in some way that changed the perspective and direction of your life. These are the stories of people who were oppressed or enslaved—physically, emotionally, or addictively—who now walk with their heads held high. They have been set free and transformed by the power of God.

This verse's reference to walking "with heads held high" speaks of more than merely being removed from the experience of slavery. This refers to the ongoing work of liberation that God worked among the Israelites during their time of wandering in the wilderness. Over time, they were liberated from an attitude of enslavement, given a new mindset, even a new worldview. Most significantly, they were given a new understanding of God. God was no longer absent or far off; He was involved in their history and their lives. And this was now the hope they had to share with the world around them.

Encounters with people who have encountered God change our understanding of Him. As well as being affected by our own experiences, we can share in the transformational experiences of others. Well-being researchers have found that our being happy can increase the happiness experienced by our friends' friends' friends—to three degrees of separation.* How much more so does God's influence in transforming our lives and changing our attitudes? And, then, even more so when we are intentional about telling our story of how God has set us free.

---

* Darren Morton, *Live More Happy* (Warburton, Victoria, Australia: Signs Publishing Company, 2017), 69.

A PEOPLE AFRAID

"As for those of you who are left, I will make their hearts so fearful in the lands of their enemies that the sound of a windblown leaf will put them to flight. They will run as though fleeing from the sword, and they will fall, even though no one is pursuing them."

—Leviticus 26:36

An encounter with God changes people—but not always positively. For those who so choose, particularly for those who stubbornly persist in their rejection of God, encountering God becomes a cause for terror. It causes extreme anxiety—even the sound of a leaf rattling in the wind can cause alarm. This was the same God who had set the Israelites free, but their freedom could be undone if they continued to reject His liberating goodness.

This was the kind of fear demonstrated when Adam heard God walking in the garden (see Genesis 3:8–10). A relationship that at one time had been loving was transformed into a fearful experience. Adam and Eve sought to escape even the sound of God's footsteps. This was the distortion that sin brought with it—the wounded relationship that would need to be healed and restored. This was the reality that God was warning the people of Israel against.

This relationship of fear was not God's intention or desire. Faced with the reality of an already broken and wounded humanity, God set out the consequences for the choices that each person—and, in this case, the nation collectively—would make. God was not coming to punish Adam and Eve in the garden; His mere presence caused their fear. He was pursuing them with a love in which they were no longer able to engage, nor could they return. God did not then and does not now want this experience for any of His people, thus His fearful warning. And even in this worst-case scenario, God assured them that He would still remember His promises and seek to restore them as His own (see Leviticus 26:44, 45).

February 1

AN ALTERNATIVE REPORT

"Only do not rebel against the LORD. And do not be afraid of the people of the land, because we will devour them. Their protection is gone, but the LORD is with us. Do not be afraid of them."

—Numbers 14:9

As the people of Israel neared the land that had been promised, Moses sent twelve men to survey the land across the Jordan River. Imagine the excitement of the people when they saw the samples of the produce of the land that these spies brought back with them! After the time they had spent traveling through the wilderness, this truly was a taste of the Promised Land.

But the report of ten of these spies was discouraging. They warned that the land was inhabited by fierce people, some of whom were giants, and all were stronger than the Israelites. "We seemed like grasshoppers in our own eyes," they said, "and we looked the same to them" (Numbers 13:33).

The minority report delivered by Joshua and Caleb gave an alternative view. Standing up to the dismay and rebellion simmering among the people, they reported that this was a good land and that if God wanted to give it to them, why should they be afraid?

Two groups of men had the same experiences, observed the same land and the same people, and even tasted the same food—yet they delivered contrasting reports. One group responded with fear; Joshua and Caleb responded with faith.

Of course, it is easier to get people excited by fear than by faith. But choosing fear has consequences. Had God not intervened, the crowd would have stoned Joshua and Caleb immediately (see Numbers 14:10). Because the people chose fear over faith on the verge of the land God had promised them, He sent them back to wander in the wilderness. The Lord said, "Not one of those who saw my glory and the signs I performed in Egypt and in the wilderness . . . will ever see the land I promised on oath to their ancestors. No one who has treated me with contempt will ever see it" (Numbers 14:22, 23).

February 2

CONFRONTING QUESTIONS

The Lord said to Moses, "Do not be afraid of him, for I have delivered him into your hands, along with his whole army and his land. Do to him what you did to Sihon king of the Amorites, who reigned in Heshbon."
—Numbers 21:34

I am uncomfortable with all the talk of conquest, wars, battles, and apparent genocide in the Bible's stories of the people of Israel moving into their new land. I struggle with the dispossession of the land's previous inhabitants in the name of God; it sounds too much like the colonization that stretched across most of the world in more recent centuries. I get even more upset by the explanations in the stories that God orchestrated these victories, which then led to mass slaughter. It seems yet another example—perhaps even the original example—of how religion has often been used in the worst ways across history, as a pretext, motivation, and rationale for conquering, oppressing, and exploiting other people and taking their lands.

Various explanations are given for these jarring stories. These kinds of narratives are common in the ancient world, it is said, in which gods compete with each other, with their respective powers being reflected in the fortunes of those who worship them. Or it is said that the stories ascribe human attitudes to God and simply use Him as an explanation or a way of narrating the nation's history. Another explanation is that God was using the Israelites as a means of exercising His judgment on wicked peoples. Or that in these battles, God was defending His people and establishing a holy nation that would be a means of working out His larger plans for our world.

Most likely, some or all of these explanations are true to varying degrees at different times. While the Bible is a special book, it leaves much incomplete, and there are many unanswered questions. Perhaps even in the midst of these questions, we can still hear the voice of God echoing from His repeated commands to Moses and the people, "Do not be afraid." When the forces—or the questions—confronting you feel overwhelming, "Do not be afraid."

February 3

WITHOUT FEAR OR FAVOR

"Do not show partiality in judging; hear both small and great alike. Do not be afraid of any man, for judgment belongs to God. Bring me any case too hard for you, and I will hear it."
—Deuteronomy 1:17

Often, the argument is made that we should not judge others because judgment belongs to God. But in appointing judges over the people of Israel, Moses used the opposite argument: Do not be afraid to judge *because* judgment belongs to God. Of course, Moses was not speaking about harsh, judgmental attitudes toward others—the kind of judging that Jesus warned against in the Sermon on the Mount (see Matthew 7:1–5). Rather, Moses was appointing leaders who would assist with administering justice among the people, settling disputes between them, and doing so in a way that was fair to all. Because God is a God of justice, His people were to be a nation of justice, and good leaders would be those who worked for justice.

So, because God is a God of justice, we should judge well and work for justice in those areas in which we have influence. As a later leader would be instructed by his mother, "Speak up for those who cannot speak for themselves, for the rights of all who are destitute. Speak up and judge fairly; defend the rights of the poor and needy" (Proverbs 31:8, 9). At its best, the system of laws and leadership given to the new nation of Israel would be a system that worked for justice—and, in this way, be a contrast to the oppressive systems of many of the surrounding nations.

This is also why promises of God's judgment throughout the Bible are good news to the poor, the exploited, and the downtrodden. Proclaiming God's judgment is a promise that wrongs will be made right, and that evil will be undone. Understanding that will change how we work to address injustice and oppression in our world today. Because God will judge, we will be unafraid to speak up for justice and to stand in solidarity with those who suffer.

LONG PROMISED

"See, the LORD your God has given you the land. Go up and take possession of it as the LORD, the God of your fathers, told you. Do not be afraid; do not be discouraged."

—Deuteronomy 1:21

The God of Abraham, Isaac, and Jacob had promised that their descendants would become a great nation and that they would inhabit the land of Canaan. Centuries later, the new nation of Israel stood on the edge of this land and looked across the Jordan River. After false starts, failed parenting, generations of nomadic living, and about 400 years of waiting, it hardly seemed possible.

Our human time spans are so short in the history of our world, much less in the eternity of our God. One of the key challenges of our faith is to live with an appreciation of God beyond ourselves, our times, and our horizon. We simply cannot fit all the promises and goodness of God within our human limitations. That is why an appreciation of history is so valuable and why our hopes for a future beyond our present lives are so necessary.

In its retelling of this story, Hebrews 11 points to each step of the Israelites' experience:

- "By faith Joseph, when his end was near, spoke about the exodus of the Israelites from Egypt" (verse 22).
- "By faith Moses' parents . . . were not afraid of the king's edict" (verse 23).
- "By faith [Moses] left Egypt, not fearing the king's anger" (verse 27).
- "By faith the people passed through the Red Sea as on dry land" (verse 29).

Many times, when they were tempted to surrender to fear and discouragement, the people in this many-generational story chose faith rather than fear.

It is not a perfect lineage, but it is a long story that moves forward whenever people choose faith rather than fear. And it is directed by a God who always has a longer view than we do and whose promises we can trust.

February 5

EXCEPT AS WE SHALL FORGET

Then I said to you, "Do not be terrified; do not be afraid of them. The LORD your God, who is going before you, will fight for you, as he did for you in Egypt, before your very eyes, and in the desert. There you saw how the LORD your God carried you, as a father carries his son, all the way you went until you reached this place."

—Deuteronomy 1:29–31

For good reason, the following is a favorite quotation for many Seventh-day Adventists. "In reviewing our past history, having traveled over every step of advance to our present standing, I can say, Praise God! As I see what the Lord has wrought, I am filled with astonishment, and with confidence in Christ as leader. We have nothing to fear for the future, except as we shall forget the way the Lord has led us, and His teaching in our past history."*

Remembering and reviewing is a principle that echoes through the Bible's stories. In the regular feasts, festivals, and holy days, God established a calendar in which the stories of His liberation and redemption would be retold from week to week, year to year, and generation to generation.

But, we also see in Deuteronomy 1 how things went wrong when the people forgot. Frightened by the reports of the giants in the land of Canaan, they forgot how God had rescued them from slavery in Egypt, the most powerful nation in the region at the time. Thus, the book of Deuteronomy is Moses' retelling of this story.

Among God's people, there is always a need for historians and storytellers to mine the experiences and teachings of our past for both their lessons for today and courage for the future. And we are called to be such storytellers—in our lives and families, as well as in our churches and communities.

---

* Ellen G. White, *Life Sketches of Ellen G. White* (Mountain View, CA: Pacific Press®, 1915), 196.

February 6

TO ANOTHER GENERATION

"Do not be afraid of them; the LORD your God himself will fight for you."

—Deuteronomy 3:22

Nearing the end of his life, Moses knew he had to pass leadership to the next generation. Regretfully, he had to leave his task of leading the Israelite people into their new land unfinished. Good leadership knows when it is time to let go and pass it on to the next generation. It celebrates what has been achieved but acknowledges that there is always more to do and that, building on what has been achieved, the next leaders will have opportunities beyond those of the current leader.

With this in mind, it is natural that leaders who have invested so much in a task, community, or organization want to ensure that the ongoing work will be in safe hands. Joshua "had been Moses' aide since youth" (Numbers 11:28) and had led Israel into battle against its enemies on a number of occasions. Even at risk to himself, Joshua had proved his faithfulness and courage, particularly in the minority report he brought back as one of the twelve spies sent across the river into the land of Canaan. Now Moses gave his final commands and prepared himself to hand over leadership to Joshua.

Moses wanted Joshua to know the ultimate Source of any success that he had achieved and any victories the people had enjoyed under his leadership. Even though Moses had worked hard leading the people for more than forty years, it had always been God who had truly led. It was He who had rescued the people from Egypt, and He had fought all their battles since. This was the foundational understanding that Joshua would need for his new role, as it is for all faithful leaders. Moses' unfinished task, as well as Joshua's new responsibilities, would be in safe hands because they were always in God's hands.

February 7

OUR GREAT AND AWESOME GOD

"Do not be terrified by them, for the LORD your God, who is among you, is a great and awesome God."

—Deuteronomy 7:21

When reading the Bible, context is important. What is the bigger picture that this is part of? Where does this fit in the Bible's larger story? Who is speaking? To whom are they speaking? In this case, Moses was giving his final exhortation to the people he had led for decades—from Egypt to Canaan. It was an important message for the people as they prepared to cross the Jordan River and for Moses to no longer be with them. Moses assured them that they had no need to be afraid because their great and awesome God would still be with them.

Again and again, Moses reminded them not only of their history but of how they had seen and experienced God in their own lives. "Do not be afraid of them; remember well what the LORD your God did to Pharaoh and to all Egypt. You saw with your own eyes the great trials, the signs and wonders, the mighty hand and outstretched arm, with which the LORD your God brought you out" (Deuteronomy 7:18, 19).

So, how might Moses address us if he had the opportunity? I am sure he would be eager to tell the stories of how he had seen God act. But he would also urge us to remember and retell the stories of how God has acted in each of our lives, in our families, and in the more recent history of our church. Then he would remind us that our God—the God both he and we have encountered—is still great and awesome and that He is with us still. And with that great and awesome God among us, why would we be afraid of anyone or anything that might attack or challenge us?

February 8

ARGUING WITH GOD

"I feared the anger and wrath of the Lord, for he was angry enough with you to destroy you. But again the Lord listened to me."
—Deuteronomy 9:19

In the Bible stories, arguing with God seems to be one of the common experiences of those who spoke directly with God. Abraham argued with God in an extended negotiation about the fate of Sodom and Gomorrah (see Genesis 18:16–33). Jacob wrestled with God Himself, both physically and spiritually, it seems (see Genesis 32:22–32). Moses argued with God about His call to return to Egypt and lead the Israelites out of slavery (see Exodus 4:1–17). Arguing with God seems to be an important element of a healthy and fearless relationship between God and His people.

But perhaps more important are the many times that Moses interceded with God on behalf of the people of Israel. Moses recalled their idolatry with the golden calf soon after they had encountered God at Mount Sinai when He gave them the Ten Commandments (see Deuteronomy 9:7–13). "You also made the Lord angry at Taberah, at Massah and at Kibroth Hattaavah," Moses continued. "You have been rebellious against the Lord ever since I have known you" (Deuteronomy 9:22, 24).

On each occasion, God's anger threatened to destroy the people. And on each occasion, despite Moses' own anger and frustration and God's offer to make a nation of Moses and his family, Moses argued with God, appealing to His goodness and mercy, and reminding Him that these were *His* people (see Deuteronomy 9:25–29). On each occasion, God changed His mind and withdrew His threats.

A relationship with God includes arguing with Him, voicing our questions and disappointments, appealing to His love and grace, and advocating for others and for our world. It seems a relationship with God gives Him more options.

February 9

FALSE PROPHETS

"If what a prophet proclaims in the name of the Lord does not take place or come true, that is a message the Lord has not spoken. That prophet has spoken presumptuously. Do not be alarmed."

—Deuteronomy 18:22

History is littered with prophets of all kinds—some divinely inspired, some insightful, some deluded or misguided, some downright fraudulent. For those longing to hear from God or simply to gain some insight into a seemingly uncertain future, the words of a prophet can be intriguing, even alluring. Moses accurately predicted that there would continue to be prophets among God's people, both true and false. As did Jesus, urging both the surety of prophecy and that there would be false prophets all the way to the end of time (see Matthew 24:24).

Today, it seems we have more aspiring prophets than ever. Anyone can start an online page, channel, or site and put any kind of message out into the world. Not only can this easily gain viewers and followers, but such an online presence can also be a way of making money through supporter donations. The more sensational, alarming, and critical voices—those that most exploit anger and stoke fear—are the ones that inevitably attract the most attention, and they are amplified by the algorithms of social media. For many of them, there is almost no filter and little accountability. Online and TV preachers and websites that specialize in conspiracies and peddle fear receive far more attention than their messages deserve, even in Adventist circles.

Both Moses and Jesus predicted the work of false prophets, providing evidence of their prophetic inspiration. But Moses also offered a simple test for the claims of would-be prophets or interpreters of prophecy: If what they predict does not come true, ignore them and "do not be afraid of them." Practice discernment, using Jesus' teachings and the Bible as a whole. Hold preachers and "prophets" accountable for the irresponsible and irrational things they say, and do not support "ministries" that exploit people's fears. Instead, seek out, support, and share preachers and messages who point us to Jesus and to serving others and that offer hope.

WEIGHING THE ODDS

"When you go to war against your enemies and see horses and chariots and an army greater than yours, do not be afraid of them, because the Lord *your God, who brought you up out of Egypt, will be with you."*
—Deuteronomy 20:1

When Jesus used a simple parable to prompt His followers to think about the costs of the choices that we make, He made a lot of sense. He said, "Suppose a king is about to go to war against another king. Will he not first sit down and consider whether he is able with ten thousand men to oppose the one coming against him with twenty thousand?" (Luke 14:31). In our everyday human terms, that makes sense. For the point that Jesus was making—that we should consider the costs of following Him before we choose to become His disciples—it makes sense.

But in Moses' understanding of what it means to have "God with us"—an understanding based on his many years of experience leading the people of Israel through the wilderness and against various armies—these are not the odds that God's people should consider when confronting an enemy or an obstacle. By Moses' reckoning, the technology, power, and people working *against* us are never a match for the God who is working *with* us—or, more correctly, the God with whom we are working.

In Jesus' example, He suggested that if the odds seemed overwhelming, the king would take the prudent step of seeking to negotiate a peaceful resolution "while the other [king's army] is still a long way off" (Luke 14:32). Humanly speaking, there is wisdom in such a response. Yet to the people of God, Moses would say, "Do not be afraid. The God who has rescued you in the past will continue to be with you. However unlikely victory might seem, and however much you are tempted to feel overwhelmed, do not be afraid." There is courage and wisdom in this response when we have chosen to be on God's side.

February 11

WHAT THE PRIEST SHALL SAY

"When you are about to go into battle, the priest shall come forward and address the army. He shall say: 'Hear, O Israel, today you are going into battle against your enemies. Do not be fainthearted or afraid; do not be terrified or give way to panic before them. For the Lord *your God is the one who goes with you to fight for you against your enemies to give you victory.' "*
—Deuteronomy 20:2–4

Deuteronomy 20 gives a fascinating insight into the war culture of the people of Israel. It sets out various speeches required from different leaders who would address those soon marching out to battle. One might imagine the solemn ceremonies that could accompany these speeches as the soldiers prepared for battle. An important observation is the seriousness with which war was undertaken, talked about, and embarked upon. A key message is, "Do not be afraid," even when setting out on such a grim assignment.

But what if we applied this same logic and commitment to the task of making peace, as Jesus taught (see Matthew 5:9)? Rarely has humanity invested in nonviolence or peacemaking at anything like the scale we have invested in war, violence, and their macabre industries and technologies. Perhaps, borrowing a phrase from philosopher William James, this calls for a personal and social investment in nonviolence with the "moral equivalence of war," meaning that those who seek peace, justice, and freedom through nonviolence must be equally prepared to live, invest, train, and die for the cause as their militaristic counterparts.*

Imagine if we embarked on peacemaking with the same kind of heroic self-sacrifice, comradeship, and discipline that are lauded on the battlefield. Again, the key message is "Do not be afraid." In the name of Jesus, let us take this assignment seriously, stepping out into our communities and our world with courage, hope, and love, knowing that our God is with us, and He will be victorious.

---

* See Ronald J. Sider, *Nonviolent Action: What Christian Ethics Demands but Most Christians Have Never Really Tried* (Grand Rapids, MI: Brazos Press, 2015), 175–177.

February 12

SEND THE AFRAID HOME

Then the officers shall add, "Is anyone afraid or fainthearted? Let him go home so that his fellow soldiers will not become disheartened too."
—Deuteronomy 20:8

Many of our parents warned us to be careful about the people we might choose to spend time with. As someone who had converted to the Christian faith and had written much on this process, as well as defended and explained the faith to wide audiences, it seems C. S. Lewis would have agreed: "The society of unbelievers makes Faith harder even when they are people whose opinions on any other subject are known to be worthless."* We need to be careful not to cut ourselves off from neighbors and friends who believe differently from us, but we also need to be conscious of the influence that time spent with others can have on our own thinking and believing.

This would be an important reason why the officers in the army of the Israelites would invite those who were afraid to return home as they were about to go into battle. One frightened soldier would discourage their fellow soldiers, and the ripple effect could undermine the courage of the entire army.

Again, we should not be cut off from people around us, but what about those people who are always fearful, who seem to spread fear wherever they go, whether in personal interactions and conversations or by what they share online? It is difficult to be courageous if we regularly hear and see the fears of others. It seems both Moses and Lewis would counsel discernment in the time and attention we give to the fearful and the fearmongers among us, whether in battle or in our everyday lives of faith. Perhaps we can offer them, instead, the message of the priest: "Do not be afraid. God is with us."

* C. S. Lewis, "Religion: Reality or Substitute?" *Christian Reflections* (London: Fount, 1981), 62.

February 13

CHOOSING FEAR?

"Among those nations you will find no repose, no resting place for the sole of your foot. There the LORD will give you an anxious mind, eyes weary with longing, and a despairing heart. You will live in constant suspense, filled with dread both night and day, never sure of your life."

—Deuteronomy 28:65, 66

Nearing the end of his transcendent summary of the Israelites' experiences and their possibilities as the people of God, Moses was blunt in setting out two alternative futures for the people. Obedience to God and His ways would bring blessings; disobedience would be a curse to them. This equation is not always obvious in our unjust world. The psalmists and others throughout the Bible repeatedly lamented the fact that evil people seemed to prosper while good people were suffering. But there is an underlying truth to this formulation that Moses and the witness of the Bible as a whole insisted upon.

This is the pattern we saw in the Garden of Eden as the elemental human condition. When humanity chooses to disobey God, relationships are broken, and fear is the result. This outcome is not always immediate, but it is inevitable. While Moses attributed this anxiety, despair, and dread to the judgments of God, they could as easily be described as consequences of the broken relationships described in Genesis 3. Moses concluded his exhortation by telling the people that the commands of God that he passed on to the people "are not just idle words for you—they are your life" (Deuteronomy 32:47). Stubbornly choosing against God leads to the disordering of creation, of ourselves and all our relationships, and eventually brings suffering and sorrow, despair and dread.

But there was good news, too, in Moses' dire warnings. This was always a choice for the people to make. It did not have to be this way. Tragically, many of Moses's warnings would be fulfilled in the future history of the Israelite nation, but even then, God was still with them. God was merciful, and He would seek to heal and restore.

February 14

EVER PRESENT

"Be strong and courageous. Do not be afraid or terrified because of them, for the Lord *your God goes with you; he will never leave you nor forsake you."*
—Deuteronomy 31:6

Our lives are ordered by the priorities we choose—or those that are forced upon us when we are not allowed to choose. When we do have the capacity to choose, the best choices are those that matter the most. Such was the choice set out for the Israelites on the verge of entering their promised land. Would they be afraid of the people God had already told them would be defeated? Or would they choose courage, trusting their God, who promised to be with them forever?

When we understand these vastly different timelines—the present vs. forever—it would seem absurd to give greater priority to temporary fears rather than to God's strong and enduring presence. But the human reality is that it is always easier for us to grasp and instinctively respond to what we can see and experience with our human sensibilities than to the often less tangible presence and promises of God. In the moment, a frightening headline, an alarming diagnosis, a tragic disappointment, or sorrow can feel more real to us than everything we claim to know about God. At such times, the call to "be strong and courageous" is a call to faith. It is not about what we can see or feel. This call to faith does not diminish the importance or reality of the fear or heartbreak with which we are confronted; it takes them as seriously as they truly are. But somehow, this call to faithful courage is always the larger priority, the choice that matters most.

When God goes with us, we can confront the enemies, extremities, and uncertainties of our lives without fear. And we can meet our fears without being overwhelmed. We have different priorities that shape our choices and how we respond to the world around us.

February 15

TAKING ON THE TO-DO LIST

Then Moses summoned Joshua and said to him in the presence of all Israel, "Be strong and courageous, for you must go with this people into the land that the Lord swore to their forefathers to give them, and you must divide it among them as their inheritance. The Lord himself goes before you and will be with you; he will never leave you nor forsake you. Do not be afraid; do not be discouraged."

—Deuteronomy 31:7, 8

The poignancy of Moses' last words, witnessed by all the people of Israel, was made more urgent by the task being entrusted to Joshua. And like so many of our roles in life, Joshua's task was not one but multiple responsibilities to different people or groups with different expectations and demands. Not only was he to take over from Moses as leader of the people, but it would be his task to lead them in conquering the new land, increasing the difficulty of this already difficult leadership task. Then, it would be Joshua's role to divide up the land "as their inheritance," meaning that the division of the land would set up the new nation for generations. This would inevitably be a thankless undertaking with much potential for conflict and resentment. In all of this, Joshua was charged with fulfilling the promises received and carried by the people from centuries earlier, adding a weight of history and destiny to his burdens.

There seemed to be so many ways in which Joshua could fail, so many reasons for him to undertake such a role with reluctance and fear. But Moses' command to lead with strength and courage came with the weight of Moses' own leadership experience. He could testify to the difference that the presence and prescience of God make to such a weighty role. So, his words were a gift to Joshua, offering the ultimate qualification for taking on such a complicated and contested list of assignments.

February 16

THEN GOD COMMANDED IT

The L*ORD* *gave this command to Joshua son of Nun:*
"Be strong and courageous, for you will bring the Israelites into the land I promised them on oath, and I myself will be with you."
—Deuteronomy 31:23

At the end of Moses' long recap of the history of the people of Israel—God's rescue of them from slavery in the land of Egypt and their journeys through the wilderness, along with the laws of their new nation and the consequences of obedience and disobedience—God spoke. He spoke first to Moses, confirming what He had warned the people about, and then He spoke briefly to Joshua, commissioning him to lead the people.

Moses had urged Joshua to be strong and courageous, assuring him that God would go before him and be with him. But now God *commanded* it! But does it work to command someone to be courageous? The answer to this question depends on whether we understand courage as a feeling or a choice. Of course, it is good to feel courage when facing danger or taking on a daunting task. We can be trained—even train ourselves—to quiet our fears and step forward boldly. But often courage means not the absence of fear but doing what needs to be done despite our fears.

As such, courage is better understood as a choice. Whatever our feelings in response to our circumstances or responsibilities, we can choose to respond in a way that is not dictated or directed by our fear. This can be challenging. Fear is real, which is why courage is presented so many times as a command when God speaks to His people in the Bible stories. But our choice is also real, which is why courage is presented as a command. How much more so when the God who commands our courage is also the God who promises His presence.

February 17

FULFILLING PROMISES

"Be strong and courageous, because you will lead these people to inherit the land I swore to their ancestors to give them."

—Joshua 1:6

As the people of Israel approached the lands promised to their ancestors, Moses reminded them of those promises, covenants, and oaths sworn by God. It was not an accident that the people found themselves on the borders of Canaan; it was the fulfillment of God's promises that had been passed down and renewed from generation to generation. As Joshua assumed leadership after Moses' death, God made a specific point of reminding him again of these promises and that, together with God's presence with His people, they were the foundation for faith and courage.

But God's promises were not an excuse for passivity. They were not an express lane into the Promised Land. God made it clear that His promises were to be paired with human agency, that there was work to be done, and that claiming the land that He "swore to their ancestors to give them" would require strength and courage. Indeed, taking God's promises seriously meant stepping into danger, facing uncertainties, and playing their part in actually creating the promised reality—always in partnership with God.

This dynamic of faithful living was echoed to the early Christian believers: "We want each of you to show this same diligence to the very end, so that what you hope for may be fully realized. We do not want you to become lazy, but to imitate those who through faith and patience inherit what has been promised" (Hebrews 6:11, 12). As we accept the promises of God, the covenants that He made with our spiritual ancestors, we also accept a role in making them a reality and moving them toward fulfillment. And this work will require strength and courage.

February 18

GOODNESS REQUIRES COURAGE

"Be strong and very courageous. Be careful to obey all the law my servant Moses gave you; do not turn from it to the right or to the left, that you may be successful wherever you go."

—Joshua 1:7

God's message to Joshua as he began his leadership repeated the command to "be strong and courageous" a number of times, each time with a different emphasis that expands our understanding of courage and fear. In most English translations, the variation in verse 7 is that Joshua was commanded to "be strong and *very* courageous." This added emphasis was paired with the instruction to obey the law Moses had passed on to him and the people.

To do what is right requires courage. "Courage is not simply *one* of the virtues, but the form of every virtue at the testing point, which means, at the point of highest reality."* When we are tempted to take shortcuts or look for easier options, to compromise what we know to be right, or to bend the truth, particularly when sticking to what we know we ought to do will cost us in some way, doing what is right demands courage; it demand that we be *very* courageous. Any real goodness requires real courage.

God assured Joshua that this might not always be the easiest path, but it was the way to true success. Being successful is doing what is right, even when it might not look or feel like success. In a world with so many temptations and distractions, in a role with so many critics and challenges, Joshua could be true to God and to himself only with courage and strength. But God was also offering Himself and His promises as the source of that courage. It's the same offer He makes to us.

* C. S. Lewis, *The Screwtape Letters* (London: Fount, 1998), 115.

February 19

COURAGE—OR DISCOURAGED?

"Have I not commanded you? Be strong and courageous. Do not be afraid; do not be discouraged, for the L*ORD* *your God will be with you wherever you go."*

—Joshua 1:9

We often think of fear as an immediate response to a threat or danger. As such, it can be more of an instinctive reaction rather than a well-thought-out response, and such fear often dissipates quickly. But fear can become chronic. It can be based on ongoing threats or danger, but it can also become an attitude to life, its perils, and the world around us. If fear is a perpetual, longer-term state of being, it will damage our physical and emotional well-being in serious ways.

Perhaps a lesser but no less chronic form of fear is discouragement. While not so immediately severe, discouragement is the destructive grind of our lives and our world that wears on our hearts, minds, and bodies, eroding our faith, hope, and love.

God's "Do not be afraids" are applicable to both our immediate fears and longer-term discouragement, wherever we are and wherever we go. This is the grace God offers to all, a standing invitation to walk with us through all our lives. "The grace of God means something like: Here is your life. . . . Here is the world. Beautiful and terrible things will happen. Don't be afraid. I am with you. Nothing can ever separate us. It's for you I created the universe. I love you."*

As they were for Joshua, God's instructions, promises, and presence are the foundation for life-long faithfulness amid the beautiful and the terrible things. But there are also so many days in between on which God's grace is quietly present, offering courage in place of discouragement.

* Frederick Buechner, *Wishful Thinking: A Seeker's ABC* (New York: HarperCollins, 1993), 39.

February 20

THE PEOPLE'S RESPONSE

"Whoever rebels against your word and does not obey it, whatever you may command them, will be put to death. Only be strong and courageous!"
—Joshua 1:18

Reading this verse extracted from its context—as above—might lead to some troubling conclusions. This was not Joshua promising to grimly defend the name and word of God with violence as "necessary." Neither was this God giving Joshua free rein to invoke His name in enforcing a potentially tyrannical rule. Instead, this was the people—particularly the people of the tribes of Reuben, Gad, and Manasseh—committing to follow Joshua across the river and into the Promised Land.

Leadership is a perennially popular topic in publishing, conferences, workshops, and other church training and discussion. We are all leaders in our own ways and in our particular spheres of influence. But we should also spend more time talking and thinking about what it means to follow well. As much as we focus on and value godly leadership, we should also learn and commit to faithful followership.

It is not about the people merely serving the needs or demands of the leader. Nor should a leader be exploited only for what he or she can offer to those they lead. The dynamics of healthy leadership will always include mutual commitment and will support the community as a whole in achieving their goals together.

In doing this, we will discover that good followers can make their leaders better and encourage them to live up to the calling God has given them. As we see in this story, the response of the people committing to follow and support Joshua echoed the command of God: "Be strong and courageous." They recognized that God would be with Joshua as He had been with Moses, and the people's commitment to God was expressed in their support of Joshua and the task to which God had called all of them.

February 21

CROSSING THE RIVER

"When you see the ark of the covenant of the LORD your God, and the Levitical priests carrying it, you are to move out from your positions and follow it. Then you will know which way to go, since you have never been this way before."

—Joshua 3:3, 4

Crossing the Jordan River was a deeply symbolic moment for the long-wandering people of Israel, but it was also something much more than that. They had stood on the banks of this river previously, but they had turned away, afraid of the challenges they might face on the other side and not trusting that God would be with them. But now they were really crossing into their long-promised Promised Land. They had never been this way before, but they knew now that God was leading them.

Only a small number of the people had been part of that group of newly freed slaves who had crossed the Red Sea, but God gave this new generation their own experience of His miraculous intervention. Following God's instructions, the priest carrying the ark of the covenant, followed by all the people over the course of that day, stepped into the dry bed of the Jordan River at the time of year when it was flooding (see Joshua 3:15–17). If they needed it made more clear, Joshua pointed out to the people that this was a sign "that the living God is among you" (Joshua 3:10).

And this experience was to be remembered. A representative of each tribe was to take a large stone from the riverbed, which would then be used to build a memorial as a cue for retelling the story. "In the future when your descendants ask their parents, 'What do these stones mean?' tell them, 'Israel crossed the Jordan on dry ground.' . . . He did this so that all the peoples of the earth might know that the hand of the LORD is powerful and so that you might always fear the LORD your God" (Joshua 4:21–24).

February 22

DEFEATED BY FEAR

Now when all the Amorite kings west of the Jordan and all the Canaanite kings along the coast heard how the LORD had dried up the Jordan before the Israelites until they had crossed over, their hearts melted in fear and they no longer had the courage to face the Israelites.

—Joshua 5:1

The arrival of the people of Israel was not unnoticed by the people of the land. This report regarding the Amorite and Canaanite kings echoes the encounter that the Israelite spies had with Rahab in Jericho. "I know that the LORD has given you this land and that a great fear of you has fallen on us, so that all who live in this country are melting in fear because of you," Rahab told the spies, recounting how God had led them and fought for them in their journey from Egypt. "When we heard of it, our hearts melted and everyone's courage failed because of you, for the LORD your God is God in heaven above and on the earth below" (Joshua 2:9–11).

Such is the power of fear that the people of Canaan were defeated before any battles were fought. The power of God was so evident that the stories of what He had done were sufficient for the next battles. For the people God was with, remembering what God had done was key to facing the future with courage. For those who did not know this God, they had a choice to make. Rahab sought safety for her family, even if she did not fully understand this new God. For the kings who would not relinquish their power or lands, their fear led them to despair and defeat. While the power and presence of God can be daunting for those who seek to walk with Him, it is overwhelming for those who would stand opposed. The fear is real, but how we respond to it makes all the difference.

February 23

RETURNING TO THE SCENE OF DEFEAT

Then the Lord *said to Joshua, "Do not be afraid; do not be discouraged. Take the whole army with you, and go up and attack Ai. For I have delivered into your hands the king of Ai, his people, his city and his land."*

—Joshua 8:1

It takes a particular kind of courage to return to a place or experience of defeat. Brimming with confidence after "their" siege of the city of Jericho and "their" remarkable victory, the people of Israel had anticipated that the town of Ai would be just as easy. The spies that they sent to this neighboring town came back with exuberance, urging Joshua that only a few thousand soldiers would make short work of their defenses (see Joshua 7:2, 3). They forgot that it was God who was really fighting their battles. They did not pause to seek His guidance, and they underestimated the importance of the commands God had given. And the people of the "easy target" of Ai beat them soundly. "They chased the Israelites from the city gate as far as the stone quarries and struck them down on the slopes. At this the hearts of the people melted in fear and became like water" (Joshua 7:5).

The people did the right thing in turning back to God for an explanation. They learned they had to account for Achan's sin. But they also had to overcome their fear and return to the place of their defeat. They made some changes, adjusting their self-confident attitude—a painful defeat will often help us with that—and changed their strategy, this time taking with them ten times the number of soldiers as before to take the same small town. But it was more than a strategic shift; God again gave them the command to not let their fear hold them back. And overcoming their fear was their first victory in this battle.

February 24

GATHERING OPPOSITION

The Lord said to Joshua, "Do not be afraid of them; I have given them into your hand. Not one of them will be able to withstand you."
—Joshua 10:8

As the people of Israel continued their march across the land, their successes brought a unity of desperation to the groups of people, tribes, and nations that were being displaced. Five kings in the south united their armies (see Joshua 10:5). Then the nations of the north brought together "all their troops and a large number of horses and chariots—a huge army, as numerous as the sand on the seashore" (Joshua 11:4). Whatever conflicts existed between these diverse peoples and their kings, they were put aside in their common opposition to the advance of the people of Israel.

If the Israelites had been confronted by these large armies when they first crossed the Jordan River, they might well have melted away themselves. But their courage grew with successive smaller victories and their growing experience, as did their trust in God. Facing these increasing numbers and increasing desperation, God's message was the same: "Do not be afraid of them" (see also Joshua 11:6). Against the southern armies, God caused confusion among these armies, then sent a severe hailstorm and caused the sun to stand still to allow the battle to continue. In the north, the battle was summarized: "The Lord gave them into the hand of Israel" (Joshua 11:8).

Although these were daunting armies, Israel's two victories were decisive in bringing an end to the military campaign sooner than might have otherwise been possible. While the kings conspired in fierce opposition to the Israelites, their unity meant they were all defeated together, and the plan that God had outlined to both Moses and Joshua was completed. This was a significant milestone in the Bible story. The land was given to the people as had been promised to their ancestors centuries before, and "then the land had rest from war" (Joshua 11:23).

February 25

SAID THE ANGEL

The Lord *said to him, "Peace!*
Do not be afraid. You are not going to die."
—Judges 6:23

Some years ago, I was part of a team leading a camp program for young people. Reflecting on the dominance of fear in our world, we chose "Do not be afraid" as our theme for the week. Among our team, we developed an extra element to this phrase so that every time someone would say "Do not be afraid," someone else would respond with ". . . said the angel."

Often in the Bible stories, this is the next phrase because almost every time an angel appeared to someone, the angel first had to help that startled person get over their fright. But the fear came from more than just the fact that angels often appeared in dramatic and radiant forms. There was more to this message than momentary fear. This was a more existential message, an encounter between God and a human being that crossed the divide of their broken relationship, as well as speaking to the broader circumstances of that character and the daunting task that the angel's message would give them.

In Gideon's experience, the "Do not be afraid" came at the end of his interaction with the angel. The angel appeared to Gideon while he was threshing grain in secret and greeted him as "mighty warrior," assuring him that God was with him despite appearances (Judges 6:12). Argument, assignment, and then more argument was followed by Gideon offering food to this mysterious messenger. Then the angel touched the food. It burst into flames and he disappeared. With the angel gone and Gideon in shock, God's voice brought the reassurance, "Do not be afraid" with all its meanings: Do not be afraid of what you have just experienced. Do not be afraid of the task you have been given. Do not be afraid of the Midianites and their oppression of your people. Do not be afraid of your lowly place in your family. Do not be afraid of what you have to do next. Do not be afraid of Me.

February 26

TOO MANY MEN?

The Lord *said to Gideon, "You have too many men. I cannot deliver Midian into their hands, or Israel would boast against me, 'My own strength has saved me.' Now announce to the army, 'Anyone who trembles with fear may turn back and leave Mount Gilead.' " So twenty-two thousand men left, while ten thousand remained.*

—Judges 7:2, 3

At least three nations had combined their armies and crossed the Jordan River to attack the people of Israel. Their armies would be described as settling in the valley of Jezreel "thick as locusts. Their camels could no more be counted than the sand on the seashore" (Judges 7:12).

In response, Gideon sounded the ram's horn and sent messages to the surrounding tribes of Israel "so that they too went up to meet them" (Judges 6:35). While the Israelites might have still felt outnumbered, it is easy to imagine Gideon's confidence growing as the groups from each of the tribes and clans marched into the camp and the Israelite army assembled.

It took God's prompting to remind Gideon of the instruction given to Moses that the officer leading the army of Israel should announce that "anyone afraid or fainthearted" should return to their homes (see Deuteronomy 20:8). But God urged Gideon that this battle was not about numbers; if it were, the army of Israel would always be outnumbered. Instead, the soldiers who remained would need to fully place their trust in God's strength and His presence with them.

It is easy to imagine Gideon's confidence being tested as his army melted away. More than 20,000 men left that day, and more were sent home after God tested them further, leaving only 300 of the original 32,000. Less than one percent seemed to be enough for God's plan. Counter-intuitively, God urged that 300 men who were forced to rely fully on Him, having no reasonable expectation of victory apart from His intervention, were a greater army than 30,000 or more who thought their numbers and their own strength might be enough.

February 27

IF YOU ARE AFRAID . . .

"If you are afraid to attack, go down to the camp with your servant Purah and listen to what they are saying. Afterward, you will be encouraged to attack the camp." So he and Purah his servant went down to the outposts of the camp.

—Judges 7:10, 11

From his first arguments with the angel, through the wet-and-dry fleeces, and the army that grew and then shrank dramatically, Gideon's responses to the task to which God was calling him ranged from resistance to uncertainty—and not much beyond that. But God persisted with him. God did not dismiss his fears or lose patience with his questions and objections. He continued to respond to Gideon's requests for yet another sign and continued giving him assurances of His presence and power.

Now, on the eve of battle, God offered yet another opportunity for reassurance—and another reminder that this really was His battle after all. Perhaps God's invitation was a little tongue-in-cheek: "If you are afraid . . ." God had more evidence of Gideon's fears than Gideon had of God's trustworthiness. He knew Gideon still had questions and doubts, but He had Gideon listen in on the fears and uncertainties to be found among the army that had assembled against them. He put the words into the mouth of one of these soldiers: "God has given the Midianites and the whole camp into his hands" (Judges 7:14).

This would not only encourage Gideon and his small army but would also be the means by which the battle would be won. Gideon's men surrounded the camp, blowing trumpets, smashing pitchers, holding their torches high, and shouting into the night. The fears of the enemy were transformed into panic among their armies, who turned on each other and ran for their lives. On this battlefield, the difference between the two armies was not the unequal numbers but the unequal fears—and it was God who had shifted that balance.

February 28

THE EVER-GRACIOUS GOD

"Do not be afraid," Samuel replied. "You have done all this evil; yet do not turn away from the Lord*, but serve the* Lord *with all your heart."*
—1 Samuel 12:20

It was never God's intention that the people of Israel would have a king. The leaders God had appointed had not wielded king-like power. When the people came to the aging Samuel, who had served as a priest, prophet, and judge, and asked him to "appoint a king to lead us, such as all the other nations have" (1 Samuel 8:5), both Samuel and God were offended. But it was God who claimed the greater anger. He assured Samuel that "it is not you they have rejected, but they have rejected me as their king" (1 Samuel 8:7).

Samuel warned them about what they were doing and predicted the dangers that a king would bring—all of which were fulfilled within three generations. Nonetheless, acceding to their request and with God's guidance, Samuel appointed Saul as the first king of Israel and then gave a farewell speech to the people of Israel. He recounted his lifelong service for the people and how God had led them over centuries, urging them to continue to follow and obey even with a newly installed king. It was a speech punctuated by thunder and a rainstorm—and the people got the point, crying out in fear and asking Samuel to pray for them.

Samuel reminded them that God had always been gracious to them and that He would continue to be gracious, even when their unfaithfulness brought consequences. And Samuel took this same gracious responsibility on himself: "As for me, far be it from me that I should sin against the Lord by failing to pray for you. And I will teach you the way that is good and right. But be sure to fear the Lord and serve him faithfully with all your heart; consider what great things he has done for you" (1 Samuel 12:23, 24).

March 1

A FRIGHTENED LEADER

Then Saul said to Samuel, "I have sinned. I violated the Lord*'s command and your instructions. I was afraid of the people and so I gave in to them."*
—1 Samuel 15:24

Fear marked the life and reign of Saul, the first king of Israel. From the day on which he was proclaimed king, when he was found hiding among the supplies (see 1 Samuel 10:22), to his ongoing struggle with "a tormenting spirit that filled him with depression and fear" (1 Samuel 16:14, NLT), from his relentless pursuit of David to his tragic death in battle, Saul struggled with a sense of inadequacy. While he did lead the army of Israel to victory on a number of occasions, on the whole, his temptations to uncertainty and fear did not work well for him as a leader or for the nation he was trying to lead.

Samuel—and God—persisted with him, encouraging him to be more steadfast in his calling and faithfulness. They urged that God had chosen him to be king, and that should be sufficient grounding for him to become a true leader. "Although you were once small in your own eyes, did you not become the head of the tribes of Israel?" (1 Samuel 15:17). But by this time, when Saul confessed that his fearfulness included fear of the men he was trying to lead, Samuel made clear to him that God was already looking for someone else to be the next king—which probably didn't help Saul with his insecurities, self-doubt, and despair.

Had God made a mistake in choosing Saul to be king? He had moments of victory, of being connected and committed to God, and of strong leadership. But it seems Saul chose to place his trust—more correctly, his lack of trust—in himself rather than in the God who would have helped him grow in the leadership role He had given him.

MORE THAN A DAVID-AND-GOLIATH CLICHÉ

David said to Saul, "Let no one lose heart on account of this Philistine; your servant will go and fight him."
—1 Samuel 17:32

The story of David and Goliath is so well known that it has become a cliché, an overused metaphor of a small person or group of people, an underdog, taking on a much larger opponent, a corporation, a government, or a superstar team. And the expression begins to lose its punch when we also assume that the story usually ends with a seemingly unlikely victory. It can feel like the unlikely outcome was actually expected.

But that was not how the story was originally told. The story opens with extensive and detailed descriptions of the size, weight, armaments, attitude, and defiant challenge of the giant champion of the Philistines (see 1 Samuel 17:4–10). The real impact of the phenomenon that was Goliath was summed up succinctly: "On hearing the Philistine's words, Saul and all the Israelites were dismayed and terrified" (1 Samuel 17:11). The fact that this went on for forty days without any Israelite challenger stepping forward shows how daunting Goliath really was (see 1 Samuel 17:16). And the situation became all the more dispiriting through repetition. By the time David arrived at the battlefield, "Whenever the Israelites saw the man, they all fled from him in great fear" (1 Samuel 17:24).

This is where young David entered the scene. Sent by his father to deliver food to his older brothers serving in the army, he heard Goliath's challenge and was indignant that the giant's belligerence was going unanswered. Due to his growing trust in God, David ignored the concerns of those around him, including King Saul, and drew on his experience, remembering how God had helped him in his shepherding past. "The Lord who rescued me from the paw of the lion and the paw of the bear will rescue me from the hand of this Philistine" (1 Samuel 17:37). With his dependence on God and not buying into the fears of his countrymen, David rescued all Israel.

March 3

A COMMUNITY OF SAFETY

"Stay with me; don't be afraid. The man who wants to kill you is trying to kill me too. You will be safe with me."

—1 Samuel 22:23

David did not choose to be a fugitive, much less some kind of outlaw leader. But, driven away by Saul's threats against him, he found safety in the wilderness. In turn, a community started to grow around him. "All those who were in distress or in debt or discontented gathered around him, and he became their commander. About four hundred men were with him" (1 Samuel 22:2). Imagine how this group would have been regarded by most of the members of the court of Saul—the "respectable" people of Israel's society.

In a sense, this is a model for the church—a community of safety and resistance against the world around us. But the church can also become part of the powerful mainstream in its own right. We should be looking to the margins and the marginalized for additional insight into understanding our faith and how to live as an alternative humanity—as the people of God in contrast to the world today. "I suspect that it is from the edges of the Church that true gospel hope is explored. Likewise, it is from the margins of society that dominant institutions and powerful ideologies must be tested."*

When Saul killed the family of priests, Abiathar found refuge with David's band. It might not have looked like it at the time, but this band of outlaws included the surviving members of the nation's family of priests as well as the man who had been anointed to be the next king of Israel. When we find ourselves left out and seemingly on the margins, we should look at those around us and work to build communities of safety with them and for those who will join us.

---

* Tim Costello, *Streets of Hope: Finding God in St Kilda* (Sydney, Australia: Allen & Unwin, 1998), 233.

March 4

FRIENDSHIP WITHOUT FEAR

"Don't be afraid," he said. "My father Saul will not lay a hand on you. You will be king over Israel, and I will be second to you. Even my father Saul knows this."
—1 Samuel 23:17

In the most unlikely circumstances, David and Jonathan formed one of the pre-eminent friendships of the Bible story. As the son of King Saul, Jonathan had to choose between loyalty to his father and family or friendship with David. As an heir of King Saul, Jonathan had to choose between his claim to the throne or acceptance of David's anointing as the next king of Israel. Jonathan gave up much and risked much to be friends with David.

For his part, David had to trust Jonathan's information and advice for survival (see 1 Samuel 20, for example). Somehow, it seemed that these two men had overcome their mutual suspicion and distrust, forging a friendship as they overcame their fears.

Sadly, the future they imagined, with David as king and Jonathan as his second-in-command, would not happen if it had ever been possible. After the disastrous battle at Mount Gilboa, David was left to mourn the loss of his friend and the possibility that they could have been friends for much longer had circumstances been better.

How the mighty have fallen in battle!
Jonathan lies slain on your heights.
I grieve for you, Jonathan my brother;
you were very dear to me.
Your love for me was wonderful,
more wonderful than that of women (2 Samuel 1:25, 26).

Trusting people without fear is key to healthy friendship. It is more difficult and more necessary when the stakes are raised, such as they were in the story of David and Jonathan. Such friendships are to be treasured while they last and mourned when they come to an end. And they are glimpses of our world without fear, as it was intended to be.

March 5

WHAT FEAR DOES

When Saul saw the Philistine army,
he was afraid; terror filled his heart.

—1 Samuel 28:5

Here is another story for the "Fear makes us do crazy things" file. Saul knew the law; as king, he had issued the decree that "expelled the mediums and spiritists from the land" (1 Samuel 28:3), drawing on commands in the law of Moses (see Deuteronomy 18:10–14). But the prophet Samuel was dead, and God seemed to be silent. The Philistine army was readying to attack, and Saul was terrified.

He asked his advisors to find someone whom he could consult, a medium who might be able to give him some kind of answer. They directed him to a woman at Endor. Despite Saul's disguise, she was rightly suspicious of this strange visitor. Of all things, it took Saul swearing an oath in God's name—"As surely as the Lord lives, you will not be punished for this" (1 Samuel 28:10)—for her to agree to his request.

But the message Saul received from the apparition of Samuel had no hint of encouragement. Instead, it recapped all his past failures, confirmed that God had left him, and predicted that Saul and his sons would die in battle the next day. Saul heard the message loud and clear. "Immediately Saul fell full length on the ground, filled with fear because of Samuel's words. His strength was gone, for he had eaten nothing all that day and night" (1 Samuel 28:20).

The only decent thing the woman of Endor did for Saul was to cook him a meal, which he ate only at his advisors' coaxing. But by looking for answers in all the wrong places, Saul's fear was only confirmed and compounded, and he went out into the night with an even greater sense of dread, knowing what the next day would bring. If only he could have grasped the truth about the God whom he had so desperately sworn by in seeking another voice. If only he had sought after God to calm his fears.

A NATION PARALYZED BY FEAR

When Ish-Bosheth son of Saul heard that Abner had died in Hebron, he lost courage, and all Israel became alarmed.
—2 Samuel 4:1

Fear is not only a personal feeling. It is something that can become pervasive across a community, in a nation's collective psyche, and sometimes even felt around the world, particularly in our age of mass communication and social media. After the death of Saul, the survivors of his family and household sought to defend their claims to the kingdom against David, who had been anointed as the next king, and his supporters. It was a time of turmoil and unrest, violence and widespread fear: "All Israel became paralyzed with fear" (2 Samuel 4:1, NLT).

Tragically, in some parts of the world today, this kind of pervasive fear is an everyday reality. All of us have experienced times when some threat, mass killing, or other national disaster has dominated the conversations and interactions with people around us, becoming a hum of anxiety underlying everything in a community or society. Those fears often extend beyond the actual threat itself and are amplified by their loud and repeated broadcast over various forms of media. But as it was in ancient Israel, such fear can have a profound and distorting influence on a community or the life of a whole nation.

While there are often real reasons for such pervasive fear, there is also truth in President Franklin Delano Roosevelt's oft-quoted line that "the only thing we have to fear is fear itself."* This is why "Do not be afraid" is not so much about changing our circumstances but choosing to respond differently. Because of our trust in a God who promises to be with us always, we have a meaningful and hopeful alternative to the fear-filled cultures around us.

---

* Jean Edward Smith, *FDR* (New York: Random House, 2008), 278, quoting a speech given on March 4, 1933.

March 7

ANOTHER ARGUMENT WITH GOD

David was afraid of the Lord that day and said, "How can the ark of the Lord ever come to me?"

—2 Samuel 6:9

Like many of the Bible characters who walked closely with God, David also had times of argument and even anger with God at some points. As part of establishing the city of Jerusalem as his capital, David wanted to see the symbols of God's presence with Israel in the city. So, with a large group of people, including a 30,000-strong army, he set out to collect the ark of the covenant from where it was being kept. It was a time of celebration, music, and worship—until it wasn't.

As he tried to steady the ark on the cart that was carrying this precious object, a man named Uzzah was struck dead, and the celebrations suddenly ceased. There are different explanations of why God was justified in His action, but regardless of any, David was angry at God. In his mind, he and his people had been trying to do the right thing, seeking to worship and honor God by moving this symbol of His presence and law to the new capital of the nation. David's anger soon turned to fear. He left the ark at the nearby home of Obed-Edom for the next three months.

It seems that there must have been further arguments between David and God during those three months. But after that time, David was convinced to try again. He took the added precaution of making a sacrifice after every six steps taken by those who were carrying the ark. Albeit slow, this journey turned into another celebration. Something had changed. David began "dancing before the Lord with all his might, while he and all Israel were bringing up the ark of the Lord with shouts and the sound of trumpets" (2 Samuel 6:14, 15).

FOR THE SAKE OF FRIENDSHIP

"Don't be afraid," David said to him, "for I will surely show you kindness for the sake of your father Jonathan. I will restore to you all the land that belonged to your grandfather Saul, and you will always eat at my table."
—2 Samuel 9:7

A healthy friendship will help us treat other people better. For the sake of that friend and for the sake of that friendship, we will be able and prepared to help someone with whom we otherwise might not have a connection. Every friendship expands our connections with the communities around us. It makes our world larger and a place to be less afraid of.

As part of David's ongoing grief over the death of his friend, Jonathan's crippled son Mephibosheth becomes the recipient of his kindness. This was despite the fact that the kingdom of Israel had already adopted the political thinking of the surrounding nations, as Samuel and God had warned. That meant that the usual way a king would treat members of a rival royal household would be to kill them all to remove the risk of an uprising or conspiring with enemy nations.

David's "Do not be afraid" was a reassurance that Mephibosheth was safe from any such threat. For the sake of his friendship with Jonathan, he rejected the common practice of kings and chose to show kindness—even making Mephibosheth part of his household. More than that, rather than claiming all of Saul's lands for himself and effectively ending the "house of Saul," he restored those lands to Mephibosheth, extending the legacy of the family of his long-time pursuer, would-be murderer, and royal rival. All this was done for the sake of friendship, honoring the memory of Jonathan.

It was an act of grace that began with a "Do not be afraid" between a grieving king and his friend's crippled son.

March 9

GOD'S WILL BE DONE

"Be strong, and let us fight bravely for our people and the cities of our God. The LORD will do what is good in his sight."

—2 Samuel 10:12

As well as a strategic planning meeting between two military leaders, this was a conversation between two brothers—Joab and Abishai. They drew up a plan for dividing their forces to attack both the Ammonites and the Arameans simultaneously, with one army in front of them and the other behind them. If one group was being overwhelmed, the other would come to its aid. With the military strategy in place came the brotherly exchange: "Be courageous! Fight bravely." That was their part of this undertaking, but there was another element: "May the LORD's will be done" (2 Samuel 10:12, NLT)

It sounds like the prayer Jesus gave to His disciples: "Your kingdom come, your will be done on earth as it is in heaven" (Matthew 6:10). It is an expression of submission, perhaps surrender—if that is not too inappropriate a term for military leaders marching into battle. These brothers had assembled their men, surveyed the forces of those coming against them, and made their plans. They encouraged each other to be brave in carrying out those plans. But they recognized that the outcome was in mightier hands than theirs.

The wisdom of the book of Ecclesiastes sets out this same pattern. "Whatever your hand finds to do, do it with all your might" (Ecclesiastes 9:10)—while acknowledging that "the race is not to the swift or the battle to the strong . . . but time and chance happen to them all" (Ecclesiastes 9:11). The best of our human effort is necessary and good, but it gives no guarantee of success. Instead, we should look for and pray for God's presence and His will to be done. This means that sometimes success might look different than we imagined.

March 10

BUILDING THE TEMPLE

"Now, my son, the LORD be with you, and may you have success and build the house of the LORD your God, as he said you would. . . . Then you will have success if you are careful to observe the decrees and laws that the LORD gave Moses for Israel. Be strong and courageous. Do not be afraid or discouraged."
—1 Chronicles 22:11–13

When David proposed the temple building project, God's first response was, "When did I ever ask for this?" (see 1 Chronicles 17:6). But we can understand David's logic: "Here I am, living in a palace of cedar, while the ark of the covenant of the LORD is under a tent" (1 Chronicles 17:1). After negotiation, it seems that God accepted the project, but insisted that Solomon, not David, would be the one to build it.

David responded graciously to this rebuff (see 1 Chronicles 17:16–26), then set about doing the preparation work for Solomon and ensuring that his son recognized the importance of the task. It became the focus of David's later years: "The house to be built for the LORD should be of great magnificence and fame and splendor in the sight of all the nations" (1 Chronicles 22:5). He ordered stones and timber, bronze and iron (see 1 Chronicles 22:2–4). He also gave a number of speeches to Solomon and the people of Israel, urging the priority of this project.

For all the attention given to this building project in the stories of David and Solomon, the Israel Museum in Jerusalem makes a surprising admission: Apart from the detailed descriptions in the Bible, "we have no archaeological evidence for the Temple in Jerusalem" from Solomon's time. While God seemed to bless this project at the time, perhaps it was not the priority and legacy that David had hoped it would be. An emphasis on building Solomon's courage and faithfulness for the duration of his reign might have brought better, more lasting results.

March 11

DO THE WORK

David also said to Solomon his son, "Be strong and courageous, and do the work. Do not be afraid or discouraged, for the LORD *God, my God, is with you. He will not fail you or forsake you until all the work for the service of the temple of the* LORD *is finished."*

—1 Chronicles 28:20

The priorities and projects of one generation are not always those of the next, but Solomon could not ignore the pressure—or the pile of building materials accumulating on the hilltop above the palace. For David, this was an expression of faithfulness to God, and the temple would be a witness to the surrounding nations.

But he had his misgivings about Solomon undertaking such a large project: "My son Solomon is young and inexperienced" (1 Chronicles 22:5). David urged him not to be afraid or discouraged and to focus on God, who would be with him throughout this project. But Solomon also had to "do the work." His trust in God would give him strength and courage, but he also had to apply himself, give it his time and energy, and do all that he could to ensure the project would be completed.

Sometimes, the Bible's "Do not be afraid" is about standing back and watching God remove or overcome the obstacle or challenge confronting us. But more often, "Do not be afraid" is the qualifier to step up and actually do the work. "Do not be afraid" is the command to do what is right, to do what needs to be done. Even if the outcome is uncertain, we can leave that in God's hands.

"Do not be afraid" is an invitation to partner with God in all aspects of our life. The work we do is important and necessary, but it is always done within God's realm and in His presence. That frees us both to work courageously and to trust in His power and provision.

March 12

WHERE THE HOUSE OF DAVID WENT WRONG

"I am about to go the way of all the earth," he said. "So be strong, act like a man, and observe what the LORD your God requires: walk in obedience to him, and keep his decrees and commands, his laws and regulations, as written in the Law of Moses. Do this so that you may prosper in all you do and wherever you go."

—1 Kings 2:2, 3

After a tumultuous life, including remarkable highs and tragic lows, from time spent as a shepherd boy to the leader of a band of outlaws to forty years as king of Israel, David gave his last advice to his son, Solomon, newly crowned to succeed him as king of Israel. From the mouth of Israel's psalmist, we would expect poetry and wisdom in these final words.

David started this final charge well, urging Solomon to have courage and walk in the ways of God. But he quickly veered off into a list of scores that he felt still needed to be settled. He finished with his wish for revenge against Shimei, son of Gera: "You are a man of wisdom; you will know what to do to him. Bring his gray head down to the grave in blood" (1 Kings 2:9). The end of David's story deserved better, and the beginning of Solomon's reign needed better.

The rot had already begun in the house of David, but this transition could have been so much better. Conflating courage and obedience to God with his own list of royal favors and grievances was the kind of kingly thinking that would precipitate the further decline of the kingdom during the life and reign of Solomon and its demise in the following generations. It seemed that Solomon tried to rise above it, but if David had stopped speaking at the end of 1 Kings 2:3 or if Solomon had embraced the courage and true wisdom that David urged, their history might have been different.

March 13

TO A STARVING, FOREIGN WIDOW

Elijah said to her, "Don't be afraid. Go home and do as you have said. But first make a small loaf of bread for me from what you have and bring it to me, and then make something for yourself and your son."
—1 Kings 17:13

Centuries after the time of Elijah, Jesus would reference this story in His first sermon in His hometown synagogue: "I assure you that there were many widows in Israel in Elijah's time, when the sky was shut for three and a half years and there was a severe famine throughout the land. Yet Elijah was not sent to any of them, but to a widow in Zarephath in the region of Sidon" (Luke 4:25, 26). Jesus also quoted from Isaiah 61, announcing "good news to the poor" and "freedom for the prisoners" (Luke 4:18, 19) but omitted "the day of vengeance" against Israel's enemies (see Isaiah 61:2).

Jesus was echoing Elijah's "Don't be afraid" to "outsiders." However, He broadened the invitation originally given to one starving, foreign widow to include all nations. The people in the Nazareth synagogue that Sabbath morning knew what He was saying, which is why, in their national pride, they became furious and tried to kill Him (see Luke 4:28–30).

But what was going through that hungry, anxious widow's mind when confronted by this strange, "hairy" prophet (see 2 Kings 1:8)? And what did she think of his presumptuous request as she was preparing the last meal for her son? Maybe she figured she simply had nothing to lose, or maybe there was something about the confidence with which Elijah made his request.

Whatever the case, she chose to trust Elijah's "Do not be afraid" and the God he introduced her to. Not only did this choice ensure her survival through the remainder of the drought, but it also gave her a place in the teachings of Jesus. Centuries after it happened, her act of faith became a model for the countless outsiders who would be invited into the kingdom of God that Jesus announced on that Sabbath morning in the synagogue in Nazareth.

THE LIFE OF A PROPHET

The angel of the L*ORD said to Elijah, "Go down with him; do not be afraid of him." So Elijah got up and went down with him to the king.*
—2 Kings 1:15

The life of a prophet was not an easy one. For Elijah, it involved confronting a succession of kings with their failures and their wrongdoing, announcing the judgments that were coming on them. It meant challenging priests and calling down fire from heaven—a number of times. It also meant running for his life and hiding out in the drought-ravaged wilderness. It was also filled with times of doubt and despair.

Soon after what seemed to be Elijah's greatest victory—at Mount Carmel—Queen Jezebel threatened retaliation. Elijah had an immediate response: "Elijah was afraid and ran for his life" (1 Kings 19:3). Ending up slumped under a solitary tree in the wilderness, God did not lecture him. Instead, an angel woke him from his exhausted sleep and simply fed him. "Get up and eat," said the angel, "for the journey is too much for you" (1 Kings 19:7). It was one of the many times that God provided Elijah with his most basic needs.

Elijah continued running until God met up with him at Mount Sinai. Elijah claimed he was the only one left standing for God, but God pointed out that there were still more than 7,000 people in Israel who were as faithful as Elijah. He was not alone (see 1 Kings 19:14, 18).

Nearing the end of his ministry, Elijah was instructed to confront a new king with a message predicting his death. After two groups of soldiers were sent to arrest the prophet, and both were consumed by fire, Elijah was assured that he could go down to the king without fear and deliver the message God had given to him. This was another example of the difficult and courage-testing life of a prophet, but Elijah's was a life that culminated with a fiery chariot sweeping him up to heaven (see 2 Kings 2:11).

March 15

AN ALMOST-FORGOTTEN GOOD KING

The fear of the LORD fell on all the kingdoms of the lands surrounding Judah, so that they did not go to war against Jehoshaphat.
—2 Chronicles 17:10

Jehoshaphat was one of the few good kings of Judah, ruling for about twenty-five years amid a list of lesser kings in the divided land of Israel during the ninth century B.C. His reign was largely overshadowed by the exploits and infamy of Ahab and Jezebel, who ruled in Israel at the same time. Jehoshaphat's greatest failure of leadership came when he arranged for his son to marry Ahab's daughter, and he was drawn into an ill-advised war against the Arameans, in which Ahab was killed (see 1 Kings 22).

However, Jehoshaphat was a good king. His faithfulness was expressed not only in his personal integrity, but he also worked to make this more of a reality in his kingdom. He removed paganism with its ubiquitous idols and altars, and commissioned a group of officials and priests to travel from town to town to teach the people the laws of God: "They taught throughout Judah, taking with them the Book of the Law of the LORD; they went around to all the towns of Judah and taught the people" (2 Chronicles 17:9).

The story of Jehoshaphat is a reminder that the good guys do not always get the headlines—not even in the Bible! But this kind of integrity and faithfulness is noticed by those around us. Sometimes, it can be the reason we are attacked in some way, but at other times—as it was for much of Jehoshaphat's reign—it is a reason for others to respect us and, more important, the God we serve. In Joshua's time, the surrounding peoples were afraid because of God's miracles and the fact that many of Israel's enemies had been defeated, but Jehoshaphat's God was "feared" because "his heart was courageous in the ways of the Lord" (2 Chronicles 17:6, NLT, margin).

JUSTICE WITH COURAGE

"Consider carefully what you do, because you are not judging for mere mortals but for the LORD, who is with you whenever you give a verdict. Now let the fear of the LORD be on you. Judge carefully, for with the LORD our God there is no injustice or partiality or bribery."
—2 Chronicles 19:6, 7

After his misguided venture with Ahab, Jehoshaphat was chastised by the prophet, Jehu, on his return to Jerusalem. He accepted the criticism and recommitted his efforts, traveling throughout his kingdom to encourage the people to turn back to God (see 2 Chronicles 19:4). As well as his leadership and innovations in growing the faith and spirituality of the nation of Judah, Jehoshaphat also reformed its legal system and appointed judges in every city, with a charge to serve fairly and in harmony with the principles God had given them.

"In his careful safeguarding of the rights and liberties of his subjects, Jehoshaphat emphasized the consideration that every member of the human family receives from the God of justice, who rules over all. . . . And those who are appointed to act as judges under Him, are to 'defend the poor and fatherless;' they are to 'do justice to the afflicted and needy,' and 'rid them out of the hand of the wicked.' "*

As with Moses' appointment of judges in the book of Deuteronomy, taking on the task of administering justice in Jehoshaphat's Judah required both discernment and courage. It was not enough to know what was right. Judges needed courage to deliver just judgments and to ensure they were acted upon. As Jehoshaphat charged the members of his newly appointed judiciary: "Act with courage, and may the LORD be with those who do well" (2 Chronicles 19:11).

* Ellen G. White, *Prophets and Kings* (Mountain View, CA: Pacific Press®, 1917), 198, quoting Psalm 82:1, 3, 4.

March 17

RESPONDING TO FEAR

Alarmed, Jehoshaphat resolved to inquire of the Lord,
and he proclaimed a fast for all Judah.
—2 Chronicles 20:3

After enjoying peace for much of his reign, King Jehoshaphat received news that an alliance of three nations had massed their armies and had marched around the Dead Sea to attack Judah. It is hardly surprising that "Jehoshaphat was terrified by this news" (2 Chronicles 20:3, NLT). But while fear can sometimes cause us to do strange things that seem out of character, it can also be a catalyst for revealing our true selves—perhaps these can even be moments when we rise above ourselves. In Jehoshaphat's fear, he sought God.

Jehoshaphat also asked all the people to join him in seeking God. This is where the work he had done earlier in his reign brought results. The people had been taught the ways of God, and in a time of crisis, "the people of Judah came together to seek help from the Lord; indeed, they came from every town in Judah to seek him" (2 Chronicles 20:4). We often do not see immediate results from the work we do in building up others, encouraging their faith, teaching them faithfulness—but then we might. That was Jehoshaphat's privilege. When he was gripped by fear, his people joined him in seeking God and His guidance, even as their enemies continued to march closer.

Leading his nation in prayer, Jehoshaphat drew on the history of the people of Israel, claimed God's promises, and sought His intervention. "Our God, will you not judge them?" he prayed. "For we have no power to face this vast army that is attacking us. We do not know what to do, but our eyes are on you" (2 Chronicles 20:12). Even in his alarm, Jehoshaphat knew where his focus should be, and he was able to lead his people there as well.

NOT YOURS, BUT GOD'S

He said: "Listen, King Jehoshaphat and all who live in Judah and Jerusalem! This is what the Lord *says to you: 'Do not be afraid or discouraged because of this vast army. For the battle is not yours, but God's. . . . Take up your positions; stand firm and see the deliverance the* Lord *will give you, O Judah and Jerusalem. Do not be afraid; do not be discouraged. Go out to face them tomorrow, and the* Lord *will be with you.' "*

—2 Chronicles 20:15–17

In response to the earnest and urgent prayers of Jehoshaphat and the people on the eve of this seemingly inevitable battle, God's Spirit inspired Jahaziel to speak. As unlikely as it might have seemed, he gave them their battle strategy but introduced and concluded his remarks with "Do not be afraid." The people needed to march out to battle, take up their positions, and stand firm. Each of those things would take courage. But they could take courage in the truth that this was not their battle. By turning up and standing up, they would be in position to see God act.

With these words, the prayer meeting became a worship service. The enemy army was still advancing towards Jerusalem from the Dead Sea, and there were still vastly more of them than there would be of the Judean army. But the people had the assurance that they were God's people and that this was God's battle. Jehoshaphat had reminded God of His promises—and God reminded Jehoshaphat of His promises. Jehoshaphat and all the people bowed in worship.

"Then some Levites from the Kohathites and Korahites stood up and praised the Lord, the God of Israel, with a very loud voice" (2 Chronicles 20:19). What a worship service that must have been—fear mixed with faith, perhaps in almost equal parts! They had a plan for battle, but they could not imagine how that plan might play out. They were readying to fight tomorrow, but today, they would sing.

March 19

HAVE FAITH IN HIS PROPHETS

Early in the morning they left for the Desert of Tekoa. As they set out, Jehoshaphat stood and said, "Listen to me, Judah and people of Jerusalem! Have faith in the Lord *your God and you will be upheld; have faith in his prophets and you will be successful."*

—2 Chronicles 20:20

When we think of a prophet today, most often it is an image of someone who might be a little odd, either mumbling or shouting messages of doom and destruction. They might be preoccupied with the end of the world or some coming calamity that they have somehow foreseen. It seems it is too easy to be a prophet of doom, and people tend to be taken more seriously when they make predictions of disaster. After all, it seems there are always bad things happening or threatening to happen in our world; they are the things that dominate our news feeds and headlines, and it is easy to make people afraid.

So perhaps the real prophets—those who speak with the greatest courage and foresight, and certainly those we should pay the most attention to—are the ones who actually inspire courage, grow our confidence in the God we serve, and help us to live with greater faithfulness and focus. A prophet with a message from God who can inspire an outnumbered and frightened army to march out to battle while singing about the holiness and love of God is a prophet worth listening to. And Jehoshaphat also put things in the right order—first, have faith in God, then have faith in the prophet who points to this God.

As God's people marched out to battle praising the Lord, God used their singing to unnerve and panic the invading armies, who began fighting among themselves (see 2 Chronicles 20:22, 23). Faithful courage has a power to it that should not be underestimated. May we look to—and even become—voices who share and inspire such courage.

March 20

OPENING OUR EYES

"Don't be afraid," the prophet answered. "Those who are with us are more than those who are with them."

—2 Kings 6:16

The Bible is alert to the times when we feel overwhelmed and surrounded by enemies, challenges, and troubles, when the fear is real, and there doesn't seem to be any reasonable way out. Both Elisha and his servant found themselves in such a situation. They woke up one morning to find the city of Dothan surrounded by an Aramean army equipped with horses and chariots. To make matters worse, this army had come specifically to capture Elisha.

But it was Elisha's servant who seemed most alarmed. Elisha himself had a different understanding of the situation. In answer to his servant's frantic questions, Elisha asked that God would open his eyes to what Elisha could see—or perhaps it was simply what he could see by faith. "Then the LORD opened the servant's eyes, and he looked and saw the hills full of horses and chariots of fire all around Elisha" (2 Kings 6:17).

Particularly when we are afraid or overwhelmed, our attention is monopolized by the source of that fear. Just when we need a bigger view, our vision narrows, our focus sharpens on the problem or threat, and the world around us seems darker. This is when our prayer—and the prayers of our friends—should be for open eyes, a clearer recognition of the power and presence of God in whatever our circumstances. Vision born of faith is one of the antidotes to fear.

The miracle experienced by Elisha and his servant was less about rescue than about vision. Elisha already knew that he was on the side with the greater strength. He had seen the fiery "chariots and horsemen of Israel" (2 Kings 2:12), so it was a vision he was able to share with his frightened servant. After Elisha's prayer, his servant also saw what was already there.

March 21

FEEDING THEIR ENEMIES

"Do not kill them," he answered. "Would you kill men you have captured with your own sword or bow? Set food and water before them so that they may eat and drink and then go back to their master."

—2 Kings 6:22

Equipped with the courage and confidence of their vision of their heavenly defenders, Elijah and his servant did something unusual; they led the enemy soldiers into the city of Samaria. Responding to Elisha's further prayer, God had caused these soldiers to be blinded. When Elisha prayed again that their eyes be opened, we can imagine their fear, finding themselves in Samaria, Israel's capital city. The king of Israel reacted as many kings throughout history would if presented with a helpless battalion of enemy soldiers. "Shall I kill them?" he asked Elisha (2 Kings 6:21).

Based on the assurance of God's presence with them, Elisha had a better suggestion. He urged the king to bring them food, and a "great feast" was prepared for the soldiers. This was a story illustrating the proverb: "If your enemy is hungry, give him food to eat; if he is thirsty, give him water to drink. In doing this, you will heap burning coals on his head, and the Lord will reward you" (Proverbs 25:21, 22). Based on an understanding of the power and presence of God, we can disarm ourselves and our enemies with kindness as simple as a meal.

When we choose to respond without fear, we can transform our enemies—as in this case: "So the bands from Aram stopped raiding Israel's territory" (2 Kings 6:23). Even if our enemies persist in their attacks or take advantage of our courageously kind response, we are transformed by becoming people who practice mercy, and we can continue to trust God, who is with us still.

March 22

OUTNUMBERED

"Be strong and courageous. Do not be afraid or discouraged because of the king of Assyria and the vast army with him, for there is a greater power with us than with him. With him is only the arm of flesh, but with us is the Lord *our God to help us and to fight our battles." And the people gained confidence from what Hezekiah the king of Judah said.*

—2 Chronicles 32:7, 8

In many of the Bible's stories, God's people seem to be outnumbered. While God loves all people, it seems He prefers to identify with the underdog, the outsiders, the "least of these," the poor, and the outnumbered. He has a special interest in those who need special attention, at least partly because they recognize their urgent need for help.

This should comfort us at those times when we find ourselves outnumbered, particularly when standing with God and for His truth. Feeling outnumbered does not indicate a lack of faithfulness. This threat from the Assyrians came "after all that Hezekiah had so faithfully done" (2 Chronicles 32:1), including the ways in which he had "sought his God and worked wholeheartedly" (2 Chronicles 31:21). But how we respond to the feeling of being outnumbered is a reflection of our faith.

When we make our stand with God, as Hezekiah urged the people to do, we are never truly outnumbered. From reading many of the Bible stories, it could be argued that it is precisely when we feel outnumbered that God is especially ready to stand with us. Because of the time Hezekiah had spent working faithfully with God and His purposes, he was well-fitted to deliver this message of strong encouragement to the people of Judah. Based on his confidence in God, he spoke with the kind of experience and assurance that instilled confidence among the people.

March 23

DON'T BE AFRAID OF THEIR BLASPHEMY

When King Hezekiah's officials came to Isaiah, Isaiah said to them, "Tell your master, 'This is what the Lord *says: do not be afraid of what you have heard—those words with which the underlings of the king of Assyria have blasphemed me. Listen! When he hears a certain report, I will make him want to return to his own country, and there I will have him cut down with the sword.' "*

—2 Kings 19:5–7

"What makes your God different from any of the other gods, whose nations we have defeated?" was the challenge from the messengers of the king of Assyria as they stood outside the walls of Jerusalem, readying to attack (see 2 Kings 18:19–35). It seems Hezekiah and his officials were as distressed by the ridicule directed at their God as they were by the threat of attack. It felt like it raised the stakes. This was no longer merely a military encounter but a battle between their God and the gods of the Assyrians. But what if they were not able to defend the honor of their God? Hezekiah and his leaders wore sackcloth to show their distress.

They sought out the prophet Isaiah, who urged them not to be so concerned about defending God. God was strong enough to defend Himself, and He would be able to look after them in the process. Those who had blasphemed His name would be defeated without the efforts of Hezekiah or his armies.

When people understand faith differently than we do or have negative responses to our faith, we are often tempted to feel we need to defend God. This can create a heavy burden for us, one that God does not need us to carry, and tends to present a small understanding of God. Our God is strong enough to defend Himself when and how He needs to. It is another reminder that the battles are God's, even when we are called to play a part or take a stand.

HOW TO DERAIL GOOD WORK

Then the peoples around them set out to discourage the people of Judah and make them afraid to go on building.

—Ezra 4:4

Doing good or seeking justice and serving others—in our faith and church contexts, in our working lives, in our communities, and in creative endeavors, requires hard work. It needs careful thinking, learning, listening, collaboration, and perseverance. One of the frustrations with seeking to do good work is that it is so easy for good work to be frustrated, subverted, or undone by others.

Those who would oppose good work, for whatever reason, do not need to make a rational case against the work being done. While there are those who work hard against goodness, they usually do not need to work as hard as those who seek goodness. They do not have to comply with the principles or expectations that come with seeking to promote goodness. All they need to do is create prejudice, confusion, discouragement, or fear. Those seeking to frustrate good work need only to raise questions and foster doubts; they do not need to answer questions or have any courage themselves. If they can make others afraid—even for no good reason—they will be recruiting others to do their insidious work, and the good work will grind to a halt.

The enemies who opposed the work of Ezra and the people did not need to do anything as hard as rebuilding a ruined temple. If they could discourage the people and create fear, the work would stop. They could bribe officials and send dishonest reports to the kings of Persia, and for a time, they were successful (see Ezra 4:23, 24).

Doing good work in our world requires courage and resisting the temptation to become discouraged or afraid. We must also commit to doing good work without causing contention: "Be careful to do what is right in the eyes of everybody. If it is possible, as far as it depends on you, live at peace with everyone" (Romans 12:17, 18).

March 25

AFRAID, BUT . . .

I was very much afraid, but I said to the king, "May the king live forever! Why should my face not look sad when the city where my ancestors are buried lies in ruins, and its gates have been destroyed by fire?"

—Nehemiah 2:2, 3

I think we all know the feeling. We have something important to say, but our mouth feels like it is full of sand, and we can barely form the words. Our heart is beating fast and seems so high in our throat that we are concerned it might actually stop us from breathing. We might have practiced the words we want to say over and over in our minds, but we are not sure that the sounds coming out of our mouths make any sense at all. In our nervous state, we might have caught the attention of the person we want to speak to by our awkwardness or distraction. It does not feel like this is the moment to say something so important, but it is precisely the importance of what we have to say that causes our anxiety.

As Nehemiah prepared to speak to the king, we can imagine him experiencing all of these symptoms of fear. It is hardly surprising that he committed the offense of failing to look happy as he served the king that morning. When the king noticed his distraction, it would have caused his heart to thump even louder. He was terrified, *but* . . . he spoke up anyway.

Struggling to get out the first few words, he relied on a phrase he would have said countless times in the service of the king, and as that familiar phrase rolled out of his mouth, his voice gained confidence. He was able to catch his breath, and he began to make his request. As the king asked a follow-up question, Nehemiah breathed a quick prayer (see Nehemiah 2:4) and continued the conversation that would change his life and renew the work of God's people at that time.

BRAVE ON BEHALF OF OUR PEOPLE

After I looked things over, I stood up and said to the nobles, the officials and the rest of the people, "Don't be afraid of them. Remember the Lord, who is great and awesome, and fight for your families, your sons and your daughters, your wives and your homes."
—Nehemiah 4:14

When they had begun to make real progress, the people's work of rebuilding the walls of Jerusalem caused resentment and opposition among nearby groups. Sympathizers warned them that they were likely to be attacked. The building work was hard enough in itself, but these threats added extra difficulties, including the need for the builders to be armed as they went about their work. The building progressed slowly.

As the leader of the project, it fell to Nehemiah to encourage the people in their work and in their defense of the re-established community. He urged them to remember their great and awesome God, but he also pointed to their families, children, wives, and homes as a motive.

There will be times in all of our lives when we are faced with defeats, threats, disappointments, and fear. "When those times come, your obligation is to look toward others as witnesses of God's goodness, to remember your responsibilities to care for others, and to remember that you are always a witness, whether you want to be or not."*

There are always people who need us to be brave, whether it is in helping them to grow their courage for the things they must do or in doing acts of service and support for them. Even when we are not feeling strong in our courage, we might be motivated to be brave on behalf of our families and friends.

* Alan Noble, *On Getting Out of Bed: The Burden and Gift of Living* (Downers Grove, IL: InterVarsity Press, 2023), 35, 36.

March 27

BUILT AMID THE RUINS

When all our enemies heard about this, all the surrounding nations were afraid and lost their self-confidence, because they realized that this work had been done with the help of our God.
—Nehemiah 6:16

Amid ongoing opposition, threats, and undermining, the work on the city walls was completed. The success of the people was noticed by the surrounding nations, and their opposition subsided into a grudgingly respectful silence. In Israel's past, their God-led military victories had caused fear in the surrounding nations and set them up for their next battles, but this achievement was different. The people had worked together and had overcome persistent obstacles and opposition, and the walls stood as a testament to their work and to the help they had received from God.

As the people began the task, they soon realized that the job might be too great for them. "The strength of the laborers is giving out, and there is so much rubble that we cannot rebuild the wall" (Nehemiah 4:10). They were not only looking to build; they had the disadvantage of trying to rebuild amid the ruins of the previous wall. But God's provision was commensurate with the degree of difficulty.

Whatever our responsibility, task, or project, we rarely get to begin with a clean slate. We work with people and in places that have rubble, history, and scars. We often have to spend much time cleaning up the ruins and damage of the past before we can build or create anew. And we bring our own past disappointments, pain, and fears to whatever our next task might be. However, those challenges are never larger than the provision of God. Any success, any achievement—anything built—testifies to our God and His willingness to work with wounded people in broken places. That's something people around us will notice and pay attention to.

IN THE BEWILDERED CITY

The couriers went out, spurred on by the king's command, and the edict was issued in the citadel of Susa. The king and Haman sat down to drink, but the city of Susa was bewildered.
—Esther 3:15

While the powerful shared a drink, the people of the city were bewildered. While the processes of bureaucracy were moving with a sense of inevitability and implacability, the powerful men were plotting together and against each other, as personal resentment was being turned into an empire-wide priority. While the edict was being read in the city squares, the people were trying to work out what this was all about and how they should respond, albeit with the limited opportunities that the common people had to work with. While the powerful men sat down to drink, hurried and whispered conversations were seeking to recruit Esther to speak up as the one hoped to undo this potential massacre.

The spotlight and the headlines tend to focus on the powerful men in the palace, but the Bible's story is alert to the confusion and despair of the common people. Their collective anxiety spread across the empire with the progress of the king's couriers: "In every province to which the edict and order of the king came, there was great mourning among the Jews, with fasting, weeping and wailing. Many lay in sackcloth and ashes" (Esther 4:3).

A biblical worldview begins at street level, noticing the distresses and disturbances of the people in our communities and in so many communities beyond our own. It recognizes the effects that the politics and plots of the powerful have on people who have little influence in return and sometimes only a limited understanding of how these systems work. These Bible stories show us that we should be prompted to adjust our ways of seeing and responding to the world around us—and to the people who most need our world to be different.

March 29

"IF I PERISH, I PERISH"

"Go, gather together all the Jews who are in Susa, and fast for me. Do not eat or drink for three days, night or day. I and my attendants will fast as you do. When this is done, I will go to the king, even though it is against the law. And if I perish, I perish."

—Esther 4:16

This is one of the statements in the Bible most likely to be offered as an example of courage. Urged by Mordecai to accept that she could not—and should not—hope to rely on her privileged position to avoid risks or responsibilities to her people, Esther acknowledged that she might well have been put in her position "for such a time as this" (Esther 4:14). She asked for the earnest prayers of the people and committed to fasting and praying herself. Then, she would risk her life by going to see the king uninvited. "And if I perish, I perish," she concluded.

It was commitment and faith, compassion and compulsion, all in one act of courage. It took courage, but it was part of a larger plan. It began with the prayers of the people—there was a whole community praying behind her. Then, there was her personal and spiritual preparation, coordinated with the prayers of her people. Even in appearing before the king, Esther adopted a careful, perhaps strategic, approach to making her request. She took her time, first inviting the king and Haman to eat with her on consecutive days and only then telling the king of her real request.

Undoubtedly, this was a statement and an act of courage by Esther. There was much to admire in what she did, risking herself for the sake of her people. But her courage was covered in prayer and enacted with careful and creative thinking. As such, this is rightly remembered as an example of what courage can be—and the difference it can make.

March 30

THE SUM OF OUR FEARS

"What I feared has come upon me;
what I dreaded has happened to me."

—Job 3:25

We all have those fears that grab us in our darker moments. They are the things that could go wrong in our lives, but these fears also reflect what we hold most dear. For most of us, these would include things like the death of family members, loss of our own health, serious financial setbacks or uncertainty, loss of our place in our community, and even doubts about the sustainability of our faith. All of these things happened to Job in quick succession.

Significantly, this is how we are introduced to Job. He "was blameless and upright; he feared God and shunned evil." He had a large family. We are given a list of his wealth, assets, and household. And just in case we are still unconvinced, we are offered this summary: "He was the greatest man among all the people of the East" (Job 1:2, 3).

Then, it is all taken away in a blunt seven-verse description of the tragedies that befall him in a single afternoon (see Job 1:13–19). Soon after, his health is attacked, and his wife is quick to call his God and his faith into question (see Job 2:7–9). These circumstances, Job's culpability, and God's role in all of it become the topic of the next thirty-five chapters as Job wrestles with his sorrow, confusion, and anger while his sincere but less-than-helpful friends try to set him straight.

We wince with Job as he endures blow after blow because all his losses are our fears—if not also our current experiences. This is why Job's story is important. In his fear and dread, his suffering, and his urgent questions, there is so much with which we can identify. But the story of Job also gives us an insight beyond what Job was able to see—the argument between God and Satan that precipitated and perhaps necessitated Job's trials. His suffering did not make sense to him, but it mattered in ways he could not imagine.

March 31

THE TEST OF EXPERIENCE

"Your words have supported those who stumbled;
you have strengthened faltering knees.
But now trouble comes to you, and you are discouraged;
it strikes you, and you are dismayed."

—Job 4:4, 5

On our best days, we can be a voice of encouragement, hope, and help to others who are going through hard times. In our times of suffering, grief, and doubt, our own words of faith and hope can seem to taunt us. But it is precisely these times when we need those words most. And it is in these times that they will be tested by the urgency of our experience.

This was the accusation made by Eliphaz—that Job had been able to give comfort and hope to others, but his fine-sounding words had collapsed under the weight of Job's own experience. It was a challenge that his faith needed to be more than mere theory.

Christian author C. S. Lewis wrote extensively on the theological problem of pain—in a book called *The Problem of Pain*. Later in his life, when his brief marriage ended with the painful death of his wife, he reflected on the difference between theory, even if explained as carefully reasoned arguments, and our actual human experiences of pain and grief. "The stakes have to be raised before we take the game quite seriously. I know this is the opposite of what is often said about the necessity of keeping all emotion out of our intellectual processes—'You can't think straight unless you are cool.' But then neither can you think deep if you are. I guess one must try every problem in both states."*

Good theology, understanding, and insight are important elements of sustainable faith, but they are not the same thing as trusting God when those formulations do not feel like they make sense. It seems the life that is both faithful and human has both theology and trust.

---

* C. S. Lewis, *Prayer: Letters to Malcolm* (London: Fount, 1998), 42, 43.

April 1

AN UNFAIR ARGUMENT WITH GOD

"Then I would speak up without fear of him,
but as it now stands with me, I cannot."

—Job 9:35

Like others in the Bible story, Job wanted to argue with God. He was confident that God would have a case to answer if they could somehow turn up in a courtroom and if he could get a fair hearing. But even if God would give him a hearing, Job also seemed well aware of the unequal nature of any such argument. He recognized that any appearance of God would be simply overwhelming, that in his own strength, he could not stand up to God in any meaningful way.

This was the same fear that sent Adam and Eve to hide among the trees at the sound of God approaching (see Genesis 3:8), the same fear that hinders our deeper engagement with and understanding of God. Job's solution was a mediator. "If only there were someone to mediate between us, someone to bring us together, . . . so that his terror would frighten me no more" (Job 9:33, 34).

This is a remarkable theological insight into what is traditionally believed to be one of the Bible's oldest stories. While the stories of the patriarchs include experiences of direct encounters with God, and conversations and arguments with Him, much of Job's reflection is about God's seeming silence and unapproachability. As such, his argument is for those of us and those times in our lives when we feel the absence of God while at the same time recognizing that His potential appearance is also a cause for fear and suspicion that it might also be a way for God to sidestep our questions.

But Job's request for a mediator also points us to another part of our story of God. The Bible insists that God *has* provided a mediator—Jesus, who is the "one mediator between God and mankind" (1 Timothy 2:5). As Job suggested, our questions, doubts, and fears find their first answer in Jesus.

April 2

PUSHING BACK BAD THEOLOGY

"Then, free of fault, you will lift up your face;
you will stand firm and without fear.
You will surely forget your trouble,
recalling it only as waters gone by."

—Job 11:15, 16

The arguments found in the book of Job are a strong critique of many of the glib arguments that are still popular in much of Christianity today. Interestingly, the book of Job stands as a counterbalance to the sometimes simplistic assumptions that we read in the book of Deuteronomy, for example. There, the formula seems straightforward—if we are faithful to God, we will be blessed; if we turn away from God, curses will follow. There is truth in this formula. But it is also difficult to align with the experiences of many of God's people throughout history. It is difficult to fit them with the experience of Job, who we have already been told was "blameless and upright; [who] feared God and shunned evil" (Job 1:2).

Deuteronomy's explanation was the explanation of Job's troubles repeatedly argued by his friends as they sat with him amid the ruins of his life. Zophar, the Naamathite, urged Job to repent, confess his sin, and seek God more earnestly—and then his suffering would end. With enough prayer, Zophar argued, Job would be able to overcome his fear and forget his troubles.

Such arguments miss so much of the experience and nuance of faithful living in a fallen world, as well as ignoring the cosmic realities that readers of the book of Job are aware of in the argument between God and Satan. But these arguments are also of little use or comfort to those, like Job, who experience loss and suffering, with the risk of adding a sense of guilt to what they are already enduring. As Job put it, "How can you console me with your nonsense? Nothing is left of your answers but falsehood!" (Job 21:35).

BRACE YOURSELF

"Who is this that obscures my plans
with words without knowledge?
Brace yourself like a man;
I will question you,
and you shall answer me."

—Job 38:2, 3

It takes courage to face and acknowledge our human limitations, including the many things we don't know and don't understand. After thirty-five chapters of Job's protests and his friends' arguments, God spoke. Job had been pressing God to get a hearing; now God responded with questions of His own. God's first words invited Job to brace himself and to admit what he didn't know—but also simply to have the courage to hear directly from God after so much arguing about Him and to have the courage to recognize his own smallness in comparison with the majesty and power of God.

Notably, God did not answer many of the questions Job and his friends had been wrestling with. Instead, He pointed to the wonders of the created world and the universe beyond. He pointed out the power and wisdom, insight, and oversight with which He created and cared for the world, challenging Job with example after example of things he did not understand and could not control. But even more significantly, God simply spoke.

Ultimately, God's response to Job's urgent questions was His presence—the reality that He had seen and heard Job's predicament and protest. Even as He gently rebuked Job and less gently rebuked Job's friends—thus giving some resolution to their arguments—His presence was affirmation in itself.

Job understood this message, and he had the courage to respond. "You asked, 'Who is this that obscures my counsel without knowledge?' Surely I spoke of things I did not understand, things too wonderful for me to know" (Job 42:3). In this sense, courage is an element of trust. Only when we are brave enough to admit our limitations will we allow ourselves to trust the One who made us, who made it all, and who has already seen and heard all our questions and doubts, even those we can barely bring ourselves to admit.

April 4

SLEEPING AMID A COUP

I lie down and sleep;
I wake again, because the LORD sustains me.
I will not fear though tens of thousands
assail me on every side.

—Psalm 3:5, 6

Despite his status as one of the Bible's great heroes, much of David's family life was messy. Murder, rape, and intrigue were recurring themes. But the plot by Absalom to overthrow David and take the kingdom was an extreme example (see 2 Samuel 15–17). David and many of the people loyal to him had to escape from Jerusalem as Absalom's army approached, crossing the Jordan for safety before making a stand in the wilderness beyond in a bid to retake the kingdom. Although David's forces were able to defeat Absalom's army, David was more concerned about mourning the death of his son than celebrating the military victory, causing further resentment among David's supporters.

As tragic as this history is, we gain an intimate insight into David's mindset in Psalm 3. Whether this was something written while he was on the run or as he was reflecting on his experience afterward, Psalm 3 is both a song of praise and a cry for help. Although David was well aware of the dangers that threatened him, his experience with God was primarily one of trust.

Sleep is a human need, but it is also an experience of great vulnerability. This is why stress so affects our ability to sleep. When we are under pressure or under attack, our body often does not allow us to relax into sleep. But David's understanding of God's presence with him allowed him to sleep even while under threat. And while Absalom was organizing an army that would march out against David (see 2 Samuel 17:1), David could declare that he was unafraid. Even if members of his own family and a large portion of the people of his kingdom were against him, he insisted that "the LORD sustains me."

April 5

AN EXPERIENCED SHEPHERD

Even though I walk
through the darkest valley,
I will fear no evil,
for you are with me;
your rod and your staff,
they comfort me.

—Psalm 23:4

The imagery of shepherding is a recurring theme across the Bible. This picture of care and protection was familiar to those who first heard or read these stories, psalms, prophecies, and parables. But as well as being one of its most popular expressions, Psalm 23 also came with the most experience of the life of a shepherd and his sheep.

David's first mention in scripture presents him as the youngest son of Jesse, out in the fields tending the sheep (see 1 Samuel 16:11). On the morning that he was sent to find his brothers in the army—the day he fought Goliath—David "left the flock in the care of [another] shepherd" (1 Samuel 17:20), and he drew on his shepherding experiences as he explained his confidence in going out to confront the giant (see 1 Samuel 17:34–37).

So, when David used the image of a shepherd to describe God's care for him, he used imagery that he was very familiar with and drew on the varied experiences of his life. He had experienced times of "green pastures," when God had led him "beside quiet waters" (Psalm 23:2). But he had also experienced times of living in the wilderness when death had been a constant threat. David knew that God was no less with him in those dark and difficult times than in the good and easier times and places.

Again, because of the goodness of God, David had expectations of God's continuing care and a secure future with Him. He knew God's goodness and love would continue to pursue him "all the days of my life, and I will dwell in the house of the Lord forever" (Psalm 23:6). This was the understanding of an experienced shepherd—one who had lived much of his life in the care of the Good Shepherd.

April 6

"WHOM SHALL I FEAR?"

The Lord *is my light and my salvation—*
whom shall I fear?
The Lord *is the stronghold of my life—*
of whom shall I be afraid?

—Psalm 27:1

Paul would later say it like this, in a similar rhetorical form: "If God is for us, who can be against us?" (Romans 8:31). But David's poetry holds up well. He described God as his light, salvation, and stronghold, using each of these aspects of God's provision and care as a basis for living without fear.

Light is a recurring image in the Bible. From Creation to the New Jerusalem, God is the source of light. It is one of the Bible's most powerful metaphors, with the light from God illuminating our world and the world made new. Jesus described Himself—and also those who would follow Him—as the light of the world, pushing back the darkness surrounding them (see John 8:12; Matthew 5:14). God's presence and power are portrayed both in large cosmic terms and as a light that allows us to take the next step in our ordinary lives.

Salvation tends to be a term weighted with theological significance, but for David and many other Bible characters, salvation was first more practical and immediate. God was his rescuer, and he had seen this in his life on various occasions. Of course, eternal salvation was most important—God would finally save him—but God was also saving him in the present, and David had equal confidence in this.

A stronghold was also part of David's experience. As a fugitive, whether it was a cave, a household, or a neighboring kingdom that took him in, a stronghold was a place of sanctuary and safety. This was something David had also found in God through his varied life experiences. Wherever he went and in whatever circumstances, he knew that God was with him—and that was a safe place to be.

So, in the care of God, who is all of those things, what could make him afraid?

April 7

"EVEN THEN I WILL BE CONFIDENT"

Though an army besiege me,
my heart will not fear;
though war break out against me,
even then I will be confident.

—Psalm 27:3

In most of our telling of the Bible stories, David is held up as a heroic warrior-king. Some of his battles seemed necessary, as when neighboring nations attacked Israel. But God made it clear that this was not His ideal for a leader of His people. When David suggested the idea of building a temple to honor God, it was God who brought up David's warrior past as the reason why he was not best suited to such a task. "You are not to build a house for my Name, because you have shed much blood on the earth in my sight" (1 Chronicles 22:8). God instead chose to work with David's son, Solomon, whom He hoped would be a man of peace.

The remarkable thing is that God will work with us and for us, even when we are not living ideal lives in ideal times or circumstances. This was David's experience. When we are surrounded by threats, attacks, and enemies, God is with us. And He is still with us, even when we might have provoked those attacks, made those enemies, or started that war.

The Bible's story of David is best read as a human story rather than a hero story—more a casebook than a guidebook. But we can be inspired by his assertions of faith, coming amid the messiness of his life and history. As such, they best fit our lives, with all our uncertainties, inconsistencies, and questions.

In David's experience, not only was God's care a reason not to fear a single threat or attack (see Psalm 27:1), but even an all-out attack by a whole army was still no match for the confidence and courage he had found in God's light, salvation, and stronghold. "Even then," he declared, "will I be confident."

April 8

WAITING NOW

I remain confident of this:
I will see the goodness of the LORD
in the land of the living.
Wait for the LORD;
be strong and take heart
and wait for the LORD.

—Psalm 27:13, 14

One of the accusations made against the Christian faith is that it disengages believers from the present world, promoting an escapist response to suffering and injustice rather than confronting the needs and realities in our lives and in the world around us today. While the Bible promises rescue, redemption, and re-creation, it also sends us back to our lives, our communities, and our world inspired by vision and hope, but with lives to live and work to do in our time and place.

Waiting for the Lord, as David described it, is never passive. Psalm 27 is both an affirmation of God's presence, protection, and care, and a prayer for that presence, protection, and care. David included his expectation of seeing God's actions "in the land of the living"—in his present life—not waiting only for a glorious hereafter. Waiting is about being alert to God working in our lives and around us. And it is about living with strength and courage today as an active and engaged way of waiting well. As such, waiting is about continuing to live and work in the light of our expectations of God's actions and ultimate intervention.

Even in the battle experiences and imagery that he used in this psalm, David was not advocating inaction. "Hope, however, does not consist in crossing one's arms and waiting. As long as I fight, I am moved by hope; and if I fight with hope, then I can wait."* Although it is not the only reason, faith has been criticized for disengaging people from the world around us because this is how we have misunderstood it. It seems David would encourage us to have a more active, expectant, and courageous kind of waiting.

* Paulo Freire, *Pedagogy of the Oppressed* (London: Penguin Classics, 2007), 65.

April 9

WHAT WE PLACE HOPE IN

Love the LORD, all his faithful people!
The LORD preserves those who are true to him,
but the proud he pays back in full.
Be strong and take heart,
all you who hope in the LORD.

—Psalm 31:23, 24

It has been said that we all have hope in something. But the reality is that we place our hope in many things in different ways and to varying degrees. Many of these can be good in their right place, including our relationships, families, education, career or work, physical health and fitness, and even our church and community. While we spend much of our lives investing in different elements and aspects of our lives and the lives of others, from a human perspective, many of the things that we might find hope in will inevitably be put aside, let us down, or be lost with time and advancing age. The challenge for finite human beings is to place our hope in something that will last beyond our lives. Ultimately, that "something" is found in God Himself.

According to David, putting our hope in the right thing is the true source of courage and strength. Hope in God is the one thing that endures, that does not have to change through the seasons of our lives, and that will not let us down. So, how do we put our hope in the Lord, as David urged the faithful to do?

As with other things in which we invest our lives, putting our hope in our God means that we give Him our time, energy, and focus. We re-order and reprioritize who we are and what we do, seeking God's leading and purposes in all aspects of our lives. Even when we are not fully certain of what this means, we begin with the small things we know to do. In itself, this requires courage, but it can also become a source of courage as we grow in our experience of God's plan and provision for our lives of faith.

April 10

DELIVERED FROM FEAR

I sought the LORD, and he answered me;
he delivered me from all my fears.

—Psalm 34:4

It was not David's finest moment. Escaping from Saul, he sought refuge with King Achish of Gath. Life on the run seemed to be sapping David's courage. He "was very much afraid of Achish king of Gath. So he pretended to be insane in their presence; and while he was in their hands he acted like a madman, making marks on the doors of the gate and letting saliva run down his beard" (1 Samuel 21:12, 13). The hero of Israel and its future king was being hunted by the current king of Israel as a traitor and was reduced to a laughingstock by his fear of the enemies of God's people.

Perhaps it was in the comparative safety of the Cave of Adullum (see 1 Samuel 22:1) that David had the opportunity to reflect on his fear and the fool that it had made of him. But it seems he had also had time to pray—and he received an answer from God that renewed his courage. "This poor man called, and the LORD heard him; he saved him out of all his troubles" (Psalm 34:6).

David still had the prospect of Saul and his army coming after him; he had been denied refuge in the enemy kingdom of Gath, and he and his men were hiding in a cave, but God heard David's prayer and delivered him from his fears.

Psalm 34 is the song David wrote as a testimony to a God who sees and hears the helpless and afraid. "I will boast only in the LORD; let all who are helpless take heart" (Psalm 34:2, NLT). Probably remembering his feigned insanity with some embarrassment, he emphasized that those who trust in God need never be ashamed and affirmed that "the Lord will rescue his servants; no one who takes refuge in him will be condemned" (Psalm 34:22).

April 11

WHEN EVIL PROSPERS

Do not fret because of those who are evil
or be envious of those who do wrong;
for like the grass they will soon wither,
like green plants they will soon die away.

—Psalm 37:1, 2

One of the perennial questions of Christian apologetics is why bad things happen to good people. Why do the innocent suffer? How do we explain the apparently unfair nature of evil, and why doesn't God do more to intervene? But we can also be tempted—as were many of the Bible authors—to ask the counterpart of that question: Why do so many people seem to prosper while doing evil? Why does the world seem to reward those who lie, cheat, exploit, and scam their way to success?

Both sets of questions reflect a world that is out of alignment with how it ought to be—with broken relationships and the real presence of evil in people and systems. In many of his psalms, David did quite a bit of fretting about the seeming injustice of how our world appears to work, so perhaps he was speaking to himself as much as those who would sing, hear, or read his thoughts when he said, "Do not fret." He emphasized the temporary nature of ill-gotten gain and anticipated a turn of events in which the apparent success of those who do evil will wither away, whether through their own hubris, by their inevitable death, or because of the direct judgment of God.

Anticipating Jesus' teachings in the Beatitudes, David urged that "the meek will inherit the land and enjoy peace and prosperity" (Psalm 37:11). The psalm goes on to describe, affirm, and celebrate the reversal that God will bring—an expectation that should refocus how we live and where we put our hope. "Better the little that the righteous have than the wealth of many wicked; for the power of the wicked will be broken, but the Lord upholds the righteous" (Psalm 37:16, 17).

April 12

PROCLAIMING GOD'S SALVATION

I proclaim your saving acts in the great assembly;
I do not seal my lips, LORD*,*
as you know.
I do not hide your righteousness in my heart;
I speak of your faithfulness and your saving help.
I do not conceal your love and your faithfulness
from the great assembly.

—Psalm 40:9, 10

The book of Hebrews employed Psalm 40:6–8 to describe the sacrifice and mission of Jesus (see Hebrews 10:5–10). The writer of Hebrews asserts that those words were spoken by Jesus, explaining His sacrifice in "a body you prepared for me" (Hebrews 10:5).

When read in this way, verses 9 and 10 are the psalmist's response to humanity's rescue through the sacrifice of Jesus. God heard his cries for help and "lifted me out of the slimy pit, out of the mud and mire; he set my feet on a rock and gave me a firm place to stand" (Psalm 40:2).

The remainder of Psalm 40 is a "new song" (verse 3) celebrating God's redemption and restoration. David urged that an important element of responding to God's goodness and salvation is to proclaim what God has done. "I have told all your people about your justice. I have not been afraid to speak out" (Psalm 40:9, NLT).

David suggested that God's salvation and goodness in our lives are never only for our own benefit. When God rescues us, He is also always working in proximity to the people around us, especially if we are prepared to share that testimony and make that evidence available. Although speaking of God's saving help might take courage, it can help and encourage others. Our lives and our stories are among the ways in which God's love and faithfulness can be revealed, even in the great assembly. So do not be afraid to speak out and speak up for the saving work of God as you have come to know and experience it.

REFUGE AMID UPHEAVAL

God is our refuge and strength,
an ever-present help in trouble.
Therefore we will not fear, though the earth give way
and the mountains fall into the heart of the sea,
though its waters roar and foam
and the mountains quake with their surging.
—Psalm 46:1–3

There is much in our world that can make us afraid. As we look back and read the accounts of peoples and nations in the past, we see that there has been much in world history that has made people afraid in their respective times and places. Among these, the first few verses of Psalm 46 describe upheaval in the natural world—things like earthquakes and landslides, storms and tsunamis. It is similar to the language that Jesus used in describing the fearful events in the world at the end of time: "On the earth, nations will be in anguish and perplexity at the roaring and tossing of the sea" (Luke 21:25).

That this was a reality written about in the poetry of ancient Israel, in the teachings of Jesus, and in His expectation of the end times reminds us that our world has been much less stable than we often imagine and that disasters of different kinds have been experienced in all societies across history. They have been something that all people have had to reckon with, live with, and try to explain across human history. People have had to find ways to live well amid the uncertainties of our planet and its sometimes destructive forces.

While Jesus seemed to indicate that there would be a greater intensity of natural and unnatural disasters as the time of His return neared, these are not new experiences for human beings. We can learn from the faith of our spiritual ancestors, who encountered these unnerving phenomena themselves yet found refuge and strength in the same God we follow and serve today. These psalmists would insist that, in the midst of seemingly ever-present trouble, we have an "ever-present help," so we will not fear.

April 14

OUR FORTRESS

The Lord Almighty is with us;
the God of Jacob is our fortress.

—Psalm 46:7

Psalm 46 also acknowledges the reality of human disasters—such things as political instability, clashing empires, wars, and violence. "Nations are in uproar, kingdoms fall; he lifts his voice, the earth melts" (Psalm 46:6). Like the implacable forces and disasters in the natural world, the tides of civilizations and the atrocities of the powerful have similarly destructive effects on human lives, impassive about the toll they take on the weakest, poorest, and most vulnerable.

Amid these realities of human history, God is a refuge and our fortress (see Psalm 46:7, 11). He alone can bring peace. His power is greater than all the armies, weapons, war machines, and nefarious technologies that humanity can assemble, invent, or stockpile. When we look back over the victims and devastation of war and violence, even just in recent decades, it can feel overwhelming to our humanity and our hope. But the assurance offered repeatedly in the Psalms—and elsewhere in the Bible—is that the scale of the evils and outrages of humanity are always dwarfed by the reality and power of God. Even when His power is not yet fully exercised or realized, the assurance of God undermines the enormity of evil.

While we do not know the specific circumstances that inspired this psalm, God is the fortress that the psalmists had found and that they now offered to those who would sing their song. Even amid the tragedies and disasters of our world, their assurance was found in pausing to remember the reality of God and His supremacy over the nations and all the earth. "He says, 'Be still, and know that I am God; I will be exalted among the nations, I will be exalted in the earth' " (Psalm 46:10).

Whatever you are confronting this week, whatever is on your news feed today, whatever is making you feel afraid or uncertain, be still and know that He is God.

REVERSAL

Why should I fear when evil days come,
when wicked deceivers surround me—
those who trust in their wealth
and boast of their great riches?

—Psalm 49:5, 6

The Bible's theme of reversal can be unnerving to those who are relatively well-off and comfortable. It is too easy to begin trusting in our own resources, assuming our security is found in the things we have or what we are able to earn—and when that happens, the voices of the psalms and the prophets, among others throughout the Bible, will sound like a threat to us.

To others, promises of reversal are good news. This was expressed in Mary's song when she visited Elizabeth soon after they had received the good news from the angel about the sons they would have. Speaking of God's action and intervention in our world that would be embodied in the lives and ministry of these two boys, Mary sang her own prophetic psalm: "He has brought down rulers from their thrones but has lifted up the humble. He has filled the hungry with good things but has sent the rich away empty" (Luke 1:52, 53).

How we hear these words will depend on our relative position in the world. This is good news for the humble and the hungry. While this feels like a warning to the rich and the rulers, it is reassuring for those who follow God, relying on His promises and provision.

So, the Bible's promises of reversal insist that history and society are not always how they appear. Those who look like winners but have gained wealth and power by deception and wickedness are not as fearsome as they might seem. "People, despite their wealth, do not endure; they are like the beasts that perish" (Psalm 49:12).

Similarly, those who have been exploited and oppressed are not as defeated as they appear. With God as their agent of reversal, they need not be afraid. "His mercy extends to those who fear him, from generation to generation" (Luke 1:50).

April 16

SINGING ABOUT FEAR TOGETHER

My heart is in anguish within me;
the terrors of death have fallen on me.
Fear and trembling have beset me;
horror has overwhelmed me.

—Psalm 55:4, 5

The honesty and humanity of the Psalms are two of their significant features. Described as a song, perhaps for use in worship, Psalm 55 even incorporates the all-too-familiar physical symptoms of fear: "My heart pounds in my chest. The terror of death assaults me. Fear and trembling overwhelm me, and I can't stop shaking" (Psalm 55:4, 5, NLT). We know those feelings and the effects they can have on us.

We all have those experiences—circumstances or periods in our lives when fear threatens to overwhelm us. People of faith and the communities they are part of should not pretend that life with God is, or ought to be, fear-free. Indeed, as a psalm "for the choir director" (NLT), Psalm 55 was a song to be sung together, a communal acknowledgment of the reality of fear in our lives. While few of our hymns or worship songs today seem to have this same kind of raw honesty, the Bible models this kind of human expression as legitimate among the community of faith.

But while many of the psalms express the reality of fear, few leave us there. Acknowledgment of fear and the weight of threat and attack that might overwhelm us is most often offered in the context of cries for help to God as our Rescuer, Protector, and Defender. Additionally, most of those psalms describe the progression from fear and anguish to a renewed trust in God. "Cast your cares on the Lord and he will sustain you; he will never let the righteous be shaken" (Psalm 55:22).

Voicing our fears—even in a general collective sense—need not mean that we are overwhelmed by them or surrender to them. Rather, it can be a way of acknowledging them together, calling for God's help, and giving them to God as an act of trust in Him, His response, and His power.

WHEN I AM AFRAID . . .

When I am afraid, I put my trust in you.
In God, whose word I praise—
in God I trust and am not afraid.
What can mere mortals do to me?

—Psalm 56:3, 4

Like Psalm 34, Psalm 56 is linked to David's experience among the Philistines in Gath, when he feigned insanity because he was afraid of what the Philistine king might do to him (see 1 Samuel 21:10–15). David had escaped to the Philistine city to elude Saul's relentless pursuit but found himself in a potentially more dangerous situation. He knew what it was to be pursued by enemies "all day long" (Psalm 56:2).

Not only can fear prompt us to do things that are uncharacteristic, but it also can cause us to look for relief and rescue in the wrong places. David had sought refuge among the enemies of God's people. Given his growing infamy among the Philistines, this was not going to end well. And if they had not driven him away, it is likely he would have been compromised in other ways.

But reflecting on this experience, David could be confident about where he could turn for help—where he *should* have turned for help earlier. Note the sequence in these verses: "When I am afraid, I put my trust in you . . . and [I] am not afraid." Being "not afraid" does not change the circumstances—the initial and perhaps ongoing cause for fear—but the response to those circumstances is different.

Because it is based on God's promises, such a response is independent of circumstances and is beyond the reach of "mere mortals," no matter how they might threaten the author of the song. Thus, this song is a note of praise even amid potentially fearful circumstances.

April 18

WHEN GOD BOTTLES OUR TEARS

In God, whose word I praise,
in the Lord, *whose word I praise—*
in God I trust; I will not be afraid.
What can man do to me?

—Psalm 56:10, 11

One of the recurring calls in the Psalms is the challenge to God to notice, hear, see, and respond to the suffering, anguish, and injustice experienced by the psalmist and observed among God's people. At the same time, there is a sense of confidence that God is aware of their suffering and would intervene. This was the "God who sees," described in language that was more poetic and intimate: "You keep track of all my sorrows. You have collected all my tears in your bottle. You have recorded each one in your book" (Psalm 56:8, NLT).

This is a powerful image. Jesus later taught His disciples that not a sparrow can fall without God noticing (see Matthew 10:29), but David insists that not a single tear can fall without God collecting and recording it. Our smallest sorrows are listed in the memory banks of heaven.

This assurance was why David was so prone to praise, even while the tears were still falling. If God noticed and every tear was counted, He would be sure to act, to bring justice, and to set wrongs right. Those who trust in Him will be vindicated, and one day, there will be no more cause for tears. "He will wipe every tear from their eyes" (Revelation 21:4). Not only are our tears noted, but we are assured that the sorrow and the suffering that they represent will be undone.

Every tear matters. As our tears are collected in heaven, we can trust the One who makes such careful observations. In Him, our fears are undone, and those who would cause our tears are rendered less threatening. If God is collecting our tears, what can other people do to us to make us afraid? Nothing is bigger than God's intimate attention.

THE GOOD NEWS OF JUDGMENT

Make vows to the LORD your God and fulfill them;
let all the neighboring lands
bring gifts to the One to be feared.
He breaks the spirit of rulers;
he is feared by the kings of the earth.

—Psalm 76:11, 12

On first reading, some of us might be surprised at the excitement and longing for God's judgment expressed repeatedly in the Psalms. While many Bible readers today consider judgment something to be feared, the ancient Hebrew perspective should give us pause for further reflection.

> Hundreds and thousands of people who have been stripped of all they possess and who have the right entirely on their side will at last be heard. Of course they are not afraid of judgment. They know their case is unanswerable—if only it could be heard. When God comes to judge, at last it will. . . . When God 'arises to judgment' he will 'help all the meek upon the earth' (76:9), all the timid, helpless people whose wrongs have never been righted yet.*

Interestingly, when God takes the side of the oppressed, downtrodden, and afflicted (see Psalm 76:9), the Psalms describe not only individuals, such as rulers and kings but also larger unjust powers and systems of injustice, including surrounding nations and neighboring lands. As unlikely as it might sound initially, this is why God's "wrath against mankind brings [Him] praise" (Psalm 76:10).

We assume that fear is the lot of the afflicted and oppressed. So often, that is the reality in our world. But God has announced His intention to help the meek and judge on their behalf. Those who ought to be most afraid are those whose power and position will be under threat of God's judgment. As Jesus said, "Blessed are the meek, for they will inherit the earth" (Matthew 5:5).

---

* C. S. Lewis, *Reflections on the Psalms* (London: Fount, 1961), 16, 17.

April 20

TELLING THE STORY AGAIN

He brought his people out like a flock;
he led them like sheep through the wilderness.
He guided them safely, so they were unafraid;
but the sea engulfed their enemies.

—Psalm 78:52, 53

One of the recurring praises of the faithful people of Israel was to tell and re-tell the ways in which God had rescued and led them in their history. Moses had urged this as something the people should do (see Deuteronomy 11:29–31), and Psalm 78 is one of those recitations, written in poetic form: "We will not hide them from their children; we will tell the next generation the praiseworthy deeds of the LORD, his power, and the wonders he has done" (Psalm 78:4).

This particular re-telling of Israel's story recounted their deliverance from slavery in Egypt and how God had intervened to wear down their captors and defeat their pursuers, particularly in the story of crossing the Red Sea (see Exodus 14:10–31). At that time, Moses had admonished the people, "Do not be afraid. . . . The LORD will fight for you; you need only to be still" (Exodus 14:13, 14).

Retelling this story hundreds of years later was a reminder to the people of their past, but it also reminded them of God's continuing power and presence with them in the present.

Psalm 78 was also a song in praise of David, whom God brought "to be the shepherd of his people Jacob, of Israel his inheritance. And David shepherded them with integrity of heart; with skillful hands he led them" (Psalm 78:71, 72). This is an example of how David, when at his best, was identified by God as "a man after his own heart" (1 Samuel 13:14). But it was also a re-echoing of the call to not be afraid. The God who had rescued them from Egypt was their God still, whatever might assail and whoever might attack or threaten them.

AMID OUR STEALTHY FEARS

You will not fear the terror of night,
nor the arrow that flies by day,
nor the pestilence that stalks in the darkness,
nor the plague that destroys at midday.

—Psalm 91:5, 6

While we can expect to experience suffering, disease, and trouble from time to time in our lives, many of these human realities strike us suddenly. Appearing with little warning, they feel like they have crept up on us in the dark, come as a shot from out of the blue, or have taken hold of us with the silence of a virus. Although they come upon us with stealth, an accident, an attack, a medical event, or a bad diagnosis can shake our lives, our families, and our faith when they hit us. The fragility of our lives, whether our own or of those we care about, of our well-being, and of so much of what we take for granted can cause big questions and real anxiety.

But God knows and sees these stealthy threats to us and our lives as clearly as He knows and sees the more obvious ones. The Bible acknowledges the fears that we have about the uncertainty, frailty, and seemingly ephemeral nature of our lives, and God is portrayed as the source of strength, courage, and refuge amid these dangers. "His faithful promises are your armor and protection" (Psalm 91:4, NLT).

In our inevitably finite lives, we cannot rely only on finding strength or mustering courage within ourselves because our selves—as much as anything or anyone else in the world around us—will ultimately let us down. It is God who offers us hope and courage beyond our human limitations: "Whoever dwells in the shelter of the Most High will rest in the shadow of the Almighty. I will say of the Lord, 'He is my refuge and my fortress, my God, in whom I trust' " (Psalm 91:1, 2).

So we will not fear.

April 22

MORE THAN PROSPERITY

Surely the righteous will never be shaken;
they will be remembered forever.
They will have no fear of bad news;
their hearts are steadfast, trusting in the L*ORD.*

—Psalm 112:6, 7

An initial reading of many of the Psalms could lead the reader to a kind of prosperity gospel—the belief that if we follow God closely enough or trust Him truly enough, we will receive blessings, protection, and trouble-free lives. But such a reading falls down on two counts.

First, there are also many psalms that cry out for God's rescue amid despair, suffering, and trouble, and that express protest at the apparent unfairness of life and its blessings.

Second, life itself. Experiences in our lives and the lives of those around us demonstrate that blessings are not reserved only for the faithful. Similarly, safety and prosperity are not assured for those who follow and trust God, nor is trouble the lot only of the unbeliever or evildoer. God's faithfulness and blessings are not so much about protecting us from troubles but about keeping us and upholding us amid difficult times and circumstances. The promise of the Psalms—among other portions of the Bible—is that God is with us even when it does not look or feel like it. Rather than a result of circumstantial prosperity and blessings, the choice to follow and trust Him in all the happenings of our lives is reflected and realized in a different quality of life.

In a world filled with bad news, whether in the headlines or in our personal experiences, we need not be afraid. Our circumstances are not the measure of God's protection nor of our faithfulness. Instead, trusting in God offers us a steadfastness that is unshakeable and unthreatened by whatever might be going on around us or even within us. In Him, we have an eternal perspective and a present purpose. The bad news might still matter because suffering and injustice matter, but we are not overwhelmed, and we are not afraid.

April 23

SET FREE FROM FEAR

When hard pressed, I cried to the Lord;
he brought me into a spacious place.
The Lord is with me; I will not be afraid.
What can mere mortals do to me?

—Psalm 118:5, 6

It is an experience that countless people who have followed God can testify to: "In my distress I prayed to the Lord, and the Lord answered me and set me free" (Psalm 118:5, NLT). It does not necessarily mean that God intervened and immediately or miraculously changed our circumstances or that the reasons for distress were suddenly taken away. Nor does it mean that we will not face more such circumstances in our lives.

While this psalm does describe a victory over the psalmist's enemies, the larger victory is to overcome the fear that might have overwhelmed him and made any other progress or victory impossible. In similar moments or experiences, we can be set free from fear and reminded that the God who is with us is always greater than whatever threatens us, attacks us, or works against us.

But this psalm also reminds us—and models for us—the importance of praising God for setting us free and testifying to His goodness and power. The writer not only had this experience but wrote a song about it that is still read and perhaps even sung thousands of years later in many places and languages around the world. Our testimony might not be quite so enduring or widespread, but it may be no less important. Our acknowledgment of God and His goodness to us is an opportunity to invite others to join in praising Him and to encourage them to look for God's presence and intervention in their own lives.

The expression that bookends this psalm is repeated in various places throughout the Psalms: "Give thanks to the Lord, for he is good; his love endures forever" (Psalm 118:1, 29).

April 24

HOW CLOSELY GOD KNOWS US

Search me, God, and know my heart;
test me and know my anxious thoughts.

—Psalm 139:23

In Psalm 139, David praises God's intimate knowledge of each of us through all our lives. The Psalm begins with God's knowledge of David's physical circumstances, whether at home or traveling, sitting or standing (see Psalm 139:2, 3). Then, it zooms out to acknowledge God's presence wherever in life or in the world he might go (see Psalm 139:7–12). And then the Psalm returns to the intimacy of God's act of individual creation of each of us—"For you created my inmost being; you knit me together in my mother's womb" (Psalm 139:13)—and the intricate knowledge He has of us as a result.

After this overview of God's knowledge of and engagement with human beings in their bodies and lives, David turned to the circumstances of his own life—particularly the threats and attacks he faced (see Psalm 139:19–22). While the Bible regularly describes God as seeing and knowing our circumstances and hearing and responding to our cries of distress and requests for help, David asked God to come closer still, to look within him and know his heart and his "anxious thoughts." He wanted God to hear and feel his fears and anxieties—the things that kept him awake at night.

It was because of God's intimate knowledge of David, his heart, and his innermost thoughts that He could lead him—and each of us—"along the path of everlasting life" (Psalm 139:24, NLT). This understanding of God—that the Creator of the universe will come so close to us—can be daunting. But He is the Creator of each of us. With a unique intimacy, He created each of our individual lives. He knows our hearts and our fears. "How precious to me are your thoughts, God! How vast is the sum of them! Were I to count them, they would outnumber the grains of sand. When I awake, I am still with you" (Psalm 139:17, 18).

WISDOM SPEAKS

For the waywardness of the simple will kill them,
and the complacency of fools will destroy them;
but whoever listens to me will live in safety
and be at ease, without fear of harm.

—Proverbs 1:32, 33

The book of Proverbs introduces its readers—or hearers—to Wisdom as a character. "Out in the open wisdom calls aloud, she raises her voice in the public square" (Proverbs 1:20). Some commentators point to Jesus as the fulfillment of this prefiguration (see, for example, Luke 11:49); others consider this character as simply a personification of the virtue, a literary device to deliver the book's larger reflections on the role of wisdom in the life of faith and human flourishing.

Whichever way we read or think about this, Wisdom urges that choosing to live by the values and virtues she declares will have real and practical results in our lives. And her words were echoed by Jesus—at least their meaning—when He concluded the Sermon on the Mount with the parable of the wise and foolish builders. "Therefore everyone who hears these words of mine and puts them into practice is like a wise man who built his house on the rock." When storms and trouble would inevitably come, their lives and faith would endure, Jesus explained, "because it had its foundation on the rock" (Matthew 7:24, 25).

The book of Proverbs portrays the way of Wisdom as one that brings a double benefit—it will protect us from the dangers of folly, and it will guide us in the paths of righteousness and goodness. As such, Wisdom will help us avoid some of life's risks, disappointments, and sorrows—a life of greater safety and ease—and will allow us to live without fear, even when harm comes or threatens us. In Proverbs, when Wisdom speaks, she is worth listening to.

April 26

THE VOICE OF EXPERIENCE

Have no fear of sudden disaster
or of the ruin that overtakes the wicked,
for the LORD *will be at your side*
and will keep your foot from being snared.

—Proverbs 3:25, 26

Our lives can change in a moment. It might be an accident, a phone call, a diagnosis, a crime, or a disaster that engulfs us or our family. It might be something that no one but us notices, or it might capture the horrified attention of millions. But whatever and whenever it might be, "the LORD will be at your side."

In Proverbs, this wisdom is presented as advice from a father to a son or child. It is the voice of experience, perhaps reflecting on times in his own life when he recognized God's presence with Him, even while threatened by or surrounded by disaster or ruin. Ideally, this should be an important element in our relationships and friendships with older people in our families, churches, and communities. This is why we tell our stories and share our testimonies in church. It is why we publish books that tell true stories of God's protection and leading in times of war or other hardship. We borrow from each other's stories and take courage from the experiences of those around us.

In hearing such stories, we tend to hold our breath when we get to the moment of greatest peril—when the person might have been overwhelmed, defeated, or killed—even when we know how the story played out because, after all, the person is there telling the story. Particularly in our families and our communities of faith, we need to value the wisdom of those who are more experienced, especially those who can testify to the faithfulness of God in their most difficult times. These people and their stories are a valuable resource for growing an enduring courage and trust in God in our own lives. They are the voices who can meaningfully urge us to "have no fear."

CHRONIC FEAR

Anxiety weighs down the heart,
but a kind word cheers it up.

—Proverbs 12:25

Fear affects us in many ways. It can galvanize us to action or freeze us in our tracks. Fear can bring out our worst instincts, or it can summon up our truest courage. But chronic fear—even what we might describe as low-level fear, such as ongoing anxiety and worry—weighs us down and wears us out. Sometimes, this can be a serious mental health issue, can be clinically diagnosed, and requires treatment by a qualified health professional. But, even if that is not the case, I suspect almost all of us live with a persistent hum of low-level anxiety in our everyday lives, draining our energy, dulling our focus, and stealing our joy.

Such anxiety is a serious issue, part of the apparently widespread malaise of much of our world today. Despite this, we should not underestimate the opportunities we have to lift others up, that even a small kindness or word of encouragement can make a seemingly inordinate difference. It can be as simple as the response we give to someone's morning greeting. However, we could also be more intentional in imagining how we can brighten the day of the people with whom we work or otherwise share our lives.

The Bible offers simple but important wisdom. It reminds us that our faith is practical. We might be tempted to think that theology must be abstract and complicated, but the Bible is about all our lives—not only ideas that fill large, dusty books and not only our going-to-church best. The Bible acknowledges that we experience anxiety and fear, so we can admit it, too. The Bible recognizes that life can wear us down, so we should not be surprised when we feel tired. We can give more grace to the people we encounter each day. The Bible suggests that something as simple as a kind word can make a world of difference—or just enough difference for today.

That is something real we can offer those around us.

April 28

PRACTICING VULNERABILITY

Blessed is the one who always trembles before God,
but whoever hardens their heart falls into trouble.
—Proverbs 28:14

In its original Hebrew, the first part of this verse simply reads, "Blessed are those who fear." Various Bible translations treat this phrase in different ways, but the general consensus is that if fear is to be considered a blessing, it must be fear of something that is best avoided—for example, "Blessed are those who fear to do wrong" (NLT)—or of Someone who is rightly to be feared, respected, or reverenced.

Trusting in God is an act of vulnerability—or, even more, an ongoing attitude of vulnerability. It feels like we are taking a risk by trusting Someone we cannot see and perhaps only sometimes feel or encounter. As such, trusting God requires courage and an "always" perseverance. "Vulnerability is not winning or losing; it's having the courage to show up and be seen when we have no control over the outcome. Vulnerability is not weakness; it's our greatest measure of courage."*

While always requiring courage on our part, this vulnerability is not misplaced because of who God is and what we believe about Him. To be vulnerable in relation to God is to be blessed, whereas to refuse to open ourselves to His presence and leading in our lives means we are largely relying on ourselves, which will inevitably let us down and lead us into trouble.

The second part of this verse qualifies and contrasts with the fear that was encouraged. Whether Proverbs 28:14 urges us to be vulnerable in trusting God or to have a healthy fear of wrongdoing, either understanding is better than becoming hardened by our experiences of life and the further trouble a calloused heart causes. So choose fear that is blessed today.

---

* Brené Brown, *Rising Strong* (London: Vermilion, 2015), 26.

TO OUR WIVES AND MOTHERS

When it snows, she has no fear for her household;
for all of them are clothed in scarlet. . . .
She is clothed with strength and dignity;
she can laugh at the days to come.
—Proverbs 31:21, 25

Some years ago, there was a popular Christian movement that urged women to be "Proverbs 31 women," employing the detailed descriptions of "a wife of noble character . . . worth far more than rubies" (Proverbs 31:10) as a job description of the many roles that a wife and mother *ought* to fulfill. While perhaps a worthy aspiration, it also seemed to burden many already busy women with a sense of guilt about all the things they were not getting done or achieving in their lives.

So, rather than reading Proverbs 31 as a God-inspired "To Do List," we should first read it as a work of literature. In the original language, the poetic form is an acrostic, meaning that each verse begins with a successive letter of the Hebrew alphabet. In the Jewish tradition, this chapter was not read as a job description or a standard by which women would always be found wanting but as a psalm of praise using lyrical descriptions to recognize so many of the good things that the women in our lives are already doing and how they have worked and provided for their families.

Belying the way in which these verses have been used as a prescription, they are better read as a script for gratitude, encouragement, and empowerment: "She is clothed with strength and dignity, and she laughs without fear of the future" (Proverbs 31:25, NLT). Such confidence would include a refusal to be burdened with unrealistic expectations of her roles in the family or in the wider world, trusting God's leading and provision even in the daily tasks that each of us is called to do.

April 30

MEANINGLESS ANXIETY?

What do people get for all the toil and anxious striving with which they labor under the sun? All their days their work is grief and pain; even at night their minds do not rest. This too is meaningless.

—Ecclesiastes 2:22, 23

Ecclesiastes is a difficult book. It is complicated, complex, and, at times, seemingly contradictory—somewhat like the lives we live. It is worth asking how it fits in the Bible. While much of the Bible urges that our lives are meaningful in many different ways, the Preacher in Ecclesiastes seems to insist, over and over again, that everything is meaningless.

Of course, understood in the correct sense, what the Preacher says is true. One of our greatest fears is that nothing actually matters. Particularly in light of death, does all our work and worry amount to nothing? Amid the stress of our busy lives, there is a lurking sense that much of what we do contributes little to any greater good and is unlikely to last any longer than our attention to it. But we must do many of these things nonetheless.

Even our anxieties, worries, and fears—the things that keep us awake at night—are considered suspect by the Preacher. If our pleasures and joys are fleeting, so too are our griefs and sorrows. Those things that we spend so much time preoccupied with or even necessarily and legitimately attending to can seem as ephemeral as the lives we devote to them.

Ecclesiastes is a contemplation of priorities, not nihilism. Those things that we spend so much of our time and energy trying to overcome or working toward will come to an end. But a life lived with God *does* matter, even if we might not always understand exactly how. "Now all has been heard; here is the conclusion of the matter: Fear God and keep his commandments, for this is the whole duty of man" (Ecclesiastes 12:13).

A TIME TO BANISH ANXIETY

So then, banish anxiety from your heart
and cast off the troubles of your body,
for youth and vigor are meaningless.
—Ecclesiastes 11:10

It's probably not a biblical instruction that we have paid much attention to: "Young people, it's wonderful to be young! Enjoy every minute of it" (Ecclesiastes 11:9, NLT). When we see others suffering, it is good that we respond with empathy, but we tend to respond more easily to the suffering of the young. Perhaps we remember our own youthful energy and idealism or simply regard our younger years as a time that ought to be relatively carefree and joyous. So it is particularly arresting when this time of life is blighted by circumstances, fear, or anxiety, as it is for so many young people in the world today.

Even for young people, anxiety can be a serious condition that requires qualified medical care. There are some who experience difficult family and life circumstances that cause anxiety and fear. But many young people today feel increasingly pressured to achieve, to pursue detailed life plans and goals, to look and act in certain ways, to compete, acquire, and post their way into the world. This is the kind of pressure and anxiety we should encourage young people to question and "banish."

Youth is a time of life to experience, discover, and relish the goodness of life, albeit with reasonable limits and guidance. Important choices and influences are developed in these years, but they are often not those that feel most important at the time. To say that "youth and vigor are meaningless" means that they are to be enjoyed, but they are not the things that give meaning to our lives. Either slowly or suddenly, they will be lost, so our lives need to have more substance than merely the strength and enthusiasm of youthfulness. So "don't let the excitement of youth cause you to forget your Creator" (Ecclesiastes 12:1, NLT).

May 2

REMEMBER YOUR CREATOR

When people are afraid of heights
and of dangers in the streets.

—Ecclesiastes 12:5

Remember your Creator in the days of your youth" (Ecclesiastes 12:1) begins one of the most quoted passages from the book of Ecclesiastes, a memory verse that many of us learned growing up in church for its educational and spiritual imperative. But the extended passage seems more focused on aging than on youthful faithfulness, poetically describing the various diminished capacities that often come with advancing age.

Listed among these is the tendency to become more fearful as we age: "Remember him before you become fearful of falling and worry about danger in the streets" (Ecclesiastes 12:5, NLT). One cause of our fears is the physical risk that comes from things that simply were not a challenge to us when we were young. Perhaps there is also the fear of aging itself, losing some of the vitality and confidence that—rightly or wrongly—we assumed when we were younger.

Often, there also seems to be an attitude of fearfulness among older people. Some may be afraid of what they do not know or understand, but some fear comes from experience, from recognizing our human frailty and fragility. "You have to be old to understand that verse, to see your whole life, from early heedlessness to present regret for heedlessness. . . . Was the particular admonition addressed to young people, to remind them that age will come for them too? Or reserved for grey heads who would hear it with the ears of experience?"*

As much as it was a memory verse for us when we were young, this passage also speaks to us when we are older and begin to identify with some of the creative descriptions of the experiences of aging. When older, it is just as important to "Remember your Creator . . ."

* Doris Lessing, "Introduction," in *Ecclesiastes* (Melbourne, Australia: Text Publishing, 1998), x.

A FEARFUL CALLING

"Woe to me!" I cried. "I am ruined! For I am a man of unclean lips, and I live among a people of unclean lips, and my eyes have seen the King, the LORD Almighty."

—Isaiah 6:5

Across the Bible's story, many of the leaders, prophets, parents-to-be, and apostles were called to their specific roles in the context of some kind of revelation of God. These experiences were attention-grabbing, transformative, and terrifying.

This moment of revelation and calling came to the soon-to-be prophet Isaiah in the year King Uzziah died—about 740 B.C. He "saw the Lord, seated on a throne, high and exalted, and the train of his robe filled the temple" (Isaiah 6:1). Above Him, angels flew on multiple wings, shouting their praises to God repeatedly and so loud that it shook the building.

Isaiah responded in a way that we can regard only as entirely understandable—he cried out in fear. "Revelation occurs against the will of the prophet. It is not a favor to him, but a burden of terror. To Isaiah the perception of God is a venture fraught with shock, peril, and dismay, something which is more than his soul can bear."*

When God asked specific people to take on difficult assignments, He often gave them a glimpse of His glory and power by which to remember their calling. This assured those who were called of His ability to uphold and guide them whatever circumstances they might face, and it also had the intended side-effect of reminding them of their sinfulness and unworthiness of His gracious attention. It was a necessary humility that fitted them for their task, causing them to rely on God even more and reminding them that, while they had an important role to play, God's larger plan was not primarily about them.

This experience moved Isaiah past his initial fear to his humble response to God's call: "Here am I. Send me!" (Isaiah 6:8).

---

* Abraham J. Heschel, *The Prophets* (New York: Harper Perennial, 2001), 458.

May 4

IGNORING AN INVITATION TO FAITH

Say to him, "Be careful, keep calm and don't be afraid. Do not lose heart because of these two smoldering stubs of firewood—because of the fierce anger of Rezin and Aram and of the son of Remaliah."

—Isaiah 7:4

Soon after the death of his father, Jotham (see 2 Kings 15:32–34), Ahaz was faced with the threat of attack from the neighboring kings of Aram and Israel. They likely saw the transition to the newly crowned, twenty-year-old king as a moment of weakness they could exploit—and they were right. Ahaz and his army were able to repel the first attack on Jerusalem, but he feared that another attack was coming.

As Ahaz looked for backup, Isaiah came to him with a message of comfort delivered on the instructions of God. "Be careful" with whom you seek alliances. "Keep calm" rather than being panicked into unwise decisions. And ultimately, "Don't be afraid." This was a call for Ahaz to trust God more than he feared his attackers. God concluded His appeal to Ahaz by saying, "If you do not stand firm in your faith, you will not stand at all" (Isaiah 7:9).

But Ahaz ignored the warning. He took silver and gold from the temple to pay Tigleth-pileser, king of Assyria, to protect Israel. The Assyrian king attacked Damascus, the capital of Aram, and killed their king (see 2 Kings 16:7–9). In the short term, the plan seemed to have worked. But Ahaz traveled to Damascus and was drawn into the pagan worship he witnessed there (see 2 Kings 16:10–20), and Judah continued to pay tribute to Assyria throughout the remainder of Ahaz's reign and beyond.

During the reign of Ahaz, the faithfulness and independence of the nation were compromised because of his failure of faith and courage, despite the warning and the reassurance that God offered to the young king through Isaiah.

"DO NOT THINK LIKE EVERYONE ELSE DOES"

This is what the Lord says to me with his strong hand upon me, warning me not to follow the way of this people:

"Do not call conspiracy
everything this people calls a conspiracy;
do not fear what they fear,
and do not dread it."

—Isaiah 8:11, 12

After Ahaz had entered into an unhealthy alliance with the king of Assyria, God warned the people that Assyria would soon overwhelm the nation of Judah. But even then, His message to Isaiah and to those who remained faithful to God was that they need not be afraid. "The LORD has given me a strong warning not to think like everyone else does" was the message Isaiah delivered (Isaiah 8:11, NLT).

In a world dominated by fear and a culture in which conspiracy theories spread like a virus online and through social media—a culture in which even some preachers trade on sensationalism and fear—this seems to be a voice we need to hear again: Do not "think like everyone else does." Fear is not a feature of our faith; rather, our faith must always be larger than our fears. When conspiracy thinking panders to our pre-existing fears and prejudices, we need to be particularly discerning.

Fear is a powerful motivation, but it usually dissipates quickly, so it needs to be constantly stoked and heightened by those who want to use it. However, fear is not a good motivator and does not bring out our best. Fear does not make us more loving, joyful, peaceful, peacemaking, patient, kind, good, faithful, gentle, or self-controlled (see Galatians 5:22, 23). So, do not think like everyone else does. Do not waste time and energy on supposed conspiracies. Do not fear what other people fear.

Instead, "make the LORD of Heaven's Armies holy in your life. He is the one you should fear. . . . He will keep you safe" (Isaiah 8:13, 14, NLT).

May 6

REMEMBERING DELIVERANCE PAST

Therefore this is what the Lord, the LORD Almighty, says:

". . . My people who live in Zion,
do not be afraid of the Assyrians,
who beat you with a rod
and lift up a club against you, as Egypt did."

—Isaiah 10:24

Through Isaiah's prophecies, God had foretold that the Assyrians, whom Ahaz had trusted to protect Israel, would, in turn, attack them and that God would use this foreign power to punish the nation and its leaders for their collective lack of faith. Yet God assured Israel that He would have a remnant among the people (see Isaiah 10:20–22), and He still described them as "my people," expressing tenderness and care. God's judgment would be—and always is—tempered by mercy.

Though the Assyrians would have their moment, they were still subject to God's larger plans, so those who were truly His people need not be afraid of them. As evidence, God offered the story of His intervention in Israel's history when He had seen their oppression in Egypt and brought them out of slavery. Although this had taken place centuries earlier, it was a touchstone of their identity as a people and as a faith. As Moses had instructed, this was a story that was to be retold repeatedly in the life of the people of Israel, but it seemed it was also to be relived at key points in their history.

At the time of the exodus, Egypt was the most powerful nation in the world. At the time of Gideon, the Midianites had overrun Israel (see Isaiah 10:26). Now, the Assyrians seemed to hold sway. But God insisted that, with Him, the remnant had less reason to be afraid than these seemingly dominant powers who were against Him. "The lofty trees will be felled, the tall ones will be brought low" (Isaiah 10:33).

Although Israel was outnumbered, overpowered, and beaten down, God was with them still, so God said, "Do not be afraid," even of those who were doing the oppressing.

A VISION OF CREATION RENEWED

They will neither harm nor destroy
on all my holy mountain,
for the earth will be full of the knowledge of the Lord
as the waters cover the sea.

—Isaiah 11:9

While warnings seemed to dominate Isaiah's pronouncements, his messages also had a persistent note of hope. The people he was addressing were under threat, and he expected their circumstances to get worse. They had been attacked and would be attacked all the more. The nation would be largely destroyed; many of the people would be killed, and most of those who remained would be exiled. But, Isaiah insisted, that would not be the end of their story as a nation or as the people of God. Indeed, their future would be even brighter than the glories of their past.

Isaiah pointed forward to One who would come. "A shoot will come up from the stump of Jesse" (Isaiah 11:1)—One who would have world-changing significance and impact (see Isaiah 11:4). He would change everything—all the way back to His original intention for all of creation.

Today, we might read this as confusing the first and second comings of Jesus, but this was Isaiah's expectation of the Messianic age, and it is helpful to consider his perspective that the transformation and re-creation resulting from these two comings should not be so isolated or distinct. There is important truth in understanding Jesus in His incarnation and Jesus in His promised return, but He is the same Jesus in both, and the effects are part of the same plan—the same redemption and restoration.

So Isaiah's descriptions of justice for the poor and judgment against those who oppress them (see Isaiah 11:3, 4), of unlikely animal companions (see Isaiah 11:6–8), and of a world of peace filled with the knowledge and glory of God can be read and celebrated as what God has done, is doing, and will do in the coming(s) of Jesus. In Jesus, these are a growing reality, a present task, and a certain hope.

May 8

IN THAT DAY

Surely God is my salvation;
I will trust and not be afraid.
The L*ORD*, *the* L*ORD himself, is my strength and my defense;*
he has become my salvation.

—Isaiah 12:2

The promise that Isaiah passed on to the people was that, after they had been exiled by the Assyrians, God would act again. "There will be a highway for the remnant of his people that is left from Assyria, as there was for Israel when they came up from Egypt" (Isaiah 11:16). Just as God had intervened on behalf of His people in their history, particularly in leading them out of Egypt and making a way through the Red Sea, so He would intervene again to lead His people back to their land and back to His plan for their nation.

"In that day" (Isaiah 12:1), songs of praise would again resound toward God as they had after the people of Israel had passed through the Red Sea to safety (see Exodus 15:1–21). "In that day," when God resumed His role of bringing salvation to His people, trust would be restored, and fear would be removed. While their present circumstances made it difficult to sing such a song, it was an expression of faith and hope to anticipate and expect that such a day would come, a day on which singing such a song would again make sense.

God's promise also revealed His nature. Centuries after Isaiah, the apostle Paul insisted, "I am convinced that nothing can ever separate us from God's love" (Romans 8:38, NLT). But Isaiah had already made this case, arguing that even God's occasional anger at the nation, even the punishment that He apparently brought through foreign invaders, could not separate the people from God's love. For the people at that time, it was yet a statement of faith. But in that day, it would be again celebrated in all its reality.

A WREATH FOR THE REMNANT

In that day the LORD Almighty
will be a glorious crown,
a beautiful wreath
for the remnant of his people.
He will be a spirit of justice
to the one who sits in judgment,
a source of strength
to those who turn back the battle at the gate.

—Isaiah 28:5, 6

According to Isaiah's prophecy, the glory of Samaria would soon fade like a flower, and "that wreath, the pride of Ephraim's drunkards, will be trampled underfoot" (Isaiah 28:3) when attacked by the Assyrian king Shalmanezer. By contrast, God Himself would be the glorious crown and unfading wreath of the remnant of the people of Judah (see Isaiah 28:5). God's promises were not merely nice poetry or a hopeful sentiment. The restoration of Israel would make practical differences in their lives and in their society in that day.

First, God's presence and power would mean that their society would work toward greater justice. "He will give a longing for justice to their judges" (Isaiah 28:6, NLT). Because of what God had done for them, they would seek to live by the principles of justice that God had given to the people in the laws of Moses. They would set right injustices, judge fairly for the poor, and care for the widows, the orphans, and the foreigners living among them.

God's presence and influence would also be a source of courage for those who would defend the people against attacks from their enemies. "He will give great courage to their warriors who stand at the gates" (Isaiah 28:6, NLT). This could include both their political and military leaders. By relying on God, more courageous leadership would foster a more confident, hopeful society. For the people in Zion—the city of God—He would be "a precious cornerstone for a sure foundation; the one who relies on it will never be stricken with panic" (Isaiah 28:16).

May 10

THE TEMPTATION TO GO BACK

This is what the Sovereign L*ORD, the Holy One of Israel, says:*

"In repentance and rest is your salvation,
in quietness and trust is your strength,
but you would have none of it."

—Isaiah 30:15

Many times during Israel's wilderness wanderings, the people complained about their circumstances and revolted against the leadership of Moses. Remembering the fish, cucumbers, melons, and onions that they enjoyed amid their slavery (see Numbers 11:5), their temptation was to turn back toward Egypt rather than relying on God's protection and provision as He had led them. So strong was this impulse based on their selective memories that Moses gave the people a specific commandment that they were never to go back to Egypt (see Deuteronomy 17:16).

In the understanding of the people of Israel and Judah, Egypt was a symbol of a faithless empire, similar to the symbolic role that Babylon and then Rome have come to occupy in the minds of God's people in subsequent centuries. All of these powerful empires oppressed the people of God and sought to replace the worship of God with the worship of their gods. So, for the people of Judah to seek to make an alliance with Egypt to protect them from the threats of Assyria was a serious betrayal of their national identity—and their trust in God. "But Pharaoh's protection will be to your shame, Egypt's shade will bring you disgrace" (Isaiah 30:3).

Fear tempted them to go back to Egypt to seek safety in the protection of that human empire. Isaiah warned that their turn to Egypt would not end well. As do most responses driven by fear, it would actually exacerbate their fears (see Isaiah 30:16, 17). But he also offered an alternative, calling them back instead to "the Holy One of Israel." In the face of an advancing Assyrian army, "repentance and rest . . . quietness and trust" might not sound like strength, but it was the invitation and promise of God.

CHOOSING THE GREATER POWER

This is what the Lord says to me:

"As a lion growls,
a great lion over its prey—
and though a whole band of shepherds
is called together against it,
it is not frightened by their shouts
or disturbed by their clamor—
so the Lord Almighty will come down
to do battle on Mount Zion and on its heights."

—Isaiah 31:4

By the length of their protest, we can understand something of the outrage of God and His prophet at the suggestion that the people of Judah would make an alliance with Egypt. As Isaiah—and God—continued to rail against this plan, they made the case that relying on human strength was foolishness compared to trusting in God. As powerful as their armies might seem, "the Egyptians are mere mortals and not God; their horses are flesh and not spirit" (Isaiah 31:3).

In contrast, God describes Himself as a great lion. As a powerful and eternal Being, He is unafraid of whatever the surrounding nations—any or all of them—might threaten against Him or His people. If the people would choose Him, He would "do battle" on their behalf, taking up a defensive position on the heights of Mount Zion. Their growling God would be fierce in their defense but gentle in their protection.

In phrasing that would be echoed by Jesus as He lamented over the city of Jerusalem, its history, and its people (see Matthew 23:37), God describes His care for the people of the city in Isaiah's day using the image of a mother bird. "The Lord of Heaven's Armies will hover over Jerusalem and protect it like a bird protecting its nest. He will defend and save the city; he will pass over it and rescue it" (Isaiah 31:5, NLT).

Isaiah urged the people to return to the God they had rebelled against. Their fearless God would be the One to defeat their enemies, and He would again be the God of Jerusalem.

May 12

IN A RIGHTEOUS KINGDOM

The fruit of that righteousness will be peace;
its effect will be quietness and confidence forever.
My people will live in peaceful dwelling places,
in secure homes,
in undisturbed places of rest.

—Isaiah 32:17, 18

When God would intervene to protect and ultimately restore the people of Judah—as Isaiah prophesied—a new kind of kingdom would be established. This would be a kingdom of righteousness, a kingdom in which evil and injustice would be reversed and set right. It would also be a kingdom of personal and courageous transformation. "The fearful heart will know and understand, and the stammering tongue will be fluent and clear" (Isaiah 32:4).

Like later descriptions in the Bible of a restored and re-created world, the details were often more about what would *not* be in this new kingdom. However, justice and righteousness were the active ingredients that God would restore to creation (see Isaiah 32:16), and they would result in peace, confidence, and rest.

Describing the fruit of God's righteous intervention in this way, it is clear that God's kingdom has both personal and social implications. Living together as the transformed and fearless people of God, trusting God's power and presence with them, meant not only protection against would-be enemies but was also a recipe for peace and rest between people within the nation itself. Restoring their relationship with God would restore their relationships with each other.

While we tend to read descriptions like this as looking forward to God's coming kingdom, Jewish readers would have recognized this as a description of the Messianic age. In a sense, this was fulfilled in the life of Jesus. Even the angels who announced His birth to the shepherds outside Bethlehem sang about glorifying God but also proclaimed "on earth peace to those on whom his favor rests" (Luke 2:14). In Jesus, the righteous kingdom has come. In Jesus, the righteous kingdom will come. This is why the angels could introduce themselves to the shepherds that night with, "Do not be afraid" (Luke 2:10).

THE PROPHET'S MESSAGE[S]

Strengthen the feeble hands, / steady the knees that give way; / say to those with fearful hearts, / "Be strong, do not fear; / your God will come, / he will come with vengeance; / with divine retribution / he will come to save you."
—Isaiah 35:3, 4

When we think of the Hebrew prophets, we often imagine thundering pronouncements of warning and judgment, often in the scratchy voices of these roughly dressed and wild-eyed characters. But this is a view from the top, the perspective of those most threatened by changes to the status quo. To them, these were messages that threatened destruction and despair.

For those who most desperately needed their lives and the world to be changed, the messages of the prophets sounded differently. In their ears, the prophets' voices brought messages of encouragement and hope to strengthen the weak and calm their fears. When we consider the world from the perspective of those who are oppressed in a society or culture, promises of God's "divine retribution" sound more like a message of salvation.

At the same time, these messages were an appeal to all people, wherever they might find themselves in the social structure. It was a call to repentance and an offer of hope. "Every prediction of disaster is in itself an exhortation to repentance. . . . Almost every prophet brings consolation, promise, and the hope of reconciliation along with censure and castigation. He begins with a message of doom; he concludes with a message of hope."* While the weak are offered hope directly, the warnings and judgments against the powerful also point out an opportunity for their reconciliation and redemption.

How we hear these prophets today tells us something about our spiritual standing and where we place our trust. Nevertheless, when we listen to these prophets, they remain a voice of hope and an assurance of God's concern for all people, proclaiming His recurring encouragement, "Do not be afraid."

---

* Abraham J. Heschel, *The Prophets* (New York: Harper Perennial, 2001), 14.

May 14

THE GOD OF ALL THE NATIONS

Isaiah said to them, "Tell your master, 'This is what the LORD says: Do not be afraid of what you have heard—those words with which the underlings of the king of Assyria have blasphemed me.' "

—Isaiah 37:6

This is Isaiah's retelling of the story in 2 Kings 19, and it largely replicates the text of that chapter, this time in the context of Isaiah's ongoing prophetic role. This event took place about 700 B.C., and history records that, as much as Assyria was the dominant power in the region at that time, Jerusalem was not defeated.

Nonetheless, Hezekiah was alarmed. He sent some of his officials to Isaiah as a way of seeking God. "This day is a day of distress and rebuke and disgrace," they said (Isaiah 37:3). Hezekiah asked Isaiah to pray for the nation, but his burning question was whether God had heard the ridicule the Assyrian spokesman had directed against Him and the people.

Isaiah dismissed the intimidation from the Assyrian delegation, and assured King Hezekiah and his officials that God was well aware of their situation and that He had heard the threats against them. While Isaiah's larger message was one of warning and judgment, he also consistently directed the people and their leaders back to God. Despite their history of unfaithfulness, God remained attentive, faithful, merciful, and available. Across his ministry, Isaiah insisted that the people's best political and military strategy was always to trust in "the Holy One of Israel" (Isaiah 37:23).

As Isaiah foretold, God intervened in the siege of Jerusalem, and Sennacherib was called back to his home in Nineveh, where he was murdered (see Isaiah 37:36–38). While we might not understand all the ways in which this works, Isaiah explained that this foreign king's life and even his military successes were always under the supervision and watch of Israel's God—"Long ago I ordained it" (Isaiah 37:26). Somehow, the God of the people of Jerusalem was also the God of all the nations.

A NEW HOPE

You who bring good news to Zion,
go up on a high mountain.
You who bring good news to Jerusalem,
lift up your voice with a shout,
lift it up, do not be afraid;
say to the towns of Judah,
"Here is your God!"

—Isaiah 40:9

As it has been passed down through history (the Isaiah scroll was the most complete document among the Dead Sea Scrolls), chapter 40 begins a new stage in the book of Isaiah. Possibly written closer to the time of these later events, the focus turns to promises of restoration for the people of God after they were taken into exile in Babylon. After years of silence, a new voice would be heard: "Comfort, comfort my people, says your God. Speak tenderly to Jerusalem, and proclaim to her that her hard service has been completed, that her sin has been paid for, that she has received from the LORD's hand double for all her sins" (Isaiah 40:1, 2).

This was good news to be proclaimed throughout the scattered peoples and shattered towns of Judah. That God would intervene and that He would return to live among them was most joyous news and not something to shrink back from proclaiming. This message fueled the expectation of a coming Messiah toward the time of Jesus' birth and was intensified with the preaching of John. Along with all the Gospel writers, John the Baptist agreed that this new era would herald the coming of the Messiah (see Matthew 3:3; Mark 1:2, 3; Luke 3:4–6; John 1:23).

Taking it as his personal mission statement and quoting Isaiah 40:3–6, John boldly proclaimed the coming of Jesus and the message of repentance and reformation to the nation. But there was also a strong sense that this was about more than just the national fortunes of God's people. John came announcing Jesus as "the Lamb of God, who takes away the sin of the world!" (John 1:29).

May 16

AMONG THE NATIONS

"So do not fear, for I am with you;
do not be dismayed, for I am your God.
I will strengthen you and help you;
I will uphold you with my righteous right hand."

—Isaiah 41:10

God has always wanted to make His case before the nations, to restore His relationship with all peoples. While He has chosen specific people throughout history, His is a mission, a message, and a love that always reaches out to all humanity. While He chose Abram, he insisted that this was not only about Abram and his descendants but that "all peoples on earth will be blessed through you" (Genesis 12:3). Not only were the people of Israel to be God's nation, but they would be an example to surrounding nations (see Deuteronomy 4:6–8) and a means by which God would work to reach those nations.

So, as God promised to bring the people of Judah back from exile in Babylon, He again sought to work through them to gain the attention of the whole world. God explained to the people that He had been at work in the rise of Babylon. Even as other nations had summoned their armies and called upon their gods to stand up to this empire (see Isaiah 41:5–7), they had all been swept away. But as small, inconsequential, and conquered as the people of Judah appeared, God remembered His promises to their ancestors.

Moses had explained to the people of Israel in his day, "The Lord did not set his affection on you and choose you because you were more numerous than other peoples, for you were the fewest of all peoples" (Deuteronomy 7:7). Now God was doing it again. He would restore them to the land He had given them. He would establish them as a new revelation of Himself and demonstrate the relationship that He desired with all nations: "You are my servant; I have chosen you and have not rejected you. So do not fear, for I am with you" (Isaiah 41:9, 10).

IT'S ABOUT GOD

"I am the Lord your God
who takes hold of your right hand
and says to you, Do not fear;
I will help you.
Do not be afraid, O worm Jacob,
O little Israel, do not fear for I myself will help you," declares the Lord,
your Redeemer, the Holy One of Israel.
—Isaiah 41:13, 14

It is natural that our perspectives of life and reality begin with the human view. But one of the significant contributions that reading the Bible offers us and our faith is the recurring nudge to consider our lives, our history, and our world from God's perspective—as far as possible. This is an important corrective to our assumption that the story is about us when it is always more about God.

Notice God's language in these verses. They are about Him. His assertions of His identification with and care for His people are the basis for the "Do not be afraids." Again, the emphasis is similar to Moses' explanation to the people of Israel why and how God had intervened to rescue them from Egypt: "It was because the Lord loved you and kept the oath he swore to your ancestors that he brought you out with a mighty hand and redeemed you from the land of slavery" (Deuteronomy 7:8). The power, goodness, and love of God is always the explanation for His intervention in our world and our lives.

But there is still another aspect to this: God's close identification with His people, even in their humiliation. He described "little Israel" as a worm. This was not to mock those enslaved, exiled, and insignificant people but to show His grace, mercy, and power in stooping to rescue them and lift them up. This close connection with humanity would reach its extreme in Jesus' death when He would be tortured and mocked as "a worm, and not a man" (see Psalm 22:6–8). All the way, the story is about God—His power, His willingness to be weak, and always His love.

May 18

BECAUSE YOU ARE MINE

This is what the L*ORD says—*
he who created you, O Jacob,
he who formed you, O Israel:
"Do not fear, for I have redeemed you;
I have summoned you by name; you are mine."
—Isaiah 43:1

Though Isaiah was focused on the world-shaping work that God was undertaking on behalf of His people, he was also alert to the intimacy that God sought with the people. God's purposes were not about geopolitical movements so much as they were about restoring the relationship between Himself and His people. At times, He would work in nation-shaking and nation-forming ways because those, too, were about people, but God and His prophets would never mistake the nations for the individuals.

This verse references God as the One who created and formed Jacob and Israel, perhaps suggesting both their personal, individual creation and their formation as a people, but He is also their Redeemer and the One who called them. It was not a generic calling; He called each person and each people group by name. This is remarkable attention and intimacy.

Pause for a moment to think how remarkable it is that God—the Creator of the universe—simply knows your name. Then consider His emphasis, "I have called you by name; you are mine" (Isaiah 43:1, NLT). Throughout His writings, Isaiah insisted that God was deeply involved in our world. He worked with nations and empires on the stage of history. He was intensely involved in the lives and fates of the people of Judah, whom Isaiah was primarily addressing. But He also maintained a personal interest in the lives of every individual.

Not only was this a generous overture for a renewed relationship, but it was also the basis for living without fear. Of course, the people would still experience the challenges of life, such as floods and fires (see Isaiah 43:2), but they need not be overwhelmed by them because God was with them, had called them, and personally knew them and their circumstances.

A LARGER FAMILY

"Do not be afraid, for I am with you;
I will bring your children from the east
and gather you from the west."

—Isaiah 43:5

These promises to the people of Judah in exile were heartening: "Do not be afraid. God will act again to intervene on your behalf." God would bring them back to their land and restore their nation. This would fulfill the promise Moses made to the people that even if their nation was taken into exile as a result of their unfaithfulness, God would "restore your fortunes and have compassion on you and gather you again from all the nations where he scattered you" (Deuteronomy 30:3). If they would turn back to Him, God would bring Israel's children—"your children"—back to Jerusalem.

But Isaiah also called them to a larger vision of God's family. God's promises were not only about the exiles in Babylon; His new and larger vision for the people of God included those He would bring from all points of the compass: "Bring my sons from afar and my daughters from the ends of the earth—everyone who is called by my name, whom I created for my glory, whom I formed and made" (Isaiah 43:6, 7). God would bring the children He had created—"my sons . . . and my daughters"—into His family.

This was a similar message to Jesus' description of Himself as the good shepherd. He would lead and protect, even lay down His life for His sheep. But they should not assume that His sheep were only those in the sheep pen they knew. "I have other sheep," Jesus said, "that are not of this sheep pen. I must bring them also. They too will listen to my voice, and there shall be one flock and one shepherd" (John 10:16). God was prepared to push His people to a larger understanding of who was invited to be part of His family—and whom they should seek to include.

May 20

"COURAGE, DEAR HEART"

This is what the L*ORD says—*
he who made you, who formed you in the womb,
and who will help you:
"Do not be afraid, O Jacob, my servant,
Jeshurun, whom I have chosen."

—Isaiah 44:2

In one of my favorite stories when growing up, one of the tenderest moments comes when the heroes of the journey were lost in a sea of darkness aboard their small ship. Amid their panicked efforts to escape the darkness, seemingly rowing in circles, Lucy—the main female character—whispered an urgent prayer for help. Although the darkness seemed unchanged, "she began to feel a little—a very, very little—better."

Then, one of the crew noticed a small point of light that grew to become a beam of light falling on them and offering them a way forward. At that moment, Lucy heard the voice of the Godlike character—a great lion, similar to the lion described by Isaiah earlier in his book (see Isaiah 31:4)—who had guided their journey but who seemed to have abandoned them in the darkness and amid the feelings of despair it generated. As the darkness began to lighten, the message was intimate and simple, in a whisper only Lucy could hear: "Courage, dear heart."*

Isaiah presented the voice of God with a similar intimacy and encouragement. This God was engaged in the creation of each person, their physical formation, and their ongoing sustaining. That each of us exists is already evidence of God's incredible care and provision.

But, more than this, God also has the voice of a doting parent, whispering reassurance to a child who was not only created but also chosen and dearly loved. *Jeshurun* was drawn from a Hebrew term of endearment and affection, saying in effect, "Do not be afraid, my dear child." Isaiah's God spoke to the people with a voice of tenderness and love—even in a time of exile, amid temptations to despair.

---

* C. S. Lewis, *The Voyage of the Dawntreader* (London: Fontana Lions, 1980), 143.

WHY OR WHATEVER

"Do not tremble, do not be afraid.
Did I not proclaim this and foretell it long ago?
You are my witnesses. Is there any God besides me?
No, there is no other Rock; I know not one."

—Isaiah 44:8

Sometimes, it can be hard to make sense of why things happen in our world. Whether in the natural world, in history and nations, or in our personal lives, we wrestle with cause and effect, with finding reasons for events that shape our lives and our world, and with wondering where God fits in our understanding.

If God has foreknowledge of the things that happen to us, does that mean He causes them, that He ordains them? Or simply that He is aware of them as things that happen? And does this mean that somehow He could order our lives differently? How do we try to make sense when it seems that God sometimes intervenes and at other times is silent? It is difficult to understand our lives from God's perspective, from the standpoint of eternity, or the uncertainties of how and why "time and chance happen to them all" (Ecclesiastes 9:11).

But, while we might not have full answers to many of these questions, the God portrayed by Isaiah—"I am the first and I am the last" (Isaiah 44:6)—is a God who is always with us whatever our circumstances, challenges, or trials, and whatever our questions or uncertainties.

God insists that there will always be a contrast in our world between those who worship idols—other gods or other priorities—and those who trust in Him. Part of this contrast will be how they respond to the circumstances and questions of life and our world. Those who make and follow idols "will be brought down to terror and shame" (Isaiah 44:11), while His message to those who follow Him is, repeatedly, "Do not be afraid." He is the Rock, and there is no other.

May 22

FINDING A FINDABLE GOD

I have not spoken in secret,
from somewhere in a land of darkness;
I have not said to Jacob's descendants,
"Seek me in vain."
I, the LORD, speak the truth;
I declare what is right.

—Isaiah 45:19

It might seem that God and humanity keep missing each other. It is one of the dynamics of that broken relationship between us—from God's lonely walk that evening in the garden of Eden while Adam and Eve hid to all the times that human beings have longed for God and expressed frustrations at His seeming silence or absence, particularly in times of need or trouble. While the approach of God might make us nervous, one of our greatest human fears is that we are left alone, that God either has never been more than an abstract explanation or fairy story, or that He has abandoned us to the uncertainties and fragility of our lives.

However, God insists across the Bible that He is never too hard to find. "I publicly proclaim bold promises," He told the people of Isaiah's day. "I would not have told the people of Israel to seek me if I could not be found" (Isaiah 45:19, NLT). God was available, interested, and courageous in His vulnerability to His people—and to any people who would truly seek Him.

This was also a marker of who Jesus was, what He was about, and how He conducted His ministry. At His trial, Jesus alluded to this verse in response to questions from the high priest: "I have spoken openly to the world. . . . I said nothing in secret" (John 18:20). While this might seem a careful answer to questions that were trying to draw Jesus into self-incrimination, the reality was that His answer was a claim to be God. Although His statement drew a sharp response from His questioners, even as He suffered, it was a reminder that He was "God with us" (Matthew 1:23)—a God who is not hard to find for those who seek Him and who is working to restore the relationship between God and humanity.

May 23

RIGHTEOUSNESS VERSUS INSULTS

"Hear me, you who know what is right,
you people who have taken my instruction to heart:
Do not fear the reproach of mere mortals
or be terrified by their insults."

—Isaiah 51:7

Because we assume our own permanence, we also assume the permanence of our world and of the people around us. But God has reminded us throughout the Bible that we are finite beings. Our lives and influence extend only so far and so long. Even "the earth will wear out like a garment" (Isaiah 51:6), so the advice from God to the people He was planning to bring back from their exile in Babylon was that they should invest their lives in things that would last beyond their present lives.

While it is good to "live at peace with everyone," "if it is possible, as far as it depends on you" (Romans 12:18), we need not be afraid of insults from others, "the reproach of mere mortals." As hurtful and as daunting as they can be, such insults are only as enduring as their source. It is difficult to feel isolated, ridiculed, or threatened, but we need to keep as large a perspective as possible. Just as a single moth can destroy a garment or piece of cloth (see Isaiah 51:8), even small things can undo otherwise fearsome people.

As always, God offers an alternative to our human fear of human reproach: "My righteousness will last forever, my salvation through all generations" (Isaiah 51:8). Only God and His righteousness last forever, so that is where we should focus our greatest attention. Jesus insisted that His followers would be blessed "when people insult you, persecute you and falsely say all kinds of evil against you because of me" (Matthew 5:11). As God assured the returning exiles, His blessings are always greater than the insults of those around us.

May 24

COUNTERING CONTINUING FEAR

"I, even I, am he who comforts you. / Who are you that you fear mere mortals, / human beings who are but grass, / that you forget the Lord *your Maker, / who stretches out the heavens / and who lays the foundations of the earth, / that you live in constant terror every day / because of the wrath of the oppressor, / who is bent on destruction? / For where is the wrath of the oppressor?"*

—Isaiah 51:12, 13

Like the people of Israel, after they had been rescued from slavery in Egypt, the people returning from exile in Babylon needed time to heal and readjust their ways of thinking and believing. After generations of oppression, living with fear, threats, and the realities of violence, the people required a period of rehabilitation to be able to live freely and without fear. While the physical slavery and subjugation had come to an end, their mindset and worldview needed recalibration—and that would take time.

One of the damages that fear does to us over time is that it becomes a way of thinking, an almost automatic response to whatever confronts us. Chronic fear can shape and twist us into people who "live in constant terror every day." In its more extreme form and with a variety of symptoms, this effect is often diagnosed as Post-Traumatic Stress Disorder (PTSD), but even at a lower intensity, long-term or repeated exposure to fear and threats can have a debilitating impact.

When prolonged fear progresses toward PTSD, qualified health care is vitally important, but God also offered a faith response to the people returning from Babylon. He again contrasted the temporary nature of the "mere mortals" and even the empire that had been oppressing them with His power and permanence as the One "who stretches out the heavens and who lays the foundations of the earth." Note the present tense. This was not something done only in the past but something that God continues to do. It was that God who now comforted them, restored them, and re-established them in freedom and fearlessness.

May 25

THE PUNISHMENT THAT BROUGHT US PEACE

But he was pierced for our transgressions,
he was crushed for our iniquities;
the punishment that brought us peace was on him,
and by his wounds we are healed.

—Isaiah 53:5

The description of the suffering servant in Isaiah 53 is one of the Bible's most poetic descriptions of Jesus' mission and sacrifice. Not only does it describe His suffering and death, but it also highlights the fact that Jesus' sufferings would work to bring us peace, to remove the fear that had come over us, and to bring reconciliation between God and humanity.

The importance of this reconciliation project cannot be underestimated. In the Bible's story, that project stretches from the evening in the garden of Eden described in Genesis 3:8–10 to the world re-created when"God's dwelling-place" will be among the people and "he will dwell with them" (Revelation 21:3). But, perhaps more poignantly, that restoration plan drew God's one and only Son into the history and pain of this world at great cost to Himself and even at remarkable risk to God. It is the mechanism by which our fear of God could be eradicated and our relationship restored.

As such, Isaiah 53 is not only great poetry, nor merely a foreshadowing of the cruel and humiliating ways in which Jesus would be tortured and would die, but also a manifesto for reconciliation and fearlessness in the relationship between God and human beings.

Contemporary author Douglas Coupland was once asked about his greatest fear. He replied, "That God exists but doesn't care very much for humans."* In Jesus and His crucifixion, God took away this great fear. It shows that God does care very much for humans. He was prepared to sacrifice His existence to demonstrate how much He cares and to make our eternal reconnection, rescue, and relationship with Him possible.

---

* Douglas Coupland, "P.S.: About the Author," in *Girlfriend in a Coma* (New York: Harper Perennial, 2004), 2.

May 26

MORE THAN RESTORATION

"Do not be afraid; you will not be put to shame.
Do not fear disgrace; you will not be humiliated.
You will forget the shame of your youth
and remember no more the reproach of your widowhood."
—Isaiah 54:4

The people of Judah were embarking on a process of recovery. They had experienced the loss of their nation. The years of exile had been difficult and had raised serious questions about their identity, faith, and future. Now, they were facing the work of rebuilding their nation, physically and spiritually.

This necessary work included the restoration of their relationship with God—and their capacity to trust Him and His goodness. Through Isaiah's ministry, God urged the people that they did not need to be afraid and that, in time, they would forget the shame of their exile. There even seemed to be a note of confession in God's messages to His people: "For a brief moment I abandoned you, but with deep compassion I will bring you back. In a surge of anger I hid my face from you for a moment, but with everlasting kindness I will have compassion on you" (Isaiah 54:7). It was not that their years of exile did not matter, but they would come to be considered brief in the context of the glorious restoration and future God had planned for them.

This was the larger vision that God offered His people in recovering their nation and their relationship with Him. It was about more than mere restoration. Trusting in God, their nation would be rebuilt beyond any past glories. He promised a Messiah who would come and inaugurate a new kind of kingdom for all His people. In that day, fear would be no more; their past sufferings would be all but forgotten, and God would forever be their God. "In righteousness you will be established: Tyranny will be far from you; you will have nothing to fear. Terror will be far removed; it will not come near you" (Isaiah 54:14). God's promises to His people stretched far beyond restoration to redemption and re-creation.

SHAPED BY FEAR

"Whom have you so dreaded and feared
that you have not been true to me,
and have neither remembered me
nor taken this to heart?
Is it not because I have long been silent
that you do not fear me?"

—Isaiah 57:11

We are shaped by the people, ideas, and things we fear almost as much as we are shaped by the people, ideas, and things that we follow. As we have seen in a number of Bible stories—and will notice in stories such as Peter's denial of Jesus after His arrest—fear can motivate us to do things that we would not normally do—things that are often out of character and a betrayal of what we otherwise believe.

This is the foundation for God's rhetorical question to the people of Judah: "Who are you so afraid of that it caused you to deny Me?" In that question, He included the empire of Babylon in which they had been exiled, the other surrounding nations, and even the various idols and other gods that seemed to perpetually tempt the people of Judah. So, of all of those, who or what were the people afraid of to such a degree that it caused them to be unfaithful to God, even to have forgotten Him?

Again, it seems that God was prepared to question Himself: "Is it because I have been so patient or long-suffering with you that you have mistaken my silence for not caring?" It is similar to the question Paul asked: "Do you show contempt for the riches of his kindness, forbearance and patience, not realizing that God's kindness is intended to lead you to repentance?" (Romans 2:4).

God's primary point through Isaiah was that faithfulness to Him was far better than being dominated by fear of those around them, whether of people, nations, or their gods. "Whoever takes refuge in me will inherit the land and possess my holy mountain" (Isaiah 57:13).

May 28

HIGH, HOLY, AND HUMBLE

For this is what the high and exalted One says—
he who lives forever, whose name is holy:
"I live in a high and holy place,
but also with the one who is contrite and lowly in spirit,
to revive the spirit of the lowly
and to revive the heart of the contrite."

—Isaiah 57:15

God is high and exalted. He is eternal and lives in a high and holy place. While the Creator God had a particular claim to the highest place, such claims were not unique in the descriptions of the gods of the ancient world. In the various theologies and mythologies, living high above their human subjects was the definition of a god—situated above, probably removed, and likely uncaring about the fate of the people who tried to attract his attention through religious rituals and sacrifices.

But God is also humble. Not only is He high and holy, but He is with those who are contrite and lowly. He chooses not to remain aloof and implacable, drawing near to hear and feel the suffering of humanity, with particular concern for those who suffer most. Isaiah presents a God who, somehow, was near to His people, identified with their pain and questions, and was actively working to lift them up—even before the incarnation of Jesus.

Indeed, it is probably best understood that because God stoops to come near His suffering people, He brings His holiness closer. Simply by virtue of Him drawing near, those who are most in need and most open feel His presence and influence. "I restore the crushed spirit of the humble and revive the courage of those with repentant hearts" (Isaiah 57:15, NLT).

When Jesus drew even closer to humanity, He repeated the same assurance: "Blessed are the poor in spirit, for theirs is the kingdom of heaven" (Matthew 5:3). In Jesus, God would be closer than ever to the contrite and the lowly, bringing them restoration and courage.

CALLING AND COURAGE

The Lord said to me, "Do not say, 'I am too young.' You must go to everyone I send you to and say whatever I command you. Do not be afraid of them, for I am with you and will rescue you," declares the Lord.

—Jeremiah 1:7, 8

The date of Jeremiah's call—"the thirteenth year of the reign of Josiah son of Amon king of Judah" (Jeremiah 1:2)—places the beginning of his ministry in 626 B.C. It would continue for almost forty years to the fall and capture of Jerusalem in 587 B.C. We often imagine the Hebrew prophets as old men with long beards, but for those whose prophetic ministry stretched over decades, their first "the word of the Lord came to me" experiences were as young people.

Indeed, his youth was Jeremiah's first objection. " 'Alas, Sovereign Lord,' I said, 'I do not know how to speak; I am too young' " (Jeremiah 1:6). It seemed like a legitimate concern, particularly in a culture in which age and experience were most respected.

God responded by dismissing Jeremiah's objection, assuring him that a calling from God was larger than his fears and that God would be with him, which should offer courage enough. This was an important conversation for God and Jeremiah to have. Jeremiah's forty years of ministry would be difficult. His messages were not popular; he was ridiculed and imprisoned regularly, and historical tradition suggests that he was ultimately stoned to death in Egypt. But his ministry began with the promise that God would be with him, and therefore, he should not allow fear to be an objection to God's calling, wherever it might lead or however difficult it might be.

Calling can be a difficult question for many of us, but perhaps our first calling is to not allow fear to be an objection to the good and faithful service and ministry we might otherwise do. It seems from Jeremiah's story that none of us can use the objection that we are too young.

May 30

GIRD UP THY LOINS!

"Get yourself ready! Stand up and say to them whatever I command you. Do not be terrified by them, or I will terrify you before them."

—Jeremiah 1:17

The King James Version puts this verse like this: "Thou therefore gird up thy loins, and arise." Get dressed and be prepared for action! The work to which Jeremiah was called was difficult work. The message he was assigned would first be a message of doom and judgment before it would be a message of restoration and hope. He was appointed by God, first "to uproot and tear down, to destroy and overthrow," and only then "to build and to plant" (Jeremiah 1:10).

It seems that this was not Jeremiah's natural disposition. "Jeremiah was gentle and compassionate by nature, and the mission he had to carry out was, to him, distasteful in the extreme. It made him contentious, petulant, irascible. People he had prayed for turned out to be his enemies."* Powerful people would oppose him, and he would suffer for what God told him to say. He would need fortitude, endurance, and courage. As God put it, he would need to become "an iron pillar and a bronze wall to stand against the whole land—against the kings of Judah, its officials, its priests and the people of the land" (Jeremiah 1:18).

Little wonder that God urged him—and needed to remind him—"Do not be terrified by them." If Jeremiah allowed himself to become afraid of the people and forces against him, he would be overwhelmed by them. If Jeremiah did not commit to this task and the messages he would be given, his work would look foolish to those he was so desperately trying to reach and whom God was trying to reach through him. Courage came through recognizing and remembering that God had given him this task. That realization is what drove him during the more than forty years of ministry to which he was called.

---

* Abraham J. Heschel, *The Prophets* (New York: Harper Perennial, 2001), 157.

May 31

MORE THAN SUPERSTITION

This is what the Lord says:

"Do not learn the ways of the nations
or be terrified by signs in the heavens,
though the nations are terrified by them."
—Jeremiah 10:2

There is something in our human nature that has a strong bent toward superstition. It is one of the ways our minds try to make sense of the world around us, to make links between signs or omens in the world around us and what they might mean for our lives or our nations, even when there is no obvious or likely connection.

We see this play out in things as trivial as the pre-competition or pregame routines of athletes and their fans—or actors and the traditions that surround their performances. But these become more serious in times of stress or when there are voices who want to exploit an event or occurrence to make some kind of political or religious point. For example, a natural disaster might be identified by an internet preacher as an act of judgment or warning against something he or she is particularly opposed to in society or culture.

When Jesus pointed to events in the natural world as "signs of the times," He did this with a similar message to the one Jeremiah gave to the people of Israel: "Do not be frightened. These things must happen first" (Luke 21:9). These are simply things that will increasingly happen in our world until Jesus' actual return when there will be "signs in the sun, moon and stars" (Luke 21:25). The focus of those who follow Jesus should always be on Jesus Himself.

Whether this warning from Jeremiah was in response to a specific astronomical event or a more general warning about the astrology that was popular among the Babylonians, his larger message to the people of Israel was to reject superstition and the accompanying fear that was so dominant among the nations and the peoples around them. The God who made the stars was much more worthy of their attention than the stars themselves.

June 1

TWO GOOD PROPHETIC PUNCH LINES

"Like a scarecrow in a cucumber field,
their idols cannot speak;
they must be carried
because they cannot walk.
Do not fear them;
they can do no harm
nor can they do any good."

—Jeremiah 10:5

We can appreciate the Hebrew prophets as performance artists. As well as thundering denunciations of the powerful nations and people of their day, heartfelt sermons that begged the people to turn back to their God, reminders of their history as God's people, and poetic descriptions of the restoration and future God promised, God often gave the prophets strange instructions for public stunts to get the people's attention and to act out parables of His long-suffering love.

Also, we can miss the humor found in various parts of the Bible. The limited understanding we have of a long-ago culture so unlike our own means that some of the best lines are literally lost in translation. That is why we should appreciate them all the more when they are obvious to us.

Challenging the idols of the surrounding nations that the people of Israel seemed perpetually tempted to worship by describing them as about as useful as "a scarecrow in a cucumber patch" was simply a good punch line. It is a vivid picture of an inanimate and powerless figure that could not speak, had to be moved from place to place, and could barely frighten birds. So, if they cannot frighten the birds, why should they frighten us? This was a direct rejoinder to the fear that has always been so dominant in pagan and other unhealthy religions, including our own, when it loses sight of God and who He is.

This was Jeremiah's ultimate punch line. God was not merely an alternative god to those of the surrounding nations. He was—and is—something altogether different. "No one is like you, LORD; you are great, and your name is mighty in power" (Jeremiah 10:6).

June 2

THE CREATOR AND THE CREATED

Lord, my strength and my fortress,
my refuge in time of distress,
to you the nations will come
from the ends of the earth and say,
"Our ancestors possessed nothing but false gods,
worthless idols that did them no good.
Do people make their own gods?
Yes, but they are not gods!"

—Jeremiah 16:19, 20

As the time of Judah's defeat and exile drew closer, Jeremiah continued to draw a strong contrast between the God who was his strength, fortress, and refuge and the gods that the surrounding nations had simply made up. He predicted that a time would come when these surrounding nations would come to God's people and admit, "Our ancestors left us a foolish heritage, for they worshiped worthless idols" (Jeremiah 16:19, NLT).

Jeremiah wanted to make the absurdity of following other gods obvious. How did it make sense that intelligent human beings could invent something, whether a story or a physical idol, that was in any way worthy of their worship? Jerome's fourth-century Latin translation of the Bible puts verse 20 like this: "Shall man make gods, though men themselves are not gods?" The conclusion is that the created should worship the Creator, not the other way around. Jeremiah insisted that even the pagan nations would come to recognize this contradiction. How much worse was it, then, when the people whose ancestors had passed down to them the worship of the true Creator turned their impulse to worship toward these same false gods?

Jeremiah affirmed his trust in the true God of Israel, not only in his words but also by continuing to warn of the destruction of the nation and ridicule the idols that were leading the people astray. It took courage to continue to assert that God would restore the people to their land in an act of redemption and restoration as significant as when He had led the people out of Egypt centuries earlier (see Jeremiah 16:14, 15). It was possible only because Jeremiah had found his fortress in God.

June 3

THROUGH THE SEASONS

"Blessed is the one who trusts in the LORD,
whose confidence is in him.
They will be like a tree planted by the water
that sends out its roots by the stream.
It does not fear when heat comes;
its leaves are always green.
It has no worries in a year of drought
and never fails to bear fruit."

—Jeremiah 17:7, 8

One of the most overused metaphors for our human experience of life and faith is that of a journey. We have our personal journeys, educational journeys, vocational journeys, emotional journeys, and spiritual journeys. We are told that our most significant journeys of self-discovery often come in the form of literal journeys to places of history, heritage, or spiritual significance. Many of us are taught, or absorb from the culture around us, an expectation of change and travel, and we experience a growing sense of restlessness if we remain in the same place for too long.

This image from Jeremiah, however, seems to present a better image of what it means to grow, flourish, and endure during the changing seasons of our lives. Living well requires a strong foundation of meaning and purpose, and while it is not always possible, it seems to work best when we have roots that grow ever deeper into place, community, and conviction. But this does not mean we are unchanging. Indeed, rootedness provides the possibility of growth and change. A healthy tree is always changing, growing taller, wider, thicker, deeper. If it stops, it begins to decline and decay.

However, there are also seasons in our lives. These are both predictable and fickle. Some summer days are pleasant; others are ferocious. But the seasons follow each other in turn. In each of these times, there are things to learn and opportunities to grow, difficulties to endure, and wonders to find. And after each, we will be changed. Whatever the season, the key to growing unafraid is roots that grow ever deeper in trust and confidence in God.

June 4

THE MOCKED PROPHET

I hear many whispering, / "Terror on every side! / Denounce him! Let's denounce him!" / All my friends / are waiting for me to slip, saying, / "Perhaps he will be deceived; / then we will prevail over him / and take our revenge on him."

—Jeremiah 20:10

The prophetic work given to Jeremiah was always going to be difficult. Much of his message was destruction and doom, and he was mocked for his apparent pessimism. "He is dubbed 'Terror is all around,' a nickname that is whispered as he passes by as if he were some clownish Chicken Little (Jeremiah 20:10). Jeremiah is wounded by the mockery, and he lashes out, not at those who belittle him, but at God."*

Passhur, the priest in charge of the temple, had beaten Jeremiah and put him in stocks. In response, Jeremiah's complaint against God was a fierce reaction of defensiveness, pain, and fear. He complained that God gave him only messages of "violence and destruction" that brought him "insult and reproach all day long" (Jeremiah 20:8). For a moment, it almost seemed he had taken the side of those who had been attacking him, that he saw and sympathized with their point of view. After all, he was also part of the nation that he was being compelled to prophesy against. These were his people, and this was his home.

We do not know how much time passed between verses 10 and 11. Perhaps Jeremiah simply paused for breath, regathered his thoughts and courage, and then proceeded with his writing. Or perhaps it took him longer to be able to regain this perspective: "But the Lord is with me like a mighty warrior; so my persecutors will stumble and not prevail. They will fail and be thoroughly disgraced; their dishonor will never be forgotten" (Jeremiah 20:11).

Even in this difficult task, amid mockery and insults and the growing threats to his people, Jeremiah insisted that God was still with him.

---

* Lee Griffith, *The War on Terrorism and the Terror of God* (Grand Rapids, MI: Eerdmans, 2002), 113, 114.

June 5

WHEN LEADERS LET US DOWN

"I myself will gather the remnant of my flock out of all the countries where I have driven them and will bring them back to their pasture, where they will be fruitful and increase in number. I will place shepherds over them who will tend them, and they will no longer be afraid or terrified, nor will any be missing," declares the LORD.

—Jeremiah 23:3, 4

It is not hard to find stories of pastors and other church leaders who have let their people down. There seems to be a steady stream of news reports of Christian leaders who have exploited their position, betrayed those who have trusted them, been tempted to wrongdoing, or led others into strange teachings and behavior. The response Jeremiah would deliver to such headlines seems appropriate—and is a reminder of the responsibilities that should come with such positions of leadership. " 'Woe to the shepherds who are destroying and scattering the sheep of my pasture!' declares the LORD" (Jeremiah 23:1).

God's response to His people would be much more redemptive and restorative of those who were let down or led astray by such leaders. He would be their leader, again using the image of a good shepherd who would protect and provide for His people. It was God who promised to collect the scattered flock of the people of Israel and return them to the good pasture of their homeland. And it was God who promised to appoint new leaders.

After the generally bleak tone of many of Jeremiah's messages, the promise of a time when the people would no longer need to be afraid offers a hint of hope. This is the beginning of a shift in tone for Jeremiah. He starts preaching the possibility of restoration that would be, again, greater than the Israelite's rescue from Egypt (see Jeremiah 23:7, 8). Such promises—including the promise of a Messiah to come—began to push back fear, even amid the present circumstances.

FUTURE AND PRESENT

"So do not be afraid, O Jacob my servant;
do not be dismayed, O Israel,"
declares the Lord.
"I will surely save you out of a distant place,
your descendants from the land of their exile.
Jacob will again have peace and security,
and no one will make him afraid."

—Jeremiah 30:10

What we believe about the future is not only about the future; it must also shape and transform the present. This promise from God that Jeremiah delivered to the people pointed to a time when the people of Israel would again enjoy the land God had given them and would have peace and security. For Jacob and his descendants, it would be a time when "no one will make him afraid." This is the future without fear promised throughout the Bible.

There is also an element in these promises that addresses God's proximity. In many religions and mythologies of the time, gods were linked to a particular location, and their power was often understood as being limited to that place. However, God reassured His people that wherever they might be exiled, He would still remember them. He could still reach them, and they need not fear that He might not be able to bring them home, even from the most distant lands. Across however many generations and across whatever distances, the power of the God of Israel would be undiminished.

But while the promises were written in the future tense, the commands were written in the present: "So do not be afraid . . . do not be dismayed." Like the instructions given to John at the beginning of Revelation, God instructed Jeremiah to write down His promises so they could be heard again by future generations (see Jeremiah 30:1–3). And because God had given His promise to act in the future and even put it in writing, the responses of the people in the present would be different, more assured, and less fearful.

June 7

TRUST AMID THE TRAGEDY

"I will rescue you on that day," declares the Lord;
"you will not be handed over to those you fear."
—Jeremiah 39:17

As the capture and destruction of Jerusalem drew near, King Zedekiah and his officials turned some of their fear and frustration toward Jeremiah and his seemingly endless dire warnings. Those who had led the people to this extremity now tried to lay the blame on Jeremiah, and all the more as they saw those warnings becoming reality. "Then the officials said to the king, 'This man should be put to death. He is discouraging the soldiers who are left in this city, as well as all the people, by the things he is saying to them' " (Jeremiah 38:4). So the king ordered that Jeremiah be thrown into a cistern, where he sank into the mud at the bottom of the empty water reservoir, presumably left there to die.

A foreigner by the name of Ebed-Melek, a Cushite or Ethiopian, lobbied the king for Jeremiah's release and then organized a group of men to lift him out of his muddy tomb. In the charged political and social environment of the doomed city, this was a courageous and dangerous task for Ebed-Melek to take on. While most people were focused on their own survival, Ebed-Melek was concerned for Jeremiah. And it was not without a real fear of retribution from the officials who had sought to do away with Jeremiah.

Amid the chaos of the capture of the city, Jeremiah was given a special message for his rescuer. Ebed-Melek had acted despite his fear, and ironically, the conquerors of the city would now set him free from those he had feared. In acting on behalf of Jeremiah, Ebed-Melek demonstrated courage and faithfulness. Now he would be rescued "because you trust in me, declares the Lord" (Jeremiah 39:18).

June 8

TEMPTED BACK TO EGYPT AGAIN

"Do not be afraid of the king of Babylon, whom you now fear. Do not be afraid of him," declares the L*ORD*, *"for I am with you and will save you and deliver you from his hands. I will show you compassion so that he will have compassion on you and restore you to your land."*

—Jeremiah 42:11, 12

After the fall and destruction of Jerusalem, many of the people were taken into exile in Babylon, but a small remnant remained amid the ruins of their nation. This group of survivors had to work out how to live in the aftermath of catastrophe and with so much of their society devastated. Their thoughts turned again to the possibilities of Egypt as they succumbed to what had been a recurring temptation in the experience of the Israelite people over the centuries since their escape from slavery in that land. Egypt seemed to offer a safe harbor against continuing marauding from the Babylonian invaders.

As might be expected, Jeremiah warned against this in strident terms. Such a course of action would be an even greater disaster (see Jeremiah 42:13–22). Even worse, it would be a denial of trust in God, who insisted that He was still greater than the king of Babylon and always had been. Even in their shattered city, God would be with them, so they need not be afraid of the Babylonians.

The people ignored Jeremiah's warnings, and a group of the survivors exiled themselves to Egypt. While they had been spared exile in Babylon, their fear drove them into an exile of their own making. There, they would be drawn into worshiping the Egyptian gods, and in time, the Babylonian armies would turn their attention to conquering Egypt (see Jeremiah 43 and 44). They compelled Jeremiah to go to Egypt with them, and neither he nor the people would return.

Jeremiah's message offered the people God's compassion in place of their fear. Tragically, they chose to follow their fear.

June 9

IN A DIFFERENT CONTEXT

"Do not be afraid, O Jacob my servant;
do not be dismayed, O Israel.
I will surely save you out of a distant place,
your descendants from the land of their exile.
Jacob will again have peace and security,
and no one will make him afraid.
Do not fear, O Jacob my servant,
for I am with you,"
declares the L*ORD.*

—Jeremiah 46:27, 28

These verses echoed the message delivered earlier in Jeremiah 30:10, 11. The difference was the context in which the message was delivered. This time, God was speaking to the people of Israel who had escaped to Egypt against Jeremiah's direct warnings. Amid the looming Babylonian attack against Egypt, God still had His eyes on His people. While they had disobeyed Him and chose supposed Egyptian security over God's care, God was yet compassionate.

With the departure of this additional group of refugees and the subsequent defeat of their supposed place of safety, it would have seemed that Israel's desolation was complete and final. But, because of God's compassion and promises, the defeated, demoralized people of Israel had greater hope for a brighter future than the empires of either Babylon or Egypt that were then competing for domination. "Though I completely destroy all the nations among which I scatter you, I will not completely destroy you" (Jeremiah 46:28). These powerful nations would become artifacts of history, but the people of God were yet to see their greatest prosperity.

As had been promised, God would bring their descendants back from exile, and they would enjoy peace in the land God had given them. God would return to them—and return them to their land again. Those promises were the basis of God's "Do not be afraid" delivered to the people of Israel who had returned to Egypt despite the warnings and commands they had been given. Although it was a present reassurance and encouragement, this was another promise that pointed to the coming of the Messiah and a time when no one would make them afraid.

"COME OUT OF HER, MY PEOPLE!"

"Do not lose heart or be afraid
when rumors are heard in the land;
one rumor comes this year, another the next,
rumors of violence in the land
and of ruler against ruler."

—Jeremiah 51:46

The call to come out of Babylon is more familiar today to students of the book of Revelation (see Revelation 18:4), but Jeremiah sounded it first: "Come out of her, my people!" (Jeremiah 51:45). It was a call that reminded God's people that their faith, hope, and security were always found in their God, not in their circumstances or surrounding culture.

Jeremiah had previously counseled the exiles to make their home in Babylon and to "seek the peace and prosperity of the city to which I have carried you into exile. Pray to the LORD for it, because if it prospers, you too will prosper" (Jeremiah 29:7). But God was now calling the people to recognize that their fortunes would be no longer tied to the fortunes of Babylon. They were not to be alarmed by rumors of threats, violence, and forces gathering against Babylon.

The empires and kingdoms of our world today also have their rumors, threats, and uncertainties. Ultimately, they all fail, weighed down by their quest for perpetual expansion and their own hubris, and defeated by the next kingdom to arise.

The people of God are not to be disconnected or disengaged from their surrounding communities and cultures. They should seek the peace and prosperity of the places in which they live, but their security is not dependent on their circumstances. Understood this way, "Come out of her, my people" also means "Do not be afraid." Because of the threats and uncertainties inherent in the structures of empires and kingdoms, placing our ultimate hopes in God and His kingdom gives us an alternative perspective and a firmer footing. Even as our fortunes are less tied to our contexts and cultures, we have renewed courage to serve those around us for the good of the place and culture in which we are exiled.

FROM THE DEPTHS OF THE PIT

I called on your name, O Lord,
from the depths of the pit.
You heard my plea: "Do not close your ears
to my cry for relief."
You came near when I called you,
and you said, "Do not fear."
—Lamentations 3:55–57

The book of Lamentations, although anonymous in itself, is generally believed to be further writings of the prophet Jeremiah. The book is in character with the tone of Jeremiah's ministry and records his sorrow over the destruction of Jerusalem, the temple, and seemingly the nation. Each of the first four chapters is an acrostic poem, in which each subsection begins with a successive letter of the Hebrew alphabet. Thus, these extended poems are literally expressions of grief from A to Z.

But Chapter 3 is different in its approach. It takes a more personal tone and seems to draw on Jeremiah's own experiences as a prophet of God while at the same time using those experiences as figurative of the experiences of the whole people of Israel. The conclusion is that God will be as faithful and merciful to His people as Jeremiah had found Him to be in his own life and experience.

As we have seen, Jeremiah had a literal experience in the depths of the pit: "They tried to end my life in a pit and threw stones at me; the waters closed over my head, and I thought I was about to perish" (Lamentations 3:53, 54). This was figuratively where the people of Israel now found themselves, but Jeremiah's testimony was that God had still heard and seen him when he was in the same predicament.

God's first words were, "Do not fear." God had heard, seen, and drawn near to Jeremiah in the depths of the pit. Then he says, "You, Lord, took up my case; you redeemed my life" (Lamentations 3:58). In the midst of this extended poem of lament comes the assurance that, just as God had intervened for Jeremiah, so would He intervene to rescue His people. And His first message to His grieving people was "Do not fear."

A PROPHET IN EXILE

"And you, son of man, do not be afraid of them or their words. Do not be afraid, though briers and thorns are all around you and you live among scorpions. Do not be afraid of what they say or be terrified by them, though they are a rebellious people."

—Ezekiel 2:6

In a sense, Ezekiel's prophetic ministry began where Jeremiah's left off. While some of the people remained in Jerusalem after it was conquered and finally destroyed by Babylon, Ezekiel was among the first group of exiles taken to Babylon with King Jehoiachin in 597 B.C. (see 2 Kings 24:12–17).

Called to be a prophet in "the fifth year of the exile" (Ezekiel 1:2), Ezekiel's ministry would be among a dislocated and traumatized people who were beginning to adjust to the realities of life in exile but who were still in survival mode with all its fears and uncertainties. They would have been questioning God's care for them and not likely to respond well to yet another prophet seeking to defend God and challenge their faithlessness.

Like many of the other Hebrew prophets, Ezekiel's message began with a vision of the majesty of God—"the appearance of the likeness of the glory of the LORD" (Ezekiel 1:28)—which left him flat on his face before it. Then God spoke to him, making plain the difficult task and the difficult people to which he was called. "To be a prophet means to challenge and to defy and to cast out fear. . . . The prophet's duty is to speak to the people, 'whether they hear or refuse to hear.' "*

Like Jeremiah, Ezekiel's message would be one of "lament and warning and woe" (Ezekiel 2:10). But as a result of his faithful ministry and his own courage in difficult circumstances, "whether they listen or fail to listen—for they are a rebellious people—they will know that a prophet has been among them" (Ezekiel 2:5).

---

* Abraham J. Heschel, *The Prophets* (New York: Harper Perennial, 2001), 22.

June 13

STRENGTHENED BY GOD

"I will make you as unyielding and hardened as they are. I will make your forehead like the hardest stone, harder than flint. Do not be afraid of them or terrified by them, though they are a rebellious people."

—Ezekiel 3:8, 9

If we imagine the most difficult and complicated context, calling, or task, we can never imagine—or encounter—something so challenging that God's action and intervention cannot overcome it. In a sense, the greater the challenges we undertake, the greater will be our understanding and appreciation of the potential and reality of God's power and care.

In effect, this was God's calling to Ezekiel. As difficult as it would be, Ezekiel was not to take it personally. "The people of Israel are not willing to listen to you because they are not willing to listen to me, for all the Israelites are hardened and obstinate" (Ezekiel 3:7). Instead, Ezekiel was to insist upon and recognize that God's capacity and ability are larger than the greatest challenges he could imagine—able to melt the hardest hearts.

Ezekiel's name means "strengthened by God," and that was the experience to which he was called and that he was to share with others. God was saying to Ezekiel that if the people's heads and hearts are hardened, your divine determination must be harder still. If they are stubborn in their rebellion, you are to be stubborn in your ministry. If the challenges seem great, your God and His power are all the greater.

As Isaiah had expressed it, "Because the Sovereign Lord helps me, I will not be disgraced. Therefore have I set my face like flint, and I know I will not be put to shame" (Isaiah 50:7). When it was Ezekiel's turn to take up the prophetic ministry, he did not need to be afraid. God was his strength, always stronger than any opposition, uncertainty, or fear that he could imagine or encounter.

PASTORAL AND MESSIANIC

"They will no longer be plundered by the nations, nor will wild animals devour them. They will live in safety, and no one will make them afraid."
—Ezekiel 34:28

One of the recurring themes of the Hebrew prophets was the promise of a time or place in which "no one will make them afraid." Ezekiel's version of this promise tied it to another favorite image of the Bible, that of God as the good shepherd of His people. The detail in Ezekiel's description of this shepherd was notable, prefiguring two of the famous pastoral parables that Jesus would teach to His disciples.

For those who first heard Jesus telling the story of the lost sheep for whom the shepherd searched so diligently (see Luke 15:3–7), the notable detail was that the shepherd would leave the other ninety-nine to search for a single lost sheep. Ezekiel's description had already described their shepherd God as one who would gather all of the scattered flock of Israel. "I myself will search for my sheep and look after them" (Ezekiel 34:11). God would carry them and heal their wounds. "I will search for the lost and bring back the strays. I will bind up the injured and strengthen the weak" (Ezekiel 34:16).

Ezekiel also hinted at another of Jesus' parables: "I will judge between one animal of the flock and another, separating the sheep from the goats" (Ezekiel 34:17, NLT). The basis for such judgment was whether justice was done or not done, as well as concern for helping the hungry and abused, as Jesus would urge in His parable of Matthew 25:31–46.

When Jesus said that He was "the good shepherd" (John 10:14)—as well as when He told these parables—He was claiming that He was the fulfillment of Ezekiel's prophecy. He was "the one shepherd" (Ezekiel 34:23), the protector and provider for His people, with particular concern for the weakest and the wandering, and continuing to point forward to a time when "no one will make them afraid."

June 15

EVEN IF HE DOES NOT . . .

"If we are thrown into the blazing furnace, the God we serve is able to deliver us from it, and he will deliver us from Your Majesty's hand. But even if he does not, we want you to know, Your Majesty, that we will not serve your gods or worship the image of gold you have set up."

—Daniel 3:17, 18

As exiles in Babylon, Shadrach, Meshach, and Abednego lived in a continual state of tension between their Hebrew faith, culture, and upbringing and their Babylonian reality. They had been taken from their homes in Jerusalem as young men, trained in "the language and literature of the Babylonians" (Daniel 1:4), and recognized for their wisdom and understanding in the Babylonian court (see Daniel 1:20). But we see evidence of their regular questioning of themselves, their faith, and their relationship to their host culture, from their refusal to eat the Babylonian food (see Daniel 1:8–16) to their determination not to bow to Nebuchadnezzar's golden idol (see Daniel 3).

Undoubtedly, there were many smaller tensions in between. Each such decision required both wisdom and courage. Perhaps an adapted form of the now-famous "Serenity Prayer"* would have been a helpful way of addressing such tensions: "God, grant me the opportunities to work with the surrounding culture in the ways I can, the courage to stand against it when necessary, and the wisdom to decide when cooperation, contribution, or resistance is the most faithful course of action."

For Shadrach, Meshach, and Abednego, this day on the plain of Dura was a time for resistance—and a time for courage. They knew God could deliver them from the king's fiery furnace, but they had no guarantee that God would choose to do so—or how. But by affirming God's ability, they affirmed their faith in a God who was greater than Nebuchadnezzar and all his gods. And by their submission to God's will, they demonstrated their courageous commitment to be faithful, whatever the consequences, even if God did not deliver them.

---

* Popularized by Reinhold Niebuhr.

WITH US, WITH THEM

Then Nebuchadnezzar said, "Praise be to the God of Shadrach, Meshach and Abednego, who has sent his angel and rescued his servants! They trusted in him and defied the king's command and were willing to give up their lives rather than serve or worship any god except their own God."
—Daniel 3:28

When we live our faith in public, it creates opportunities for those with whom we work or associate to see God at work. As did Shadrach, Meshach, and Abednego, we can trust that God is with us in even our most difficult circumstances. "He who walked with the Hebrew worthies in the fiery furnace will be with His followers wherever they are. His abiding presence will comfort and sustain."* And when we live our lives with others, "God with us" also draws near to them through us.

This was Nebuchadnezzar's experience at the fiery furnace. We note two elements in his testimony about what he had witnessed, two reasons he gave for praising the God these young Hebrews served.

First, Nebuchadnezzar recognized the presence of a fourth figure in the flames—one who "looks like a son of the gods" (Daniel 3:25). He did not fully understand who this figure might be, but he knew he had seen something remarkable.

Second, it seems that Nebuchadnezzar found the trust and courage demonstrated by Shadrach, Meshach, and Abednego almost equally noteworthy. He was not used to people defying his orders, and that they were unafraid to risk their lives to do so caught his attention, aroused his admiration, and prompted him to take their God seriously.

The three were seemingly doomed to suffer the wrath of the pagan king of one of the world's great empires; instead, God's miraculous intervention partnered with their courageous faithfulness to challenge Nebuchadnezzar's faith and invited his own trust in their God.

---

* Ellen G. White, *Prophets and Kings* (Mountain View, CA: Pacific Press®, 1917), 513.

June 17

AFTER TWENTY YEARS

The queen, hearing the voices of the king and his nobles, came into the banquet hall. "May the king live forever!" she said. "Don't be alarmed! Don't look so pale! There is a man in your kingdom who has the spirit of the holy gods in him. In the time of your father he was found to have insight and intelligence and wisdom like that of the gods."

—Daniel 5:10, 11

Historians believe that Belshazzar reigned for as many as seventeen years before the defeat of Babylon in 539 B.C. In the early part of Belshazzar's reign, Daniel received the visions recorded in Daniel 7 and 8, but it had been many years since he had interacted with Nebuchadnezzar, as recorded in Daniel 2 and 4. But his special insight and his reliance on God was remembered by the Queen Mother, perhaps twenty years later.

Often, people notice our faithfulness whether we realize it or not. And it can matter to people in unexpected ways. As a writer who writes mainly for church publications, I am sometimes surprised when someone who may not have had a connection with the church for many years notices and responds to an article I have written—and that it matters to them. It is the same with those around us, who might be curious about what it means to live a life of faith or who might take some comfort in the fact that they know someone who believes or who might pray for them.

When Belshazzar was confronted by that startling vision, the Queen Mother immediately remembered Daniel and his faithfulness. It was her foundation for urging the officials not to be afraid but to seek wisdom and guidance from Daniel as a man "who has the spirit of the holy gods in him"—a phrase she may have borrowed from Nebuchadnezzar (see Daniel 4:8). She probably did not fully understand Daniel's relationship with God, but she found comfort in the insight and wisdom it gave him. And she was prepared to offer that to her son.

AS HE HAD DONE BEFORE

Now when Daniel learned that the decree had been published, he went home to his upstairs room where the windows opened toward Jerusalem. Three times a day he got down on his knees and prayed, giving thanks to his God, just as he had done before.
—Daniel 6:10

After a group of jealous officials plotted to trip up Daniel by having his religious practice banned, his response was courageous and resolute. He simply kept on praying and giving thanks to God three times a day, "just as he had done before." His relationship with God was not dictated by his critics, by the decree of the king, or by the law of the empire.

However, we might wonder why he insisted on continuing to pray so publicly. God would have still heard his prayers, even without the open windows. After all, Jesus would teach His disciples, "When you pray, don't be like the hypocrites who love to pray publicly on street corners and in the synagogues where everyone can see them" (Matthew 6:5, NLT). Jesus was warning against performing a religious show, but Daniel prayed openly, knowing that his faithfulness was under scrutiny and under threat. He was not putting on a show or using his religiosity to make a political point. Instead, he was praying faithfully "just as he had done before." Yes, this required courage, but it was precisely his trust in God and his connection with Him that were the source of his courage.

Perhaps Daniel knew that the plotters would eventually catch him out in some way, but he resolved that they would not curb his devotion and witness to the God he served. It might be that he also remembered the courage of Shadrach, Meshach, and Abednego standing before Nebuchadnezzar's idol and was inspired to continue his own act of defiant faithfulness. Whatever his thinking, he continued to pray "just as he had done before."

June 19

THE TESTIMONY OF ANOTHER KING

"For he is the living God / and he endures forever; / his kingdom will not be destroyed, / his dominion will never end. / He rescues and he saves; / he performs signs and wonders / in the heavens and on the earth. / He has rescued Daniel / from the power of the lions."
—Daniel 6:26, 27

When my mother moved to a different home a couple of years ago, she found a small "book" that I had written sometime before the age of ten that somewhat creatively retold the story of Daniel and the lions, complete with crude but cute illustrations. As someone who grew up with these Bible stories, my imagination had obviously been captured by this particular incident. Rediscovering this early attempt at authorship caused me to reflect on how my life and faith were shaped by this story, by Daniel's example of courageous faithfulness and God's miraculous protection.

Notably, that experience had a similar effect on King Darius as one of the first witnesses to it. More directly than my engagement with this story, he was there "when Daniel was lifted from the den, [and] no wound was found on him, because he had trusted in his God" (Daniel 6:23). The king wrote his testimony as a decree to all the peoples of his kingdom, urging that they show "fear and reverence" to this God who had so dramatically saved Daniel and whom Daniel so courageously served.

As exuberant as Darius was in his newfound respect for Daniel's God, his understanding of faith was different from Daniel's faith. While Darius celebrated God's "signs and wonders," Daniel's everyday faithfulness was already in place long before God rescued or saved. It is good to respond to the evidence of God's goodness and power, but Daniel was committed to God even in His seeming absence. Daniel's attitude of faith and trust in God's faithfulness was later recommended to those who were suffering for their faith in the early church: "So then, those who suffer according to God's will should commit themselves to their faithful Creator and continue to do good" (1 Peter 4:19).

A PERSONAL FEAR

"Do not be afraid, Daniel. Since the first day that you set your mind to gain understanding and to humble yourself before your God, your words were heard, and I have come in response to them."

—Daniel 10:12

Like many of the Hebrew prophets, including Isaiah, Jeremiah, and Ezekiel, Daniel was deeply shaken by his encounters with God and the messengers of God that he experienced in vision. In response, he was given two "Do not be afraid" commands (see Daniel 10:12 and 10:19), each with a different significance.

The first "Do not be afraid" addressed his immediate physical fear of the grand and awesome vision he was experiencing and into which he was about to be led deeper. Even though his companions did not see what Daniel was seeing, they ran away, sensing that something big was happening. They left Daniel alone—fainting, trembling, and unable to speak. In an experience similar to that of Isaiah, a hand touched Daniel's mouth, and his speech was restored. He immediately explained: "I am overcome with anguish because of the vision, my lord, and I feel very weak. How can I, your servant, talk with you, my lord? My strength is gone and I can hardly breathe" (Daniel 10:16, 17).

Daniel's vision from God made his own weakness very clear to him. He felt human vulnerability in the presence of something so much greater. But the response from God's messenger was personal. He described how God had been with Daniel "since the first day" that he turned to Him for understanding. This experience reminded Daniel of how God had been with him over the many years since his exile to Babylon as a young man and his success in faithfully serving God and a succession of rulers as one empire had followed another. Daniel's story was remarkable; God had blessed him through many challenges and threats—and God was with him still.

June 21

AN EXISTENTIAL FEAR

Again the one who looked like a man touched me and gave me strength. "Do not be afraid, you who are highly esteemed," he said. "Peace! Be strong now; be strong." When he spoke to me, I was strengthened and said, "Speak, my lord, since you have given me strength."

—Daniel 10:18, 19

The second "Do not be afraid" in Daniel 10 was a precursor to the visions he would see in the next chapters of the book. It addressed a more existential fear—the underlying fear that marks the relationship between God and humanity. God was not against Daniel and his people. He was not a threat to them; He was for them.

The visions of Daniel 7 through 12 portray a large scope of world history, the rise and fall of empires, the battles between competing beliefs and ideologies, and the fierce conflict between good and evil. In all of this, God's people often appear as victims or, at best, collateral damage. The empires are portrayed as beasts that would continue to trample and persecute God's people. But God was with His people. God saw their distress, and God, with them, would ultimately be victorious.

This was the larger "Do not be afraid" of Daniel's visions. In his own lifetime and in his experiences of working close to the center of power in successive empires, he had experienced some of the best and the worst of political and military power. But he had also witnessed God at work on the largest stages of world history and in many of the individual lives he encountered there.

By the time that Daniel was entrusted with the task of writing out these visions, much of his work was done, and he could rest in the assurance that God was with him and would continue to work out His plans in the larger world. "As for you, go your way till the end. You will rest, and then at the end of the days you will rise to receive your allotted inheritance" (Daniel 12:13).

BECAUSE GOD LOVED THE WORLD

Do not be afraid, land of Judah;
be glad and rejoice.
Surely the Lord *has done great things!*
Do not be afraid, you wild animals,
for the pastures in the wilderness are becoming green.
The trees are bearing their fruit;
the fig tree and the vine yield their riches.
Be glad, people of Zion,
rejoice in the Lord *your God,*
for he has given you the autumn rains
because he is faithful.

—Joel 2:21–23

We tend to personalize the invitation and promise of John 3:16, yet the language Jesus used also gives it the widest possible meaning: "For God so loved *the world* that he gave his one and only Son" (emphasis added). The Greek word for "world" is *kosmos*, which can be understood and translated as "all of Creation" or "the whole created order." So, there is more profound theology in this simple, well-loved verse than we sometimes notice. God sent His Son to offer eternal life to humanity—for the sake of His love for the whole of creation. This would restore the relationship between Himself and human beings, which in turn would restore the broken relationship between human beings and the world around them.

Like the other Hebrew prophets, Joel also pointed forward to a time when God's people would be fully and ultimately restored. He offered this hope in contrast to the ravages of the enemies that had beset Israel, consuming the nation and destroying it as implacably as a swarm of locusts.

But Joel, too, offered a holistic portrayal of what God's Messianic intervention would look like—all that had been lost and broken would be restored. The land would no longer be afraid; rather, it would rejoice because of what God had done. The wild animals would no longer be afraid, and the trees and plants would flourish. Amid all of the restoration and re-creation, God's people would also rejoice at the faithfulness and abundant goodness of God.

Because God so loved the world—and His people.

June 23

ROARING WITH MERCY

When a trumpet sounds in a city,
do not the people tremble?
When disaster comes to a city,
has not the Lord *caused it?*
Surely the Sovereign Lord *does nothing*
without revealing his
plan to his servants the prophets.
The lion has roared—who will not fear?
The Sovereign Lord *has spoken—*
who can but prophesy?

—Amos 3:6–8

Called to the work of delivering messages of warning and judgment to the people of Israel and Judah, Amos had good reason to reflect on the task he had been given and the messages he delivered. What is the purpose of prophecy? And why does God seem so often to foretell such bad news?

On the surface, the language of Amos' prophetic message is among the harshest in the Bible. In sometimes lurid language, it portrays God acting to punish the people, bringing disaster and destruction, slavery, and death to them because of their sins. No matter how sinful the people might have been, this language can and should make us uncomfortable.

But Amos 3 and 4 made it clear that these pronouncements, judgments, and warnings were coming near the end of a long process through which God had sought to call the people back to Himself and His ways. These looming judgments from God were not the point of His actions toward the people nor of Amos' message. "Amos' primary mission is not to predict, but to exhort and persuade."*

As daunting as Amos' message would have sounded to the people (we can almost hear the lions roaring in his thundering proclamations), his ministry and messages were, in themselves, one more evidence of God's mercy and forbearance. If God had truly given up on these people, He would not have sent yet another prophet to call them back to repentance again. So how could Amos not continue to work and continue to prophesy?

* Abraham J. Heschel, *The Prophets* (New York: Harper Perennial, 2001), 45.

OUR ORIGINAL PURPOSE

Everyone will sit under their own vine
and under their own fig tree,
and no one will make them afraid,
for the L*ORD* *Almighty has spoken.*

—Micah 4:4

Despite other less wholesome suggestions, the world's oldest profession is that of a gardener, although perhaps it is better described as a vocation. Gardening was the primary task given to the first human beings. "The LORD God took the man and put him in the Garden of Eden to work it and take care of it" (Genesis 2:15). And this was where Micah's vision of God's future would lead us.

This passage is not intended as a description of heaven as such. It contrasts markedly with most portrayals of the future of the faithful and the redeemed. According to the Hebrew prophets, the future would be a place of vocational enjoyment: "The prophets envisage redeemed humanity as humanity at work, but in the joy afforded by the absence of warfare, the reign of righteousness and peace, and the cooperation of nature. . . . The *new* creation restores God's *original* purpose for humanity."* The reality is that working without fear or threat makes the work more worthwhile. When gardeners are assured of enjoying the results of their labor and care, the work becomes part of the pleasure.

In that time and place where "no one will make them afraid," we will be returned to our original purpose, original relationships, and original vocation. Rather than some super-spiritual sky resort, God's future for His people will see them as fully human. The new is the original. Micah would have understood this as a restoration of the people to the land of Israel, but in Jesus and in God's larger plan, this vision expands to become the re-creation and restoration of the whole earth and all of creation—and the return of humanity to all we were created to be and to do.

* Christopher J. H. Wright, *Old Testament Ethics for the People of God* (Downers Grove, IL: IVP Academic, 2004), 161, 162.

June 25

A DIFFERENT KIND OF FAITH

He has shown you, O mortal, what is good.
And what does the Lord require of you?
To act justly and to love mercy
and to walk humbly with your God.

—Micah 6:8

As the prophets so often did when talking about the relationship between God and His people, Micah begins in chapter 6 by retelling how God had led and cared for His people in the past (see Micah 6:1–5), concluding with the declaration that "I, the Lord, did everything I could to teach you about my faithfulness" (Micah 6:5, NLT).

The prophet's reflections then turn to asking what the appropriate response from God's people should be to such faithfulness. "With what shall I come before the Lord and bow down before the exalted God?" he asks rhetorically (Micah 6:6). Echoing the calls of other Hebrew prophets, Micah's suggestions came in the context of worship (compare Isaiah 58 and Amos 5:21–24, for example), but also hinted toward the fearsome demands of the surrounding nations' gods, who often seemed to need appeasement.

Micah began modestly, talking about a sacrifice of calves, but this seemed inadequate, and his suggestions quickly inflated. The next step was offering "thousands of rams and ten thousand rivers of olive oil" (verse 7) before going to the horrific extreme of suggesting the sacrificing of his firstborn child, an all-too-common practice in pagan worship of the time.

But the answer was more simple, more profound, and more worshipful: "To act justly and to love mercy and to walk humbly with your God." Rejecting the religions of fear with all their excesses, superstitions, and sacrifices, the faith and worship of God's people were about living in a way that responded to, reflected, and enacted the faithfulness and goodness of God. If their God was a God of justice, mercy, and humility, as He had insisted and demonstrated repeatedly in their history, this was the kind of people they were called to be.

June 26

OUR ORIGINAL RELATIONSHIPS

"I will leave within you
the meek and humble.
The remnant of Israel
will trust in the name of the LORD.
They will do no wrong;
they will tell no lies.
A deceitful tongue
will not be found in their mouths.
They will eat and lie down
and no one will make them afraid."

—Zephaniah 3:12, 13

The restoration that God promised to the remnant of Israel included the renewal and restoration of the relationships He intended for all people. The brokenness of these relationships—with God, ourselves, and others, as well as the rest of creation—stretches back to the story of Adam's and Eve's choice to believe the lies of the serpent. Their fear and shame led them to hide from God, so when God promised that fear and shame would be no more, He was talking about a truly restored relationship and a renewed trust between Himself and His people. "On that day you, Jerusalem, will not be put to shame for all the wrongs you have done to me" (Zephaniah 3:11).

He promised to renew their lives and their characters as His humble people. The language in Zephaniah would be echoed in the description of the 144,000 redeemed who fully trust God with their lives and who will one day stand and sing on the heavenly Mount Zion. "No lie was found in their mouths; they are blameless" (Revelation 14:5). The authenticity of the people of God restores relationships between them. No longer will they be in competition with others, with its temptations for exploitation and unfair advantage. God's people will be trustworthy and safe to be around. And with God among them, they also will be able to live in safety, enjoying the good things of God's new creation, free from all fear.

This will be a return to Eden in the relational sense, with humanity restored to the relationships in which and for which God created us.

June 27

COURAGE THAT WORKS

On that day
they will say to Jerusalem,
"Do not fear, Zion;
do not let your hands hang limp.
The L*ORD* *your God is with you,*
the Mighty Warrior who saves.
He will take great delight in you;
in his love he will no longer rebuke you,
but will rejoice over you with singing."
—Zephaniah 3:16, 17

The prophet Zephaniah was a contemporary of Jeremiah. In his much more succinct book, he also warned of the consequences of the people's unfaithfulness and rebellion, and he included God's promises of redemption and restoration. The people of Israel would suffer through a time of destruction and exile, but God's love toward them was enduring and extravagant. His love was portrayed both in His saving power and as delighting in and singing over His people. Both the strength and tenderness of this portrayal catch our imaginations and move our hearts.

These promises were intended as a source of comfort and hope for the people, even as disaster unfolded around them: "No discipline seems pleasant at the time, but painful. Later on, however, it produces a harvest of righteousness and peace for those who have been trained by it. Therefore, strengthen your feeble arms and weak knees" (Hebrews 12:11, 12).

This restoration, this renewal of courage, and this affirmation of God's generous love toward them would also renew their call to work for God and for goodness in the world. Their limp arms would regain their strength, and this would be a time of renewed action and activity.

The people of Israel were always intended to be God's partners in the work of caring for, healing, and restoring the world. This work would be part of the restored relationship between God and His people. Throughout the Bible, "Do not be afraid" was often a starting point for a new task that God gave to His people. It is also an important element of the renewal of His relationship with all humanity.

REBUILDING WITH PROMISE

"Be strong, all you people of the land," declares the LORD, "and work. For I am with you," declares the LORD Almighty. "This is what I covenanted with you when you came out of Egypt. And my Spirit remains among you. Do not fear."

—Haggai 2:4, 5

The prophecies of Haggai are dated to about 520 B.C. at the time that work was underway on rebuilding the temple in Jerusalem. This was a time of mixed emotions for the returning exiles. Haggai noted the disappointment that was felt by many of those who remembered the glory of the former temple (see Haggai 2:3), a sorrow that was also recorded in the book of Ezra: "Many of the older priests and Levites and family heads, who had seen the former temple, wept aloud when they saw the foundation of this temple being laid" (Ezra 3:12).

It should not surprise us that God reminded them of the promises He had given to their ancestors in the time of the Exodus. He also assured them of the continuing presence of His Spirit among them. And He pointed forward to a still more glorious future: " 'The glory of this present house will be greater than the glory of the former house,' says the LORD Almighty. 'And in this place I will grant peace' " (Haggai 2:9). There would be a greater glory in this lesser temple—the revelation of Jesus, the Son of God in the flesh, their long-promised Messiah, the One who would bring hope and peace to all humanity. "What is desired by all nations will come" (Haggai 2:7).

So, as they worked to rebuild among the ruins of their nation and their memories of what had been lost, God was with them still, and the message of God through Haggai was to say again to the people of God, "Do not fear."

June 29

LET YOUR HANDS BE STRONG

"Just as you, Judah and Israel, have been a curse among the nations, so I will save you, and you will be a blessing. Do not be afraid, but let your hands be strong."

—Zechariah 8:13

Zechariah was another prophetic voice around the time of rebuilding the temple in Jerusalem (see Ezra 5:1). God seemed particularly active and concerned to let the people know that He was aware of their circumstances and that He was on their side. "Two months after Haggai's last recorded message was delivered, Zechariah had a series of visions regarding the work of God in the earth. These messages, given in the form of parables and symbols, came at a time of great uncertainty and anxiety, and were of peculiar significance to the men who were advancing in the name of the God of Israel. . . . God saw that His people were in need of being sustained and cheered by a revelation of His infinite compassion and love."*

There is nothing more demotivating than fear. It really does sap our strength and weaken our resolve. God's people were recovering from the destruction of their homes and communities and a generation of exile. They were now dislocated back to their distant homeland, of which the younger generation had no memories. They were facing a massive task of rebuilding amid the ruins of their nation and were surrounded by enemies and doubters who were working to undermine their efforts. We should not be surprised that they were feeling the weight of their circumstances and the nearly overwhelming challenges of the work to be done.

But Zechariah assured the people that God was working with them. This was a message of divine encouragement: "So don't be afraid. Be strong, and get on with rebuilding the Temple!" (Zechariah 8:13, NLT).

---

* Ellen G. White, *Prophets and Kings* (Mountain View, CA: Pacific Press®, 1917), 579.

June 30

SPEAK TRUTH, DO JUSTICE

"So now I have determined to do good again to Jerusalem and Judah. Do not be afraid. These are the things you are to do: Speak the truth to each other, and render true and sound judgment in your courts; do not plot evil against your neighbor, and do not love to swear falsely. I hate all this," declares the LORD.

—Zechariah 8:15–17

As the people were setting to work rebuilding their nation, city, homes, and temple, God was also concerned about them putting in the work to rebuild their relationships and their society. The assurance that God was offering to His people—the renewal of His relationship with them and the covenant He had made with their ancestors—was not only the foundation for their building projects. A restored relationship with God would recalibrate their relationships with each other and reorder their social systems. Trusting God would help the people build trust with each other.

According to Zechariah, the "Do not be afraid" message had important and practical implications. It feels like it should have been unnecessary to warn the people not to "plot evil" against each other, but this is sometimes necessary among groups of people who have been dominated by survival and self-preservation instincts for decades. When God's people took His "Do not be afraid" seriously, they would work to speak truth and do justice in their personal relationships with each other and in the courts and other social systems they would establish.

As God had always intended, the people of Israel were again called to become a nation that would be a light, an example, and a benefit to the nations of the world: "This is what the Lord Almighty says: 'In those days ten people from all languages and nations will take firm hold of one Jew by the hem of his robe and say, "Let us go with you, because we have heard that God is with you" ' " (Zechariah 8:23).

July 1

DWELLING AMONG US

The Word became flesh and made his dwelling among us.
We have seen his glory, the glory of the one and only Son,
who came from the Father, full of grace and truth.

—John 1:14

In the story of the garden in Eden, Adam and Eve hid from the approaching God. Human sin had caused humanity to withdraw—even seeking to escape—from the presence and glory of God. But God had a plan to repair and restore this broken relationship. God would approach humanity as a human being. To overcome the human fear of God, He would, in Jesus, be subject to all the fears of what it means to be human.

As much as we like to tell them to our children, many of the stories about Jesus are not neat or "nice." Jesus lived a real human life, with all its dangers, threats, and fears—and more. "Terror surrounded the life of Jesus like great parentheses. At his birth, Herod pursued him with slaughter, and in his crucifixion, he shared the fate of the condemned slaves and others of low esteem. But Jesus was not contained by the terror, for at his birth and at his resurrection, messengers from God proclaimed for all who would hear: 'Do not be afraid.' "*

In this context, the "Do not be afraids"—and similar commands that Jesus taught, such as "Do not worry" and "Do not be anxious"—sound all the louder and reach deeper into the realities of our lives. Based on the existential "Do not be afraid," these many similar commands constitute the wholistic life of faith, a life "not contained" by the fears that press themselves upon us. Because Jesus took on our fears, He sees and hears them in a different way and offers the healing and undoing of all our fears.

* Lee Griffith, *The War on Terrorism and the Terror of God* (Grand Rapids, MI: Eerdmans, 2002), 278.

BREAKING THE SILENCE

When Zechariah saw him, he was startled and was gripped with fear. But the angel said to him: "Do not be afraid, Zechariah; your prayer has been heard. Your wife Elizabeth will bear you a son, and you are to call him John."

—Luke 1:12, 13

There had been 400 or so years during which the Jewish people had lived with the apparent silence of God. After the voices of the Hebrew prophets fell silent, Greek and then Roman armies marched across their land, with the occasional brave but doomed revolts arising among the oppressed people. Those strident prophetic voices that promised restoration and renewal with the coming of the Messiah had receded into history, replaced by occasional rebel leaders who wanted to take on the mantle to rally the people to their cause. But the occupying armies were cruel and unmoved—and God seemed to be silent.

For Zechariah and Elizabeth, their experience of God's silence was not as long but was no less real. We are introduced to this couple as righteous, childless, and very old (see Luke 1:6, 7). We can imagine their years of hopes and expectations, their earnest prayers and bitter disappointments. And worse than this was the social stigma that compounded their frustrations. As Elizabeth commented after hearing the news, God had now "taken away my disgrace among the people" (Luke 1:25). Yet, for all those years, God had seemed silent.

Then, the silence was broken. After so long, it was hardly surprising that Zechariah was startled. It might have been considered privilege enough to perform the priestly duty of burning incense in the temple, but then an angel appeared with a message that God had heard his prayers and the time had come for a response. Zechariah still took some convincing (see Luke 1:18–20)—but he could not deny that God had finally broken His silence. Zechariah's family, the nation, and the world would not be the same again.

July 3

ZECHARIAH'S SONG

"He has raised up a horn of salvation for us
in the house of his servant David . . .
to rescue us from the hand of our enemies,
and to enable us to serve him without fear
in holiness and righteousness before him all our days."
Luke 1:69, 74, 75

After nine or so months, Zechariah's silence was broken in the act of naming his new son. After his encounter with the angel in the temple, his silence gave him all the more time to reflect on the reality that God was doing something significant. Undoubtedly, he must have played the conversation with the angel over and over in his mind. We are able to read the thought-out, pent-up response in Zechariah's song recorded in Luke 1:68–79.

It was a song of praise for God's intervention in the life of his family, celebrating the birth of their longed-for son. But it was also a song of praise for God's intervention in the nation and in history. The angel had given suggestions of the significance of this son and the call to transformation he would bring to the nation (see Luke 1:16, 17). It seems that Zechariah had also noted the angel's "Do not be afraid" and figured out that it involved more than simply a response to his momentary fear at the angel's appearance. Much more than that, this new intervention of God in history would "enable us to serve him without fear."

The relationship between God and His people, between God and all humanity, was entering a new phase. Inspired by the Holy Spirit, the old priest and new father recognized that this was something to celebrate. Hearing and amplifying the angel's "Do not be afraid," he proclaimed the rescue of his people and a restored relationship with God that would shine a new light into the darkness and "guide our feet into the path of peace" (Luke 1:79).

THE ANGEL'S TROUBLING WORDS

Mary was greatly troubled at his words and wondered what kind of greeting this might be. But the angel said to her, "Do not be afraid, Mary; you have found favor with God."
—Luke 1:29, 30

Six months after the angel appeared to Zechariah at the temple, the same angel, Gabriel, appeared to a young woman in a small village in the region of Galilee, a few days' journey to the north of Jerusalem—far enough away that she had obviously not heard Elizabeth's surprising news in the six months since that message had been delivered. As startled as Zechariah was by the appearance of an angel in the temple, an angel would appear even more alarming in the everyday surroundings of a simple village home in Nazareth. But, according to the story, Mary was more troubled by what the angel said—and his announcement was the particular reason for his "Do not be afraid."

Mary had not been seeking to earn favor with God; it was simply that God had favored her. But who was she to be so favored? She was from an unlikely town and was an unlikely person to be visited by an angel or chosen by God for any kind of task. She was confused by the angel's greeting, and her first reaction to his announcement that she had somehow come to God's attention was fear.

Again, there is a larger dimension to this "Do not be afraid." The favor or attention of God was not something from which she should hide. As daunting and confronting as her task would be, this was a vital part of the plan to remove fear from the God-human relationship. "Do not be afraid" would be a message she would personally need to hear at key points in mothering the Messiah, but "Do not be afraid" was also the point of the entire plan in which she was being invited to play her part.

July 5

WORDS OF REASSURANCE

The angel answered, "The Holy Spirit will come on you, and the power of the Most High will overshadow you. So the holy one to be born will be called the Son of God. . . . For no word from God will ever fail."

—Luke 1:35–37

When we retell the story of Mary—mostly at Christmas time—we naturally focus on the awesome task Mary was taking on, the unlikely, scandalous, even dangerous nature of what was being asked of her, and her humble acceptance of it. But it is worth remembering that this undertaking was far more unlikely and hazardous from the perspective of heaven. God was risking everything on this project of reconnection and restoration. God was making Himself vulnerable, and Gabriel's "Do not be afraid" revealed the fears and threats that this assignment necessarily entailed.

Even in this immediate moment, the plan was possible only with Mary's cooperation. It seems likely that the angel Gabriel held his breath: "As he said it, he only hoped she wouldn't notice that beneath the great, golden wings he himself was trembling with fear to think that the whole future of creation hung now on the answer of a girl."*

Sometimes, the reassurance we give to others is exactly what we ourselves need to hear—and reveals our true feelings of fear. We resonate with the fears and anxieties of the other person, then seek to calm their nervousness as much as our own. In Jesus, God became human. But in a new way, the whole of heaven also became vulnerable to the risks and fears of what it meant to be human, including the fear of vulnerability and rejection.

Heaven's fear was calmed by Mary's response: " 'I am the Lord's servant,' Mary answered. 'May your word to me be fulfilled' " (Luke 1:38). We might imagine that Gabriel let out the breath he had been holding, as did all of heaven.

---

* Frederick Buechner, *Peculiar Treasures: A Biblical Who's Who* (New York: Harper and Row, 1979), 44.

THE FORGOTTEN FATHER

But after he had considered this, an angel of the Lord appeared to him in a dream and said, "Joseph son of David, do not be afraid to take Mary home as your wife, because what is conceived in her is from the Holy Spirit. She will give birth to a son, and you are to give him the name Jesus, because he will save his people from their sins."
—Matthew 1:20, 21

Joseph often seems like the forgotten hero in the story of Jesus' birth. He's there in all the nativity scenes, but he is always a support character. In many retellings of the story, he is only briefly mentioned along the way. But God was also working in Joseph's life, which is made obvious by angels appearing to him at least three times in Matthew's telling of the story.

At the time of Mary's unexpected and unexplainable pregnancy, she was engaged to Joseph. Although their culture around engagement was different than how we understand it today, the story is clear that their marriage arrangement had not been concluded—and Joseph could still have chosen to back out. Unsurprisingly, he was upset and probably wished to avoid dishonoring himself, but he also did not want to publicly shame Mary. He wanted to protect her from the accusations, gossip, and even possible threats to her life that would be directed at her in such a scandalous situation.

As Joseph struggled, God intervened. This time, an angel appeared to him in a dream, confirming that Mary's explanation for her unexpected condition was true and that he should not be afraid to stay with her. Not only did the angel reassure Joseph, giving him a way forward in this difficult situation, but he was also established in the father's cultural role and given the privilege of naming the child. Even here was a reminder of the saving significance of who Jesus would be in God's larger plan of restoration and relationship.

July 7

THOSE SHEPHERDS AND THOSE ANGELS

An angel of the Lord appeared to them, and the glory of the Lord shone around them, and they were terrified. But the angel said to them, "Do not be afraid. I bring you good news that will cause great joy for all the people."

—Luke 2:9, 10

We tell this story in hushed tones every Christmas: The quiet and chilly evening outside Bethlehem, the sounds of animals and murmured conversations around a small fire, complaints about the influx of visitors to their small town, the rough shepherds as unlikely recipients about to receive a startling interruption, a world-changing announcement, and an angel choir. For many years, I have been part of a large-scale reenactment of this story for the community in our part of the city each December. Every year, I feel again the sense of wonder that is part of the story, but also that such an unlikely story is still being retold more than 2,000 years later—and that somehow we believe that this obscure historical moment changed everything.

But there is also an undertow of danger and fear in the story. Empires and rulers were concerned with any claims to a new king or a different kind of kingdom. As such, the angel's "Do not be afraid" was not only for those shepherds startled from their evening drowsiness but was also to be a message of "great joy for all the people." It was for all who would hear or read the story in the centuries to come, inhabiting a world of fear and threat but hoping to believe that this baby changed their story and would offer a different way to live with one another and with God. Afterward, the shepherds followed the angel's instructions, found the baby, and went back to their sheep, praising God. There was a powerful effect on those who first heard the remarkable story—"all who heard it were amazed at what the shepherds said to them" (Luke 2:18).

July 8

JESUS AS A REFUGEE

When they had gone, an angel of the Lord appeared to Joseph in a dream. "Get up," he said, "take the child and his mother and escape to Egypt. Stay there until I tell you, for Herod is going to search for the child to kill him."
—Matthew 2:13

We can easily imagine the fear that would have gripped Joseph and Mary as they gathered up a few belongings in the early morning darkness, quickly packed some food, and dressed the sleepy young Jesus in clothes for traveling. Long before daybreak, they left Bethlehem and were on the road south toward Egypt, traveling as fast as they could and as far as their strength would carry them. They could only imagine the horror taking place in Bethlehem behind them (see Matthew 2:16–18), but their fear drove them onward, alert to any sound of galloping horses warning them that Herod's soldiers might be broadening their search.

Sadly, this is a scenario that has played out countless times in the history of our world. Today, tens of millions of people are displaced from their homes by fears of violence, hunger, exploitation, and persecution. Driven by these fearful realities, they risk the dangers of travel, exploitation, uncertainty as to where they might be heading, and the likelihood that they will not be welcomed when they get there—all in the hope of the relative safety of a foreign nation.

In Jesus, God identified with and experienced this fear. For those seeking refuge, this is a remarkable comfort. God has seen, heard, and felt such fears—after all, He experienced such a journey with His earthly family, living as foreigners in the land of Egypt, probably for a couple of years. For those today who might welcome refuge-seekers, the identification of Jesus with those who run in fear for their lives should challenge us to respond. In serving them, we might be most truly serving Him.

July 9

FOR GOD SO LOVED THE WORLD

For God so loved the world that he gave his one and only Son, that whoever believes in him shall not perish but have eternal life.

—John 3:16

It was not God who broke the relationship between Himself and humanity, between Himself and His children. And even when those relationships had been fractured, God's first response was love. This was the motive for Jesus becoming human. Because God loves the world so much—Jesus. Love is always God's action, God's motivation, God's explanation, God's invitation.

The word *love* is often sentimentalized, even trivialized, by much of our culture. But God's love is active, tangible, and transformative. It takes shape in our world as it shapes our world. It took shape as Jesus Himself. It is the invitation to eternal life, overcoming the fear of death. In Jesus, God's love is stronger than death for those who choose that love. And God's love is greater than our most innate human fear, always reaching out to those first humans hiding from the sound of His approach and to those of us who so often follow their example.

Throughout the New Testament, the *world* is often shorthand for evil, temptations, and distractions. These are part of our world as it is, but there is also so much that is good, beautiful, and true. And this is the world that God has loved—from the first to the last—and continues to love. In Jesus, God was worldly in the best sense of the word. He was for the world, for the sake of the world, and for the good of the world.

The eternal life offered in John 3:16 is not merely the opposite of death or overcoming it. It is a restoration of the relationship with God that gives us the eternal quality of life today—a life that matters for eternity because it is in harmony with the great, eternal, and loving God.

July 10

SALVATION, NOT CONDEMNATION

For God did not send his Son into the world to condemn the world, but to save the world through him.

—John 3:17

Ask most secular people what they think of faith, religion, church, or Christianity, and it is likely that they will mention being judgmental. Even when they do not have much contact or interaction with church people, many of these people feel they are being judged or condemned by church people. It is one of the reasons that people are afraid to venture into a church or into church contexts.

That was the dynamic in the garden after Adam and Eve first sinned. The sound of God walking toward them was enough for them to imagine that they were hearing His judgment. God had not said anything, but their consciences condemned them nonetheless. In a sense, they attributed this judgmentalism to God, and they hid from Him. Our fear of judgmentalism often reflects more about us and our state of mind than it does about God's attitude toward us.

While some churches *are* judgmental, the perception of these churches might similarly be colored by people's expectations of condemnation, partly based on experience and popular representations, but also partly a response similar to Adam and Eve's instinct to hide from the approaching God. Unfortunately, such anticipated condemnation can form real barriers for many.

This could also have been our perception about God sending His Son into the world—except that Jesus explicitly rejected this understanding of who He was and what He came to do. Jesus sought to disarm the anticipated condemnation, defuse the fear that kept people at such a distance, and repair the relationship between God and humanity as far as possible. It was not God who broke the relationship between Himself and humanity, but it is always God who is working to restore what was lost.

July 11

STEPPING INTO THE LIGHT

"Everyone who does evil hates the light, and will not come into the light for fear that their deeds will be exposed. But whoever lives by the truth comes into the light, so that it may be seen plainly that what they have done has been done in the sight of God."

—John 3:20, 21

John's Gospel uses the metaphor of light and darkness repeatedly and in several different ways. When Jesus met with Nicodemus, a member of the Jewish council, the story begins with the comment that this prominent, powerful leader "came to Jesus at night" (John 3:2), suggesting that he met with Jesus privately under the cover and anonymity of darkness. So when Jesus begins talking about light and darkness, it seems that He is inviting Nicodemus to "come into the light" with more than one possible meaning.

Many of us—all of us?—have things that we would be embarrassed to have reported publicly. But this was not quite the point that Jesus was making here. Of course, He described those who choose evil as being afraid "that their deeds will be exposed." But He described the dynamic of those who choose to "live by the truth" in a different way. It is the person himself who "comes into the light," and it is not their deeds that will be thus revealed, but that what they did was "done in the sight of God." In Jesus' description of those drawn by truth into the light, the focus shifted away from them and their deeds to the fact of God's presence with them.

This was a significant shift, but it was a gradual process for Nicodemus. When he spoke up in the council meeting (see John 7:50) and when he publicly declared his allegiance to Jesus by assisting with His burial, Nicodemus was described as "the man who earlier had visited Jesus at night" (John 19:39). That night had been a starting point, but perhaps two or three years later, Nicodemus had overcome his fears and stepped into the light as Jesus had invited Him to do.

July 12

KNOWING HIS ROLE

"He must become greater;
I must become less."

—John 3:30

For a period of time, John the Baptist was the most famous preacher in the land. Even though he was based in the wilderness, people of all kinds traveled to hear him and to be baptized by him. His power and popularity were such that it prompted questions among the leaders and the people as to whether he might actually be the Messiah for which they were waiting. If not the Messiah, they wondered, then he must at least be counted among the prophets of Israel (see John 1:19–23).

John was clear that his role was to announce the coming One; he even was able to point Him out and baptize Him (see John 1:29–34). But when Jesus began His ministry, what was next for His forerunner? It seems that John continued to preach and baptize and had disciples who stayed with him. It was these disciples who seemed most jealous for John, afraid that he was being eclipsed by this new teacher. "They came to John and said to him, 'Rabbi, that man who was with you on the other side of the Jordan—the one you testified about—look, he is baptizing, and everyone is going to him' " (John 3:26).

John's answer is one of insight and humility. Of course, it would have been foolish to think that he could "compete" with Jesus and His ministry. Because John truly believed in Jesus, he knew that Jesus was the reason for his work and even any "success" he had. He knew that the more attention Jesus received, the more effective his own work had been. He did not need to guard his ministry, compete for crowds, compare baptism numbers, or even keep his disciples.

John's remarkable example is the ministry blueprint for all followers of Jesus—"He must become greater; I must become less." Imagine what this might look like in our lives, our churches, and our ministries today.

July 13

"I UNDERSTAND"

Then Jesus declared, "I, the one speaking to you—I am he."
—John 4:26

Jesus' long conversations with unlikely people—Nicodemus, the woman at the well in Samaria, among others—are a unique element of John's Gospel. They reveal deep truths, as well as the personal interactions that Jesus had with those diverse people.

Significantly, in His conversation with an outcast Samaritan woman—the longest personal conversation in all of the Gospels—Jesus first confessed that He was the expected Messiah. In the story, their conversation is interrupted at that point, so we do not hear the woman's response, but the conclusion of the people of her town is this: "We know that this man really is the Savior of the world" (John 4:42).

But this was not the testimony the woman led with. It seems she was more affected by the personal aspect of her encounter with Jesus: "Come, see a man who told me everything I've ever done. Could this be the Messiah?" (John 4:29).

Jesus, uninvited, had recounted her troubled relationship history. But from the woman's reaction, this was not what she heard. Instead, she had met a Messiah who had seen her troubles, disappointments, and fear. What she heard from Jesus was not accusatory—"I know what you have done," but was instead, "I understand"—spoken gently and with love. This was the moment that most touched her heart and that she proclaimed to the people of her town.

Hearing that voice of Jesus—perhaps in contrast to some of the tones of voice in which Jesus has been presented in our past—can transform our faith and our lives. "We need to ask ourselves, *Do I really believe the Good News of Jesus Christ?* Do I hear His word spoken to my heart: 'Shalom, be at peace, I understand'?"*

* Brennan Manning, *The Ragamuffin Gospel* (Milton Keynes, UK: Authentic Classics, 2003), 136.

JESUS REVEALED

When Simon Peter saw this, he fell at Jesus' knees and said, "Go away from me, Lord; I am a sinful man!"

—Luke 5:8

It seems likely that Peter knew Jesus before witnessing this miraculous catch of fish—an event that Peter identified with closely as a professional fisherman. But this was a new and greater revelation of Jesus' power and led to Peter's growing understanding of who Jesus might be. His immediate response was similar to that of Zechariah, Mary, and the shepherds—fear at the appearance of God's power among humanity. Peter took this realization further, acknowledging his unworthiness to be in the presence of this power and urging Jesus to depart from him.

As we have seen, this is one of the most human of responses. "In the biblical record, the response of human beings to the appearance of God (in the guise of an angel, a burning bush, a whirlwind) is always the same—fear and terror." This was now Peter's experience: "The huge catch of fish is the occasion for a theophany. The Lord's gracious response is exactly the same as that of the biblical angels who come directly from the presence of God: 'Fear not.' Without that merciful reassurance, the human being would be annihilated by the burning holiness of God. This sense of the distance between God and His creation must always be held in tension with the intimate closeness of the personal God who draws near to us in grace."*

While acknowledging the correctness of his response, Jesus disarmed Peter's fear. This was not the end of their friendship but the beginning of a remarkable new relationship. It would be a relationship that would transform Peter and, in time, play an important role in changing the world.

* Fleming Rutledge, *The Crucifixion: Understanding the Death of Jesus Christ* (Grand Rapids, MI: Eerdmans, 2015), 521, 522.

July 15

FROM FEAR TO MISSION

Then Jesus said to Simon, "Don't be afraid; from now on you will fish for people."

—Luke 5:10

As in the previous divine appearances in Luke's Gospel, Jesus' reply to Peter's declaration sought first to allay his fear. "Don't be afraid," said Jesus, acknowledging the divine-human dynamic that Peter had suddenly recognized. At the same time, He gently rejected Peter's request that Jesus leave him alone, perhaps understanding that this was simply the instinctive reaction of the moment, not what Peter truly desired. What Peter needed was reassurance that despite what he was coming to understand about Jesus, they actually could be friends, that they could fish and work together.

Not only did Jesus seek to calm Peter's fears, but He also used Peter's confession—both of Jesus' power and his own unworthiness—as a catalyst for a closer relationship and for advancing mission. While Peter seemed to push Jesus away, Jesus drew him closer: "Seeing God's power is not a cause to fall back and withdraw from God, but is an opportunity to draw near to Him."*

Drawing on Peter's confession, Jesus called Peter and his colleagues to a different kind of life, and while the statement is brief as recorded by Luke, the result was clear in the following verse, which recorded that "they pulled their boats up on shore, left everything and followed him" (Luke 5:11). This was more than just a call; it was an affirmation that Peter's insight into who Jesus was—even as limited as it might have been at that time—was correct. The call would make sense only if Jesus was who Peter was recognizing Him to be. It was also an affirmation that Peter's humility, his sense of unworthiness, was the primary qualification for the task to which Jesus had now called him.

---

* Darrell L. Bock, *Luke 1:1–9:50*, Baker Exegetical Commentary on the New Testament (Grand Rapids, MI: Baker Books, 1994), 460.

REFUSING LIFE

"You study the Scriptures diligently because you think that in them you have eternal life. These are the very Scriptures that testify about me, yet you refuse to come to me to have life."
—John 5:39, 40

This statement of Jesus could be considered one of His most sobering warnings. His extended conversation with the Jewish leaders came in the aftermath of His healing of the man who had been paralyzed for thirty-eight years at the Pool of Bethesda. They challenged Jesus about breaking the Sabbath, which led to some of Jesus' most direct statements about His relationship with God the Father. But He also made this stark warning about the risks for committed religious people, students of the Scriptures, missing the point of their religious study—even as He was standing in front of them and they were beginning to persecute Him (see John 5:16).

As evidenced by His life and teaching, Jesus was certainly not against the study of the Scriptures and the work of learning and growing in our understanding of faith. He taught His disciples and commissioned them to teach others. But Jesus was clear that there were serious temptations and preoccupations that are unique to religious people, perhaps even more so to religious leaders and experts, as well as for those of us who have grown up in, studied in, and are employed in church contexts. Professional and highly committed religiosity has unique hazards.

However, the response to this warning is not to study harder, pray more, or be more religiously earnest. It is to come to Jesus Himself. We surrender ourselves and even our religious expertise or qualifications to Him, seeking the life that He brings and—in the context of the story in which this discussion took place—the real healing and liberation He offered. The question Jesus urged was whether our religious expectations and engagement, including our Bible study, add to, discount, or discourage the life, ministry, and service to which Jesus has called us.

July 17

CLEARING OUR VISION

"Why do you look at the speck of sawdust in your brother's eye and pay no attention to the plank in your own eye?"

—Luke 6:41

One of our perpetual temptations is that of judging others. This is not the sole province of people of faith, but it does have a unique form within faith contexts. Jesus' teaching addressed this a number of times, especially calling out the hypocrisy of many priests and leaders of His time (for example, see Matthew 23).

While some of them were using religion merely for position and power, the more earnest were desperate for the approval of God and, drawing on Israel's troubled history, were afraid that any wrongdoing or even minor failures to observe their many rules and regulations would open the nation to further occupation and dispossession. Either way, the priests and leaders were hypervigilant for the sins and failures of others, creating a social and religious environment of judgment and fear. As Jesus pointed out, this was not a blueprint for healthy faith or leadership: "Can a blind man lead a blind man? Will they not both fall into a pit?" (Luke 6:39).

Jesus taught His followers, "Do not judge" (Luke 6:37), warning that the measure we use to judge will be the measure by which we will be judged. But this was not about discernment in order to sidestep God's judgment. Rather than judging others, Jesus' followers are to live with forgiveness and generosity.

Jesus urged all leaders to view themselves and others with these same attitudes. Rather than focusing on the specks in other lives, our first task should be healthy self-reflection. Being honest about our own wounds and failures means that we can seek the healing that Jesus offers. It means our faith is not driven by fear, either of God or of others. This is the way of seeing clearly, which is the foundation for living, leading, and serving well.

July 18

REJOICE AND BE GLAD?

"Blessed are you when people insult you, persecute you and falsely say all kinds of evil against you because of me. Rejoice and be glad, because great is your reward in heaven, for in the same way they persecuted the prophets who were before you."

—Matthew 5:11, 12

The Beatitudes are remarkably simple statements that are both transformative and profoundly challenging in their application. Most of them feel like contradictions—which demonstrates how counterintuitive the kingdom of God is to most of what we are taught and assume from the culture around us. This is why the Beatitudes are so important to life as a follower of Jesus.

Throughout the Beatitudes, Jesus taught that avoiding those threats and experiences that we most fear and most want to avoid is not the highest priority in the kingdom of God. Rather, in the midst of persecution, misunderstandings, and false accusations, we are to rejoice. It seems a strange and difficult command. It reminds us that a faithful life can sometimes appear unsuccessful, even tenuous, in this broken world. But there are two important provisos.

First, persecution is "blessed" when it is "because of me [Jesus]." This does not give us license to be rude, loud, mean, or aggressive in our lives or even our faith. If people dislike or exclude us because of our offensive attitudes or insensitivity, all the pushback in the world does not prove us right. But persecution because of Jesus will come despite our faithful actions in the spirit of Jesus.

Second, the call is not to rejoice *because* we are being persecuted. That would be a perversion of Christ's point. But we are to rejoice in the larger reality into which Jesus is inviting us. In the kingdom of God, our lives are measured by something other than our current circumstances, success, social acceptance, or safety. That is why we can rejoice and be glad even amid days that seem like our worst.

July 19

LET YOUR LIGHT SHINE

"You are the light of the world. A town built on a hill cannot be hidden. Neither do people light a lamp and put it under a bowl. Instead they put it on its stand, and it gives light to everyone in the house. In the same way, let your light shine before others, that they may see your good deeds and glorify your Father in heaven."

—Matthew 5:14–16

Jesus taught His disciples that they would transform, flavor, and preserve the world—that's the "salt of the earth" metaphor (see Matthew 5:13)—and that their faithful living would shine like a light in the night for all to see for the glory of God. On a dark night, a town built on a hilltop will be seen from a long distance simply because it is there. This is not necessarily due to a special effort that is put in; it is the inevitable result of the townspeople lighting their houses and streets—of simply living their lives.

But Jesus was also talking about a collective light. The Greek word Jesus used for "you" in this description is plural, meaning groups of His followers shining together. A single small flame may hardly be visible, but when many small flames shine together, it can be seen from the surrounding countryside.

In a fear-darkened world, one of the brightest lights we can shine is to choose to live in contradiction of fear. Rather than retreating to the supposed safety of our own small communities, the light we shine for God should be visible in public, in the wider world. Living boldly and lovingly as followers of Jesus, we will shine all the brighter, particularly when we do it together. It will be noticed by those around us and will be attractive as a different way of thinking, choosing, and acting in our world.

COURAGEOUS GIVING

"Give to the one who asks you, and do not turn away from the one who wants to borrow from you."
—Matthew 5:42

One of our innate human fears is that we will not have enough. For those who have experienced financial hardship or been deprived of the resources necessary for life, that survival impulse can be all the stronger. But *enough* is also a slippery term, difficult to define, and often a measure that is more relative than fixed. So, giving is an act of courage, particularly when we give to a degree that feels like it might threaten our own financial well-being or viability. Even when we give from what feels like extra resources we have at the moment, we are pushing back against the instinct to self-preservation, the fear that we might not have enough at some point in the future. This is why giving is such a valuable practice for a life of faithful courage.

In the preceding verses, Jesus was talking about how His followers should choose to respond to those who were oppressing them. The violence and exploitation that Jesus described were part of the daily experiences of many of His listeners. In this case, a generous response was an act of resistance, creatively and non-violently seeking to overcome evil by doing good (see Romans 12:19–21). Similarly, generous giving is an act of resistance against the temptations of our culture to consumerism and accumulation and our assumption that our security is found in things.

With practice, generosity can become an attitude for every aspect of our lives. So, we need to learn how to give intentionally, thoughtfully, and regularly but also randomly and generously when specific needs arise. Both kinds of giving will push back against our fears, the culture around us, and the things that can so easily gain a hold over us. Both kinds of giving can also be valuable for helping someone who really needs the help we give.

July 21

LOVING OUR ENEMIES

"You have heard that it was said, 'Love your neighbor and hate your enemy.' But I tell you, love your enemies and pray for those who persecute you, that you may be children of your Father in heaven. He causes his sun to rise on the evil and the good, and sends rain on the righteous and the unrighteous."

—Matthew 5:43–45

In the broken relationships that the Bible describes and the fear that results from them, it is inevitable that there will be some people who are easy to love, some whom we would prefer to hate or avoid, some who frighten us, who might even wish us harm. But Jesus did not give His followers those options. He urged us to love all people, especially those we might consider enemies—and, in the worst-case example, those who are actually persecuting us. In every case—best case to worst case—Jesus' command was, and is, to love.

Love can be mistaken for some kind of nice feeling toward a particular person, which can be terribly hard to create if we take it on as a merely emotional project. But the example of God's actions that Jesus gave His disciples was much more practical and tangible. The Bible insists that in every situation and scenario, God seeks our good, whatever our relationship with Him. And this is the model that Jesus gave to His followers. Loving our enemies and praying for our persecutors is about actively seeking their good. It is not about warm emotion but practical service. This might mean that we risk rejection and ridicule—and we need to be alert to unhealthy and abusive situations, which are not good for the abuser or us—but this is the courage that love requires. And sometimes, when we work for the good of others, we can come to truly desire their good and begin to restore the relationships that are broken between us.

July 22

THE PRAYER JESUS GAVE US

"Our Father in heaven,
hallowed be your name,
your kingdom come,
your will be done,
    on earth as it is in heaven.
Give us today our daily bread.
And forgive us our debts,
    as we also have forgiven our debtors.
And lead us not into temptation,
    but deliver us from the evil one."

—Matthew 6:9–13

In the Sermon on the Mount, the Lord's Prayer is part of Jesus' general teaching on prayer and faithfulness. When Luke shared this prayer, it was introduced by a request from the disciples: "Lord, teach us to pray" (Luke 11:1). Coming after His warnings in the Sermon on the Mount about showy religion and long prayers, it is not surprising that the prayer Jesus gave to His disciples was short and practical. It also touched on the core relationships of our human lives—with God, with ourselves, with others, and with the world around us. Presented in this way, all relationships and their necessary restoration are acknowledged by God, are the subject of His care, and are to be entrusted to Him in the act of prayer.

Addressing God as our "Father" is a significant opening, reminding us that God is immanent and transcendent. This is a prayer that stretches from heaven to earth, from the coming kingdom to our everyday needs, from protection and forgiveness to relationships restored between ourselves and our neighbors. While in this sinful world, food is earned "by the sweat of your brow" (Genesis 3:19) but, in Jesus' prayer, we also acknowledge the creation and provision of God.

When the disciples asked Jesus to teach them to pray, they were asking Him to teach them what it means to live in the reality of the kingdom of God, even amid the realities of everyday life, as well as in times of unusual threat or pressure. In all of that, the simple prayer Jesus gave them—and us—is one of trust and restoration. And with praying, our lives will be shaped increasingly in the way of Jesus.

July 23

DO NOT WORRY

"Therefore I tell you, do not worry about your life, what you will eat or drink; or about your body, what you will wear. Is not life more than food, and the body more important than clothes?"

—Matthew 6:25

It can seem glib to talk about the necessary things of our physical lives—food, water, and clothing, for starters—and simply say, "Don't worry." Those who have gone without these essentials at some time in their lives know how vital they are. So, Jesus had to make His case, particularly when teaching the crowd of Galilean commoners, many of whom would have had their own experiences of hunger and need. He was not speaking glibly but was pointing them to the goodness of God and that His words were not merely a theological argument but should transform the priorities by which they lived their lives.

Jesus pointed first to the birds darting about the hillside and circling in the sky above them, seemingly without a care in the world but fed by the abundance of creation. Then, He saw the wildflowers growing on the hillside, noting their fragile and fleeting beauty, which outshines the robes of royalty even if the flowers might only last a single day. In both examples, Jesus made clear the capacity of God and His creation to supply our basic needs—and, in His abundance and generosity, so much more.

So, don't worry, Jesus said. As His followers, our lives are not to be focused on what we need or what we can get or accumulate. "The pagans run after all these things, and your heavenly Father knows that you need them" (Matthew 6:32). According to Jesus, the God who sees and responds to injustice and oppression in our world is also the God who knows our everyday needs. Like the birds and the flowers, we can live for His glory with freedom and trust.

STRESSED ABOUT BEING STRESSED?

"Can any of you by worrying add a single hour to your life?"
—Matthew 6:27

Jesus was asking a rhetorical question. Worrying doesn't add any length to our life, nor can it make us taller—as an alternative version of this verse puts it. In fact, quite the opposite is true; worry tends to grind us down, wear us out, and can have significant negative effects on our well-being. Today, we might talk more about stress than worry, but they are much the same in this context. When worry and stress come to dominate our lives, we find it difficult to live well. A little or occasional stress is a natural and inevitable part of our lives, but chronic stress becomes a threat to our health.

Worry and stress can also have a compounding effect, meaning that the more we worry, the more worried we can become about being worried. "Stress and worry seem to come too easy to us. A fascinating recent study has shown that, while stress affects our health, it is worse for people who believe that stress is damaging. The takeaway message is that how we think about stress matters and stressing about being stressed makes things worse!"*

Accordingly, Jesus was not trying to make us feel guilty about being worried, adding an extra layer of anxiety to our already-stressed lives. Instead, He was offering what might sound like a "merely" spiritual solution, but it is actually the ultimate stress-management plan, both spiritually and practically: "Seek first his kingdom and his righteousness, and all these things will be given to you as well" (Matthew 6:33). We don't have to be worried about being worried, because as citizens of His kingdom we live with different priorities, and we can choose to entrust our worries to Him.

---

* Darren Morton, *Live More Happy* (Warburton, Victoria, Australia: Signs Publishing Company, 2017), 134.

July 25

LIVING TODAY

"Therefore do not worry about tomorrow, for tomorrow will worry about itself. Each day has enough trouble of its own."

—Matthew 6:34

Jesus was not promising a worry-free or care-free life. When He said, "Do not worry," He was acknowledging the necessity of so many of the things we worry about—and that such worry has always been part of human existence. We are fragile creatures, dependent on things as simple as food and water—and so much more—for life and health. We do have to be concerned about taking care of ourselves responsibly and caring for our families, our community, and others in need. And for most of us, most of the time, we need to work to provide those things using the resources, skills, strength, and opportunities that we have been given. For most of our lives, that is the work of today.

Jesus also warned us about becoming too preoccupied with worries and fears for the future. He told His followers that they should not import tomorrow's troubles into today. Confronting the threats and stresses that we expect or imagine in the future is not the task we are given today. This does not mean that we don't make plans or work toward goals. What we do today can help shape the future for ourselves and others, but planning and working faithfully today are the focus for today.

Even with the hardest work and the most careful planning, we cannot control the future. Life is difficult, frustrating, and even tragic for so many people—but that is not how God intended or intends it to be. The answer to worry is to entrust ourselves and our futures to the God who feeds the birds and clothes the wildflowers so abundantly. He is not only a God of provision but a God of creativity and beauty. When we trust Him with tomorrow, no matter how uncertain it might feel, we are choosing to be part of God's project to restore and re-create it all. It's the biggest assurance we can have.

July 26

BUILT ON THE ROCK

"Therefore everyone who hears these words of mine and puts them into practice is like a wise man who built his house on the rock. The rain came down, the streams rose, and the winds blew and beat against that house; yet it did not fall, because it had its foundation on the rock."

—Matthew 7:24, 25

Storms come to each of our lives. While they affect us in different ways and at different times, they are an inevitable element of our human experiences. Whether as widespread and implacable as the weather itself or as individual and unique as our most private trauma or tragedy, the storms we experience can shape us in different ways. They can leave us harder or more empathetic, angrier or more understanding, defeated or more resilient, more isolated or more reliant on the help of others and the power of God. In short—as Jesus taught—such storms can reveal the foundation of our lives.

When Jesus gave this example, He was probably not thinking of coastal views and ocean frontage. Instead, His listeners would have imagined the wadis that flash flooding had carved out in the Judean and Samarian hills. At the bottom of these narrow valleys were smooth sandy flats leading down to the Jordan River. It was easy to build in these places, but everything could be swept away with a heavy shower of rain somewhere up the valley. Building on the rocky hillsides was a more arduous undertaking, but the result would be a house that was less subject to the vagaries of weather.

Jesus urged His disciples that following His teaching would not necessarily feel like the easier path, but ultimately, it was the path with less risk. They would not be immune from the inevitable challenges and tragedies of life. Storms would still come, but grounded in the teaching and promises of Jesus, those who heard and put them into practice would remain firm.

July 27

AN UNEXPECTED HEALING

Some men brought to him a paralyzed man, lying on a mat.
When Jesus saw their faith, he said to the man,
"Take heart, son; your sins are forgiven."

—Matthew 9:2

In Jesus' interactions with various people, He often seemed to be answering a different question or a different request than the obvious one. A group of men brought a paralyzed man to Jesus to be healed. Jesus noticed the collective faith of the group and, rather than healing the man, told him to be encouraged because His sins were forgiven. We can only guess at what the man's friends might have thought about that response to their obvious request. They may have even been concerned that they might be disappointed and have to carry their friend home again after all.

We might be tempted to think that Jesus was trying to make a point to the teachers of the law nearby, who were quick to express their dismay at Jesus claiming such a prerogative. But it doesn't make sense that Jesus would use a man who came seeking help in such a way. Instead, it seems more likely that Jesus somehow knew this man's real unease—or dis-ease—and that his healing would be complete, perhaps could be possible, only if his heart issue was addressed first.

Perhaps this first step of receiving forgiveness gave the man courage to even attempt a physical step in response to Jesus' later command, "Get up, take your mat and go home" (Matthew 9:6). Our bodies, hearts, and minds are intimately connected, and a dramatic healing of the body will always have mental and spiritual implications.

Sometimes, when someone gives us an unexpected response to a question or request, it makes sense in a way that we would not have imagined. In this case, it seemed that the response Jesus gave really was the unsought answer that made all the sense in the world.

July 28

AN ORDINARY JOURNEY

One day Jesus said to his disciples, "Let's go over to the other side of the lake." So they got into a boat and set out.

—Luke 8:22

It started out as an ordinary journey. And despite its risk and danger, it remained an ordinary journey because these are the risks and dangers of all of our everyday lives. From the mundane to the extreme, from the physical to the spiritual, from life to death, from the chronic to the emergency, from the inconvenient to the tragic, we can see so much of our lives in the sequence of events that Jesus and His disciples experienced in Luke 8:22–56—a storm on the lake, a demon-possessed man, a bleeding woman, Jairus with his daughter. When we read their stories together, these four miracles "reflect an escalation, since they progress from external threats to more internalized threats, culminating in the direct threat of death itself."*

But the collective picture is that of Jesus' power over all those things that attack, degrade, and destroy our lives. "Together they show Jesus' comprehensive power and authority. . . . Jesus can deal with all of these attempts to overwhelm humankind."† Whether it was weather, demonic power, disease, or even death, not only was Jesus' power demonstrated in response to each of those threats, but those who were with Jesus were repeatedly amazed at His power and authority. Additionally, they witnessed His care and concern for those who were hurt and excluded by the destructive powers.

Not every day will see us confront all of these dangers and threats, but across all of our days, we will confront each of them at different times and in various ways. And many of those days will begin as ordinary days, with us setting out on ordinary journeys. But on both our ordinary journeys and our unexpected or extraordinary journeys, we begin them with Jesus. He will be journeying with us, and we might have the opportunity to witness His power.

---

* Darrell L. Bock, *Luke 1:1–9:50*, Baker Exegetical Commentary on the New Testament (Grand Rapids, MI: Baker Books, 1994), 754.

† Bock, 754.

July 29

IN GREAT DANGER

As they sailed, he fell asleep. A squall came down on the lake,
so that the boat was being swamped, and they were in great danger.
The disciples went and woke him, saying,
"Master, Master, we're going to drown!"

—Luke 8:23, 24

A few years ago, I had the privilege of taking a boat ride on the Sea of Galilee. Conveniently designed to accommodate a coachload of tourists, the boat was larger than the first-century fishing boats in which Jesus and His disciples would have sailed on these waters. It was a perfect afternoon, warm but with an occasional breeze. When the captain switched off the engine and allowed the boat to drift for a few minutes, we could hear the gentle slap of the small waves against the hull and smell the freshness of the water.

Enjoying such a tranquil and reflective moment, it was inevitable that one of our tour group would ask the captain about the reality of storms on the lake. It was probably not a unique question, and the captain responded by showing us a video on his phone of waves breaking over the boat as this larger vessel was tossed about by wind and water. In contrast to our experience, we could easily imagine the fear of the disciples on a dark and stormy night as the wind whipped across the lake and their smaller boat filled with water.

Amid that danger, Jesus was asleep, and the disciples woke Him with real fear in their voices. While Jesus would chide them for their seeming lack of faith, it wasn't until after He had addressed the threat. "He got up and rebuked the wind and the raging waters; the storm subsided, and all was calm. 'Where is your faith?' he asked his disciples" (Luke 8:24, 25). The obvious answer: their faith was in Jesus. While their faith seemed weak, it was not misdirected. In turning to Jesus, they were turning to the One who could answer their cries for help.

July 30

BE STILL!

He got up, rebuked the wind and said to the waves, "Quiet! Be still!" Then the wind died down and it was completely calm.
—Mark 4:39

It is in Mark's telling of this story that we hear Jesus' voice. For us, as readers, it must seem remarkable that the wind and waves also heard His voice. No matter how many times we might have heard this story, we should not skip over the key sequence: Jesus spoke, the wind died down, and the waves were calmed.

We also remember that this was the same voice that spoke the wind and the waves—and indeed all the world—into existence (see John 1:1–3). That voice became flesh and was small enough to be sleeping in the back of a small fishing boat on the Sea of Galilee as the wind and waves threatened to swamp it. This is the miracle of the incarnation. Then, when the voice spoke, it carried His creator power, and the sea was calmed. In some inexplicable way, the Creator had become a small, fragile, and tired creature within His creation, yet was still the Creator.

But He was not only the creator of the natural world; He was also the creator of the human beings with whom He was in the same boat—literally and in terms of their immediate predicament. "This story is much more than simply an account of Jesus' miraculous control over nature. The story demonstrates Jesus engaged in conflict with all the forces of chaos that would destroy our peace—both internal as well as external forces. . . . It is possible that Jesus' command, 'Peace! Be still,' was directed as much at the disciples' fear as it was at the storm itself."*

In this story, the voice that created our world and created us echoes in our present lives and circumstances—whatever they might be: "Peace! Be still!"

* Tracy S. Daub, *Holy Disruption: Discovering Advent in the Gospel of Mark* (Louisville, KY: John Knox Westminster Press, 2022), 59, 60.

July 31

FROM TERROR TO FEAR

In fear and amazement they asked one another, "Who is this? He commands even the winds and the water, and they obey him."
—Luke 8:25

A few years ago, I was privileged to join my wife in fulfilling one of her childhood dreams—riding a mule down into the Grand Canyon. It was an incredible experience and not something I would have ever chosen or desired to do. I have a reasonable fear of heights, so clinging to the back of a large mule as we wound our way down the narrow ledges and cliff faces of the canyon was both terrifying and amazing. I came to realize that as much as I was afraid of the heights we were traversing, it was precisely these heights and the scale of the canyon that made it such an awe-inspiring place. And obviously, I did survive the experience and even overcame my fear—to some degree.

Perhaps this was something like the experience of the disciples amid the sudden calm and quiet of the lake that night. Jesus' command of the storm would have awakened echoes in their minds of various stories from the Hebrew scriptures, demonstrating God's power over the natural world. While they were concerned with perishing as the storm raged around them and Jesus slept, it was actually after Jesus' miraculous intervention that they were described as having fear, asking who Jesus might be, and having that kind of power.

Those two kinds of fear are closely linked, but they are not the same. The fear of the storm is not the same as the fear of the One who silenced the storm. There is a goodness in the fear that comes with recognizing the power that is used for good, even if our first impulse might be to recoil or try to hide from it. If we can overcome that fear, even just a little, we experience things that are not otherwise possible. We can be amazed. And more so when we are with someone we love and the One who loves us.

AN UNLIKELY ANSWER

When Jesus stepped ashore, he was met by a demon-possessed man from the town.

—Luke 8:27

As the storm on the lake subsided, the disciples were left to whisper among themselves rhetorically, "Who is this?" amid the unnaturally sudden quiet. But as the morning light began to creep over the hills of the eastern shore of Galilee, the disciples arrived to hear a frantic and aggressive answer to their question. "What do you want with me, Jesus, Son of the Most High God?" yelled the demon-possessed man as he came to a stop in front of them (Luke 8:28).

It is easy to imagine the disciples shrinking back, perhaps preparing to jump back into the boat. It was another moment for genuine fear. But Jesus seemed undaunted in the face of this overt manifestation of evil. He engaged the man—or the demons that possessed him and spoke through him—in what would seem a strange conversation, except for our having heard this story so often.

Jesus de-escalated the situation and dramatically changed the story in a way that demonstrated the truth of the man's answer. That unfortunate man was in every way outside acceptable Jewish society—a demon-possessed non-Jew who lived in the cemetery of a community that kept pigs. Yet he was healed and restored by Jesus, and such was the magnitude of his transformation that he became a messenger of Jesus in his home community. "So the man went away and told all over town how much Jesus had done for him" (Luke 8:39).

This is a story of the ultimate restoration of a man and his relationship with God, which then led to a restored relationship between him and his community, which then led to many more restored relationships with God. Sometime later, Jesus returned to this region, and it was near there that Jesus fed the crowd of "about 4000 men" (see Mark 8:1–9).

August 2

THE OTHER REACTION

Then all the people of the region of the Gerasenes asked Jesus to leave them, because they were overcome with fear. So he got into the boat and left.
—Luke 8:37

While the formerly demon-possessed man was beginning a new and markedly different chapter of his life, the people from the nearby town were reacting in the opposite way. While the man had been set free, the large herd of pigs nearby had been suddenly possessed. "The herd rushed down the steep bank into the lake and was drowned" (Luke 8:33). The pig herders rushed to town to tell the story, and a delegation came to investigate. Despite seeing the evidence of the transformation of this locally notorious man, now dressed and in his right mind, they also had to consider the loss of their income and perhaps the anger of the wealthy farmers who owned so many animals.

Whether it was the economic threat or simply the strange phenomenon of the large herd of pigs hurling themselves into the lake, they understood that this was linked to the group of men from the other side of the lake. Responding to the people's fear of what Jesus had done and what His power might mean, they asked Him to leave. The disciples on the lake after the storm and the townspeople recognized an unfamiliar power—and both groups were afraid. For the disciples, it was a reason for wonder and for staying with Jesus. For the townspeople, it was fear of how else their lives might be disrupted, and they wanted Him gone.

In both miracles, Jesus brought peace in place of fear, but the exercise of that kind of power gave rise to different kinds of fear. The two groups of people chose to respond to fear differently. How we respond to things that make us afraid—the things we don't understand—matters.

August 3

A TIMID TOUCH

As Jesus was on his way, the crowds almost crushed him. And a woman was there who had been subject to bleeding for twelve years, but no one could heal her. She came up behind him and touched the edge of his cloak, and immediately her bleeding stopped.

—Luke 8:42–44

When Jesus landed back on the other side of the lake, in the more familiar surroundings of Galilee, a leader in the local synagogue made his way through the crowd with an urgent request that Jesus heal his sick daughter. The crowd was pressing, and their slow progress was interrupted by something no one noticed except Jesus.

In contrast to the two public miracles on the lake—calming the storm and casting the demons out of the wild man—this next miracle was a private and personal one that Jesus stopped to point out, giving the woman the opportunity to share her story and thereby affirm her faith.

Because of her condition, this woman would also have been considered unclean and would not have been welcomed as a member of the community, but her need was prioritized over the request of Jairus, the synagogue ruler. In a sense, this woman's touch was daring. She was hoping not to be noticed, but as much as she dared to hope for healing, she was also risking disappointment—perhaps nothing would happen or change. At the same time, her outstretched hand was also tentative and timid. She was risking rebuke and further public shame, but she had little left to lose.

Whatever the mix of daring and timidity, of hope and desperation, she was healed. We can imagine that whatever might have happened, she must have felt something change in that moment. Now, she was caught between her sense of healing and her desire to remain unnoticed. And, despite her best efforts, Jesus noticed her.

August 4

"GO IN PEACE"

Then the woman, seeing that she could not go unnoticed, came trembling and fell at his feet. In the presence of all the people, she told why she had touched him and how she had been instantly healed. Then he said to her, "Daughter, your faith has healed you. Go in peace."

—Luke 8:47, 48

In the same moment that all her hopes were realized, all her fears also came true. The healed woman was suddenly the center of the crowd's attention, and there was nowhere for her to hide. For a moment, the joy of her healing was swamped by the fear of being discovered. Trembling with a fear that belied the faith she had demonstrated, she fell at Jesus' feet and began stammering out her story. But her voice likely grew stronger as her story reached the climax of her miraculous healing only a few moments earlier.

Jesus stayed quiet to allow her the space to tell her story. It is easy to imagine His smile growing as her confidence grew in telling her story—giving her testimony of how her brief encounter with Jesus had transformed her. A quietness rippled through the crowd as they strained to hear her. As she finished speaking, perhaps Jesus paused for a moment to let the silence of this moment linger. Then we can imagine the gentleness in His voice as He quieted the last echoes of her fear, "Daughter, your faith has healed you. Go in peace."

In Matthew's telling of the story, it was with these words that she was healed (see Matthew 9:22). Perhaps this speaks of the larger act of healing and restoration that this physical healing entailed—restored to her community, healed of her shame and fear, and given a renewed identity as a daughter of God with a story to tell of how Jesus had changed her life.

RECEIVING BAD NEWS

While Jesus was still speaking, someone came from the house of Jairus, the synagogue ruler. "Your daughter is dead," he said. "Don't bother the teacher anymore."

—Luke 8:49

We have all received those phone calls or messages, perhaps a knock on the door or a conversation that relayed the news. Someone we loved was gone. Whatever we were planning to do that day—perhaps even some major aspect of our lives—was changed irreversibly in that single tragic moment when we received the news. Our lives would afterward be measured from that moment—before and after we received that news.

Whether we expected their death or not, whether they were old or young, whether we had the chance to say goodbye or not, every death is heartbreaking, and every time we lose someone we love, our humanity is shaken. In a world with so much death and uncertainty, and with death's apparent inevitability, it seems we could come to see death as less of an outrage, less of a shuddering, bone-jarring jolt. But it hits us every time, and each of our losses has a cumulative weight upon us. We feel instantly dislocated and disoriented. Our world tilts on its axis, and at that moment, it feels like there can be no normal beyond.

In Jairus' story, the news came while he was desperately seeking Jesus' help. His frustration with the delay caused by the healing of the woman turned to despair, perhaps anger. As the messenger from his home whispered those words in his ear, his worst fears came true, and his whole body went cold. He didn't want to accept it, but he knew the messenger's advice was right: "Don't bother the teacher anymore."

But Jesus noticed. Jairus did not get the chance to simply turn away and head home with his broken heart. Because Jesus noticed, his story would have a different ending.

August 6

FEAR AND GRIEF

Hearing this, Jesus said to Jairus,
"Don't be afraid; just believe, and she will be healed."
—Luke 8:50

No one ever told me that grief felt so like fear. I am not afraid, but the sensation is like being afraid. The same fluttering in the stomach, the same restlessness, the yawning."* It's a description that we are familiar with from experiences of grief in our own lives. The visceral, physical sensations of grief and fear dominate our thinking and threaten our prayers. Death seems to close in upon us and fill our horizons. It seems outrageous that so much of the world can simply go on, apparently unheeding, unconcerned, and unaffected by the loss we have suffered.

At such times, there seems to be nothing we can say that is meaningful. Any attempted words of comfort stick in our mouths and sound hollow in our own ears even as we say them. It is not a time for rationale or theology, even if our best responses are shaped by our best theology. It is a time for presence, but perhaps silence. It is one of our most common human experiences, something we all experience at various times in our lives in different ways, but always with shock and outrage and always uniquely painful.

Frustrated by Jesus' delay, then heartbroken by the news of his daughter's death, Jairus heard Jesus' voice cut through his grief—"Don't be afraid."

Jesus knew something important about grief, but also about this particular tragedy. Of course, Jairus had little option but to follow Jesus to the house where mourning for his daughter had already begun. Jesus demonstrated His power over death, restoring the girl to life and bringing healing to the family and the community in the face of this loss. Jairus and his wife were described as astonished at the power they had witnessed in their home.

---

* C. S. Lewis, *A Grief Observed* (London: Faber and Faber, 1962), 5.

FEAR AND PRAISE

They were all filled with awe and praised God. "A great prophet has appeared among us," they said. "God has come to help his people."
—Luke 7:16

Across the valley of Jezreel, the small village of Nain can be seen from the hilltop at the edge of Nazareth—likely the one from which the people of Nazareth tried to throw Jesus down a cliff when they became infuriated at His words in the synagogue (see Luke 4:28–30). Today, Nain is an Arab village of about 2,000 people. Despite its proximity to Nazareth, Capernaum, and the other towns and villages of Galilee, Nain's only mention in the Bible story is the miracle Jesus performed there. It was a worthwhile way to be put on the map.

Jesus was traveling with His disciples and a large group of followers and onlookers, both the committed and the curious. As they neared the village, this group was met by a group with a very different tone. A widow was burying her only son, and the people of her village had gathered to mourn.

Jesus noticed, stopped, and responded with compassion. "When the Lord saw her, his heart went out to her and he said, 'Don't cry' " (Luke 7:13). He interrupted the funeral procession and brought the young man to life, giving him back to his mother. Jesus put this village on the map, and the story of the day Jesus visited Nain is retold across the generations.

Of course, this also caught the attention of the large crowd that was traveling with Jesus. "Great fear swept the crowd, and they praised God. . . . God has visited his people today" (Luke 7:16, NLT). The people responded with equally appropriate fear and praise. Importantly, this story would also be part of Jesus' answer to the disciples of John the Baptist, whom John had sent to check on whether Jesus really was who John thought He was (see Luke 7:18–23). It also put Jesus on the map as the news of this miracle spread "throughout Judea and the surrounding country" (see Luke 7:17).

August 8

A QUESTION FROM PRISON

John's disciples told him about all these things. Calling two of them, he sent them to the Lord to ask, "Are you the one who was to come, or should we expect someone else?"
—Luke 7:18, 19

John the Baptist had a history with Jesus. Their mothers were cousins who had celebrated their unlikely pregnancies together (see Luke 1:39–45), and it seems likely that Jesus and John would have met as boys. John baptized Jesus as part of his public ministry of announcing the good news of the soon-coming Messiah (see Luke 3:1–18). But when John publicly denounced Herod for taking his brother's wife "and all the other evil things he had done, Herod added this to them all: He locked John up in prison" (Luke 3:19, 20).

It seems John was imprisoned for about a year in the lonely fortress of Machaerus on the other side of the Dead Sea. John had been among the first to proclaim Jesus as the Messiah, but his doubts and fears that perhaps he had been wrong about Jesus had plenty of time to fester. Isolated from his people, hearing only secondhand reports about Jesus, John sent some of his disciples to ask Jesus that question.

There was also the harsh reality of his circumstances. We might wonder if John's question was more a suggestion—a hint that if Jesus really was the Messiah, perhaps His forerunner, cousin, and supporter should not be languishing in Herod's prison.

Jesus' answer was to point to the practical ministry He was doing, a list that echoed what He had announced in His sermon at Nazareth (see Luke 4:18–21). But he concluded with an important addition: "Blessed is anyone who does not stumble on account of me" (Luke 7:23). Jesus urged John not to fear, not to let his circumstances get in the way of his faith, not to give in to his disappointed expectations of what he thought the Messiah should be. Interestingly, the Gospel writer also pointed out that John's ministry continued to bear fruit (see Luke 7:29).

August 9

THE FIRST MISSION TRIP

"As you go, proclaim this message: 'The kingdom of heaven has come near.' Heal those who are ill, raise the dead, cleanse those who have leprosy, drive out demons. Freely you have received; freely give."

—Matthew 10:7, 8

Mission work can often seem daunting. It seems Jesus knew that, and He took care to introduce His disciples to it step by step. After they had spent some time with Him, listening, watching, and learning how He interacted with people, He sent them out on a first training run. It was limited to the towns of Israel, which meant people, language, and a culture they were familiar with as a place to start.

The message that Jesus gave them was simple—"The kingdom of heaven has come near." And this was then to be enacted by their work in helping and healing the people in the villages and towns they visited. This was a practical proclamation of the good news of the kingdom of God. When people asked who had sent them, the disciples would tell the story of Jesus, the teacher who had changed their lives and who they were increasingly convinced was the Messiah.

Mission work need not be daunting. It does not have to begin on a large scale or with international travel. We do not have to preach a complicated sermon series or lead in-depth Bible studies. It can begin in our neighborhood, community, or city, listening to people, helping and healing where we can, and doing so in the name of Jesus, whose kingdom we proclaim by our lives, our deeds, and our words.

In short, we share freely from what has been so freely given to us. When we have experienced healing, hope, and courage, this is what we can offer to others, whether it is by how we serve with generosity and love or by the story we tell of how God gave us those in our own lives.

August 10

REASSURANCE AMID PERSECUTION

"On my account you will be brought before governors and kings as witnesses to them and to the Gentiles. But when they arrest you, do not worry about what to say or how to say it. At that time you will be given what to say, for it will not be you speaking, but the Spirit of your Father speaking through you."

—Matthew 10:18–20

Persecution has been a reality for followers of Jesus throughout the history of the church. For many Christians in the world today, it remains a reality, sometimes in large ways, sometimes in everyday smaller forms. But, whatever the disciples would face, and whatever we might face, Jesus gave reassurances when first sending His disciples to the towns and villages of Israel.

First, when they encountered persecution, they would recognize that Jesus had anticipated this. Persecution would not take Him—or them—by surprise. That Jesus understood this about the dynamics of the gospel showed His insight and understanding of the world in which the disciples were to live, minister, and serve.

Second, Jesus urged that persecution would provide opportunities to witness to powerful leaders and the wider world. Throughout history, the focus that persecution has brought to followers of Jesus has given them a platform and voice they would not have had otherwise. Not that persecution should be sought, but when it came, more people would hear the message of Jesus and see a demonstration of faith.

Third, Jesus told the disciples that they need not worry about "what to say or how to say it." Instead, the Holy Spirit would be especially close to them at such times, and they would be given the words to speak that would be most powerful to their hearers in those circumstances. Under the pressures of persecution, followers of Jesus are not asked to carry the added burden of making the perfect speech. God will be with them and shine through their faithful witness.

August 11

THE REVELATORY RESPONSE

"So do not be afraid of them. There is nothing concealed that will not be disclosed, or hidden that will not be made known."
—Matthew 10:26

We do not get to choose how people respond to us. We certainly have a role to play in how we treat others, and we must be sensitive to how our attitudes and actions can affect others, even unwittingly, but we do not choose their response. How people act and react—including how they respond to who we are and what we believe—often reveals more about them than it does about us.

An inordinately angry or hostile response might suggest that something about us has touched a sore point in their lives or sparked a twinge of guilt in their conscience. If they unjustly accuse us of wrongdoing, perhaps something in their accusation reveals a weakness in their own lives. As Jesus taught, when we notice the speck in another person's eye, we might be missing the plank in our own (see Matthew 7:3–5).

So when we are threatened or accused, we have the opportunity to notice the fear, pain, and grief of the other person as an invitation for empathy—as difficult as that can be. But we also have Jesus' promise that ulterior motives and secret plots will be revealed and undermined. As such, we do not need to be afraid of how people respond to us.

Whether in the final judgment or in the unraveling of people's secret lives, Jesus was clear that who we really are will be revealed—both in our lives and in our eternal futures. If we are seeking to be faithful, we do not have to seek vengeance on those who would threaten or accuse us. Instead, we can choose to respond with kindness and generosity (see Romans 12:19–21), revealing a truly different way of living and being in the world as followers of Jesus.

August 12

LIFE MEASURED DIFFERENTLY

"Do not be afraid of those who kill the body but cannot kill the soul. Rather, be afraid of the One who can destroy both soul and body in hell."
—Matthew 10:28

When I was embarking on this writing project, this was one of the first sayings of Jesus that jumped to mind. It is not one of the most reassuring of the Bible's "Do not be afraids," assuming as it does that we may well be risking our lives by following Jesus. Rather, it is one of His statements that challenges our assumptions about life and its purpose, urging that even life itself—as we now know it—should not be our pre-eminent value. If and when we can bring ourselves to believe this, we are truly free to live without fear, trusting our lives to the One who ultimately holds our whole being in His hand.

This is not to say that death does not matter. It matters desperately. It also serves as a test of what matters more to us. "You never know how much you really believe anything until its truth or falsehood becomes a matter of life and death to you. . . . Only real risk tests the reality of a belief."* The point is that there are things that matter more than death, as outrageous as this sounds.

Many of the disciples to whom Jesus first addressed this statement would confront their own death because they chose to follow Him. But they had also seen Jesus overcome death in the miracles He performed and in His own resurrection. They knew that the reality and power of Jesus had defeated death, so they could trust Him even in death. That profoundly changed the way they understood, measured, and valued their lives.

---

* C. S. Lewis, *A Grief Observed* (London: Faber and Faber, 1962), 20, 21.

August 13

MORE THAN MANY SPARROWS

"Are not two sparrows sold for a penny? Yet not one of them will fall to the ground outside your Father's care. And even the very hairs of your head are all numbered. So don't be afraid; you are worth more than many sparrows."

—Matthew 10:29–31

One of the many things I appreciate about my wife is her ability to notice. She notices birds and animals, flowers and trees. She knows their names and can point out their habits and habitats. She notices people and things about people that I too easily miss. When exploring the world with her, I get to see and experience more of the world than I would alone.

This is the kind of co-exploring relationship into which we are invited by God—to see the world as God sees and hears it. We can notice the abundant creativity and detail that He designed into the world, paying attention to the smallest creatures and noticing their joys and their losses. To hold a tiny bird is to feel its weightlessness and marvel at its vulnerability. Things we might be tempted to dismiss or disregard are considered by God as having great value. All He created matters.

Remarkably, without diverting His attention from the smallest bird, God's vast attentiveness is all the more directed toward us. We are worth more than many sparrows, Jesus insisted, without diminishing the value of a single bird. He also knows the minutiae of our lives. And if He is keeping a count of the hairs on our heads as that count fluctuates across our lives, how much more does He see and know our joys and griefs, disappointments and successes, hopes and fears?

In God's creation, little things matter—and you matter more. God notices even the little things, and He notices you and your life even more. May we never underestimate the knowingness and attentiveness of God. His loving attention is one more way in which He says, "Do not be afraid."

August 14

A DEEPER RESPONSE

"Whoever finds their life will lose it, and whoever loses their life for my sake will find it."

—Matthew 10:39

One of our strongest innate human instincts is self-preservation and survival. In most situations, our first reaction is: "How do I save myself?" And, perhaps those closest to us. Our next reaction is, "Can I benefit from this situation in some way?" As an instinctive reaction, self-preservation is not necessarily wrong, but neither of these responses is likely to bring out our best.

Followers of Jesus are called to a deeper response, particularly when we have opportunities to make a more intentional choice between prioritizing ourselves or the kingdom of God. Indeed, our natural instincts are why we need to be more careful, thoughtful, and prayerful in choosing how we respond to threats to our wellbeing in the world around us, seeking a deeper response than what is merely instinctive.

Jesus said that if we focus on preserving ourselves and the things that we assume make up our lives, we will lose in the end—if not sooner. But if we can shift our focus and priorities away from ourselves, we can live more freely and courageously. Many people have found this kind of freedom in the practical work of serving others. Others lose themselves—in the best sense—in creating art and beauty or some other activity that demands their best work in contributing to goodness in our world. Whatever they might be, these "losing ourselves" experiences are a glimpse of the kingdom of God.

At times, in our broken world, "losing ourselves" can mean a more serious kind of self-sacrifice. We would not choose such circumstances, but we do choose how we respond, albeit only with the grace and courage that comes from our trust in God. Even then, taking the focus away from ourselves offers a kind of freedom, reclamation, and renewal of our lives that might not otherwise be possible. We can hold on to even our very lives loosely, trusting ourselves to God and His care and provision.

August 15

"I WILL GIVE YOU REST"

"Come to me, all you who are weary and burdened, and I will give you rest. Take my yoke upon you and learn from me, for I am gentle and humble in heart, and you will find rest for your souls. For my yoke is easy and my burden is light."
—Matthew 11:28–30

I was preaching to a group of pastors a few years ago, drawing on these verses, and simply asked whether anyone in the group felt tired. From the responses, the better question would have been to ask whether anyone didn't feel tired. In our always-on world, we all feel tired.

We are worn out by our daily to-do lists, always feeling like we are struggling to keep up. We are bombarded with ideas, news, advertising, and opinions—much of it pleading its importance and urgency. We are ground down by our experiences of disappointment, sorrow, and pain. We lose more of our people without feeling like we have adequately mourned our previous griefs, and their weight seems to accumulate. We worry that we don't measure up in the present, and we are afraid of what the future might bring. We feel like we should be more spiritual, more committed, more zealous—and all of that wearies us all the more.

Nevertheless, through all this noise and inattention, distraction, and discouragement, we might just be able to hear the voice of Jesus—"Come to me, all you who are weary and burdened, and I will give you rest."

Life lived in partnership with God offers a different way of living. All of our busyness and burdens might remain, but the rest that Jesus offers for our souls can change our hearts and minds. We might be able to reprioritize some aspects of our lives as we learn from Him, but even with our current burdens, the yoke of Jesus can make them lighter and transform our weariness.

August 16

WORLD-CHANGING GENTLENESS

"A bruised reed he will not break,
and a smoldering wick he will not snuff out,
till he has brought justice through to victory.
In his name the nations will put their hope."

—Matthew 12:20, 21

To explain what Jesus was doing in healing "all who were ill" (Matthew 12:15) and ministering to the people, Matthew borrowed these lines from the first few verses of Isaiah 42. It described the gentleness of Jesus' ministry—His concern for the weakest and seemingly most insignificant—that would somehow be world-changing and bring hope to the nations. In Jesus, the vulnerable and marginalized found a sympathetic and powerful ally. At the same time, the powerful—those who oppress and benefit from injustice—were confronted with the assurance that justice would be victorious.

In effect, this is a similar description to that in Mary's song when she celebrated the news of the coming of Jesus with her cousin Elizabeth: "He has brought down rulers from their thrones but has lifted up the humble. He has filled the hungry with good things but has sent the rich away empty" (Luke 1:52, 53). This was good news to the poor and a challenge to the rich and powerful. How we hear descriptions such as these will depend on where we are positioned in our society and culture.

The Gospels have a significantly countercultural bent. They are also notably practical in their portrayal and understanding of the ministry of Jesus, and their descriptions of the anger aroused among the leaders and privileged of His day underline this dynamic of what Jesus did. Jesus was not the usual revolutionary known throughout history. His was a revolution of gentleness, kindness, and justice—but no less revolutionary or world-changing for its approach, perhaps even more so. This is the revolution we are invited to be part of as His followers.

August 17

AN UNFAIR CONFLICT?

"The seed falling among the thorns refers to someone who hears the word, but the worries of this life and the deceitfulness of wealth choke the word, making it unfruitful."
—Matthew 13:22

The way of goodness sometimes feels like an unfair struggle. There seem to be fewer ways for life and faith to go right than there are ways to go wrong. While we are saved by God's grace, maintaining our relationship with Him and growing in His grace requires the good soil of hearing and understanding (see Matthew 13:23), as well as intention, focus, and effort.

In contrast, the seeds that God plants in our lives can be ignored, die away with persecution, or be choked out by the busyness, distractions, and worries of our lives. Those who would wear away our faith and our intentions to do good in the world do not need better arguments or more attractive offers; all they need to do is keep us busy, cause confusion, wear us out, or make us afraid. We are likely to be alert to the direct challenges to our faith, but undermining our faith works best when we barely realize the effect, often in everyday kinds of ways.

This corrosive effect explains the many times Jesus told His disciples, "Do not be afraid" and "Do not worry." Fear and worry warp our thinking and shift our priorities, especially if they are allowed to dominate our lives. Jesus recognized the urgency of shifting our thinking back to the things that are most important in the kingdom of God.

This competition for our attention and our lives can feel like an unfair conflict. God has to be fair and truthful; those who would pull us down do not have to abide by any rules. Even in the parable of the sower, there are three soil types that go wrong, and only one way to get it right. But goodness brings larger results. Jesus said that the one who "hears the word and understands it. . . . produces a crop, yielding a hundred, sixty, or thirty times what was sown" (Matthew 13:23).

August 18

SMALL BUT GROWING

He told them another parable: "The kingdom of heaven is like a mustard seed, which a man took and planted in his field. Though it is the smallest of all your seeds, yet when it grows, it is the largest of garden plants and becomes a tree, so that the birds come and perch in its branches."

—Matthew 13:31, 32

We tend to measure things by the large, the dramatic, the tragic, and the alarming. It is hardly surprising that these are the things that catch our attention. "A lot of times good news happens slowly and bad news happens all at once. And so we tend to focus on the bad news that's crashing over us in waves, and not on the slow long-term work that people are doing together to try to make a better world for us to share."*

This is all the more true in our understanding of the kingdom of God. Jesus taught His followers that we should not be surprised if the kingdom of God looks small and perhaps inconsequential, particularly in contrast with the bad news, the tragedies, and the powerful systems of our world. But like that small seed, the kingdom of God continues to grow, sometimes dramatically, but often almost imperceptibly.

Over the past 2,000 years, even the story of Jesus itself has seemed unlikely to be told and retold, but it still persists as one of the most enduring influences in the world today. We should not be afraid to be small. When we seem to have little influence or support, we can still be the mustard seeds of God's kingdom and share with others. The potential for the largest of garden plants is already present in the smallest of all the seeds.

In the kingdom of God, we learn to measure things differently. Dramatic, bad news is not as powerful as quiet goodness. Things that make us afraid are never as important as those that give us hope.

---

* Author John Green, in conversation with Steve Levitt on *People I (Mostly) Admire* (podcast episode, November 11, 2022).

WALKING ON WATER

Jesus immediately said to them:
"Take courage! It is I. Don't be afraid."
—Matthew 14:27

It was another dark, stormy night on the Sea of Galilee. As the disciples struggled to keep the boat heading toward their destination through what seemed most of the night, the wind was against them—and, on this occasion, Jesus was not in the boat with them. Unlike their previous experience, when they woke Jesus, who was sleeping in the boat during a storm (see Matthew 8:23–25), they were alone with the wind and waves, as well as their fears and imaginations.

If the earlier story of Jesus calming the storm reassures us that He is with us in the storms of life, perhaps this story speaks to those times in our lives when we do not feel His presence. Sometimes, we feel alone. Sometimes, the storms and circumstances surrounding us are all that hold our attention, and our fears grow larger as the night becomes darker and the headwinds grow stronger.

We get an insight into the disciples' mindset from their reaction to the unexpected appearance of Jesus. "They were terrified. 'It's a ghost,' they said, and cried out in fear" (Matthew 14:26). We can imagine their heart rates rising even beyond the elevated levels that came with their physical exertion and existing stress. They were not trying to talk with this figure, only crying out in fear.

But we can also imagine their sense of relief when the voice that answered them was both familiar and reassuring. Even as they were still being buffeted by the wind and the waves, their understanding of their predicament was transformed by their recognition of Jesus and the sound of His voice. He hardly needed to say, "Don't be afraid." His presence and His voice would have communicated that message clearly, even amid the sounds of the storm and the beating of their hearts.

August 20

RESCUED AND REBUKED

Immediately Jesus reached out his hand and caught him. "You of little faith," he said, "why did you doubt?"
—Matthew 14:31

Walking on water is no easy task. As a child, inspired by the Bible stories I was taught at Sabbath School, I would occasionally try it at the local swimming pool—always without success. I am sure that many of us who grew up with the stories at least attempted it with some sense of curiosity.

In the Bible's telling of this story, Peter began to sink after he noticed the wind and became afraid. But I wonder if the walking on water itself might have been frightening enough. In all his years as a fisherman on the lake, he had never seen anyone walking on the water. He suggested to Jesus that he join Him amid the waves, probably without thinking much about it. But when it was actually happening, it seems that it would be unnerving in itself. I have experienced taking on a task or finding myself in circumstances that seem completely beyond my expertise or out of my control. Even when it feels like it might be working, that can become a cause for fear in itself. Fear can take hold of us when things seem to be working out almost too well, and we find ourselves suddenly outside our comfort zone.

In the moment of Peter's fear, Jesus was there for Him—to catch him, rescuing him from the waves and pulling him up so he could step back into the boat. At that moment, the wind died away, and the lake became calm. It was only after rescuing Peter that Jesus chided him for his doubts. The rescue came first. Peter did not have to resolve his doubts or get over his fear before Jesus would reach out and catch him. But we can also expect that many of his doubts and fears would have evaporated in that moment of rescue. It seems that Peter would have readily joined the other disciples in worshiping Jesus in the boat (see Matthew 14:33). Being rebuked for a lack of faith stings much less when we have already been rescued.

August 21

CHILDREN AND CRUMBS

"Lord," she replied, "but even the dogs under the table eat the children's crumbs."

—Mark 7:28

It took courage to argue with Jesus, even if it was courage born of desperation and the feeling that she had nothing left to lose. Jesus and His disciples were traveling to the north of Galilee when this Greek woman begged Jesus to heal her daughter—to drive out the demon that possessed her. Jesus' harsh reply has been explained in various ways, but to the disciples and to the woman herself, it seems that His response was not unexpected.

Perhaps it took courage to make the initial request, but it took more courage to persist and offer a retort that was both bold and self-deprecating at the same time. It is possible that she sensed a tone in Jesus' answer that invited such a witty rejoinder, something that we cannot read in the bare words on the page. But she returned His barb in a similar tone, insisting that even the crumbs of Jesus' attention and power would be sufficient to accomplish her request.

We can imagine Jesus smiling at her response. "For such a reply," he said, "you may go; the demon has left your daughter" (Mark 7:29). He honored the woman's response with His answer to her request and assured her that she would find her daughter well by the time she returned home, which she did.

Arguments with Jesus did not often end well for the other party, which is why taking Him on could only be an act of courage, foolishness, or meanness. In this case, it was born of courage. This woman was not trying to score a point or undermine Jesus. She was so desperate for her daughter to be healed that she was willing to confront this strange, foreign teacher, appealing to His generosity or pity and not afraid to risk ridicule or failure. In doing so, she helped Jesus teach His disciples a lesson about faith, courage, and the more inclusive and compassionate kingdom He was inaugurating.

August 22

THE CONCERNS OF GOD

But when Jesus turned and looked at his disciples, he rebuked Peter. "Get behind me, Satan!" he said. "You do not have in mind the concerns of God, but merely human concerns."

—Mark 8:33

Peter had just made the greatest claim about Jesus that it was possible to imagine. In response to Jesus' leading question, Peter had declared, "You are the Messiah" (Mark 8:29). It was a bold and insightful statement, one that Jesus affirmed. But Peter promptly made it clear that he did not understand what it meant.

Responding to Jesus as He began to explain to the disciples that He would be rejected and killed by the Jewish leaders, Peter rebuked Him. We can understand his thinking. If what he had just affirmed about Jesus was correct, it did not make sense that Jesus would immediately begin to talk about His suffering and death. We might also imagine Peter feeling a touch of concern that the close connection he had with this Messiah might not turn out as he expected. He was suddenly afraid of what following Jesus might really mean. So Peter expressed those concerns, urging Jesus not to talk like that.

In turn, Peter received a strong rebuke of his own. He was speaking with the voice of Satan, missing the purposes of God and replacing them with human expectations. Jesus could hear Satan's temptation in Peter's rebuke, sounding like the voice that had offered Him the kingdoms of the world by some means other than the path of suffering and self-sacrifice (see Luke 4:5–8). Perhaps Peter's fears risked sparking Jesus' own fears into life, so Jesus had to respond strongly to ensure they did not take hold and undermine His own sense of purpose.

In words that might have only added to Peter's concerns, Jesus explained further to His disciples what it truly would mean to follow Him: "Whoever wants to be my disciple must deny themselves and take up their cross and follow me" (Mark 8:34). Ultimately, this would be the way of the Messiah that Peter and the other disciples would follow.

August 23

TRANSFIGURED

When the disciples heard this, they fell facedown to the ground, terrified. But Jesus came and touched them. "Get up," he said." Don't be afraid." When they looked up, they saw no one except Jesus.
—Matthew 17:6–8

Peter, James, and John had already spent quite some time with Jesus before witnessing His transfiguration. One night, on a high mountain in the north of Israel, Jesus started to glow as His true glory was allowed to shine through. Then, two of the greatest heroes of the stories of the Hebrew scriptures appeared with Jesus, followed by a bright cloud. "A voice from the cloud said, 'This is my Son, whom I love; with him I am well pleased. Listen to him!' " (Matthew 17:5). For a moment, the three disciples were given a glimpse of heaven and heard the voice of God—and they were terrified.

Then Jesus was left to comfort them, and Jesus was all they needed. All of the other people and elements of this experience testified to the nature and significance of Jesus. So when the disciples were overwhelmed by the reality and majesty of Jesus revealing more of His divinity, He was also their comfort. Even when Peter suggested building shelters for the three citizens of heaven, he was rebuffed by the larger reality of Jesus Himself. Jesus already was God dwelling among them (see John 1:14); they did not need to add to that.

In contrast with their vision of the transcendent and glorious God, Jesus was able to simply reach out and touch them. He gently quieted their fears and gave them time to reflect on what they had witnessed for themselves without the initial burden of having to try to describe or explain it to others. And when all that was left on this now-dark mountaintop was Jesus alone with the three cowering disciples, He was enough.

August 24

BELIEF AND UNBELIEF

Immediately the boy's father exclaimed,
"I do believe; help me overcome my unbelief!"
—Mark 9:24

Too often, church people are hesitant to admit their questions and doubts, particularly in church contexts. But that leaves us who do not always feel so certain, afraid to be honest about our doubts, and not sure if we actually fit with the church crowd. This is where the story of Jesus' interaction with a father who both believed and was yet willing to admit his unbelief is helpful.

This father brought his son to Jesus but was met by some of the disciples, who were not able to help them. Eager for his son to be healed, the father was confronted with Jesus' bold statement: "Everything is possible for one who believes" (Mark 9:23). This could have been interpreted as a call for an unequivocal, unambiguous assertion of faith. And why wouldn't the anxious father have offered such a confession of faith when desperately seeking healing for his son? But it seems honesty was more important than certainty—particularly, a contrived certainty.

The father was more circumspect in his expression, even if not in tone: "I do believe," he insisted, "help me overcome my unbelief" (Mark 9:24). His response characterizes many of our honest reflections on faith. When we are confronted with the claims of Jesus, we believe; we want to believe; we try to believe, yet we must also confess our need for help overcoming our unbelief.

I imagine Jesus smiling at this father's answer as He proceeded to heal the boy amid the gathering crowd. In doing so, He affirmed the father's enthusiastic but awkward confession. It seems that honest faith is enough in Jesus' eyes—and that helps grow my belief in God, who understands our questions and doubts but also urges that we not let our fears dominate our lives, our faith, or our priorities.

THE QUESTIONS WE DON'T ASK

He said to them, "The Son of Man is going to be betrayed into the hands of men. They will kill him, and after three days he will rise." But they did not understand what he meant and were afraid to ask him about it.
—Mark 9:31, 32

Throughout the Gospels, Jesus makes many references to the fate that would befall Him, trying to prepare His disciples for the end of His public ministry that He foresaw. As we read these statements with hindsight—knowing how this story would end in both death and resurrection—it is difficult to see how the disciples could have failed to understand what Jesus was telling them. But that was because of their expectations of what the Messiah should be. Nevertheless, Jesus was careful to equip them with those insights, even though they might only begin to make sense of them after He was arrested and executed.

Despite His repeated warnings, it was clear that the disciples had little understanding of what Jesus was explaining to them. But, at least to some degree, this was their own failing. They had the opportunity to ask questions but were afraid to seek clarification. Often, we are afraid to ask questions when we suspect that we will not like the answers we might receive. Sometimes, even the questions frighten us.

Rather than asking, the disciples soon returned to arguing among themselves about who was or would be the greatest in Jesus' kingdom—again, without knowing much of what that would mean. They would have been far better served by mustering their courage and accepting the warnings that Jesus was giving them. If they had been able to understand what He was facing and why, imagine how they might have been able to support Him in His trial and suffering. Those questions and answers would have challenged their faith and understanding, but they would have transformed their relationship with Jesus.

August 26

AN INCLUSIVE MISSION

"Do not stop him," Jesus said. "No one who does a miracle in my name can in the next moment say anything bad about me, for whoever is not against us is for us."

—Mark 9:39, 40

Sometimes, those who believe almost as we do or who simply are not part of our group are those we are most likely to be suspicious of or to criticize. The disciples had encountered someone who "was not one of us" (Mark 9:38) but who was driving out demons in the name of Jesus. So they told him to stop.

We know nothing more of this person's identity, mission, or motives—what connection he had to Jesus or how he had come into his miracle-working ministry. But Jesus was quick to defend the person's ministry. The mission and message to which He had called the disciples and that He had already sent them out to practice and proclaim (see Mark 6:7) were not their exclusive territory. Instead, the mission would require the contributions of as many people as possible and would grow to include more and more diverse people than the disciples would have ever been able to imagine. There is enough mission for everyone.

Even when it comes to proclaiming the kingdom of God, our tendency is to assume some kind of restrictions on who can do it "properly" and to imagine the risks that could come with welcoming inclusivity. But Jesus' response—"Whoever is not against us is for us"—stands in contrast to many of those human attitudes. "Part of the reason we avoid associating with other Christians is that we feel insecure. Truth really should have nothing to fear. It should not make us intolerant, arrogant, and authoritarian. Instead it should develop in us openness, humility, and assurance."* In the kingdom of God that Jesus proclaimed, all are invited, and every honest contribution is valued.

---

* Sakae Kubo, *The God of Relationships* (Hagerstown, MD: Review and Herald®, 1993), 127.

UNQUESTIONING FEAR

But no one would say anything publicly about him for fear of the leaders.

—John 7:13

Everyone had an opinion about Jesus, and no one wanted to say anything. Much of the nation's population was gathered in Jerusalem for the Festival of Tabernacles. Rather than having open conversations, people whispered quietly among themselves. Jesus' unbelieving brothers urged Him to go to Jerusalem to "show yourself to the world" (John 7:4), while the Jewish leaders were on the lookout for Jesus and any trouble He might cause. Among the people, some thought He was a good man; others thought He was a deceiver. All these ideas and agendas were swirling around, but everyone was too afraid to talk about Him openly, even as they were all celebrating a festival that remembered how God had led their people in the past.

Fear that inhibits or ends conversations is an unhealthy thing. Faith communities should be the places in which people can most afford to ask questions, work through disagreements, and even express doubts and fears, all as part of learning and growing in our faith and knowledge. Different perspectives and positions should be shared with gentleness and respect, and our discussion groups, even between churches, should also move beyond continual debates. But if we are unable to ask questions and wrestle with important ideas together in church contexts, where could we do it any better?

Leaders or members who seek to restrict questions and honest doubts and who define faithful thinking more and more narrowly are echoing the Jewish leaders of Jesus' day. Despite their best attempts to keep Him contained, Jesus kept bursting through their walls of fear, rules, and traditions.

When Jesus arrived at the Festival a few days later, His teaching and boldness stood in refreshing contrast to that of his persecutors. "The Jews there were amazed and asked, 'How did this man get such learning without having been taught?' " (John 7:15). The public debate grew all the louder as Jesus presented a faithful and freeing alternative to the regime of fear maintained by the Jewish leaders.

August 28

THE LIGHT OF THE WORLD

When Jesus spoke again to the people, he said, "I am the light of the world. Whoever follows me will never walk in darkness, but will have the light of life."

—John 8:12

In His teaching, Jesus did not ignore the reality of darkness and dark times in our lives in this world. In His own life, He experienced darkness. He knew what it was like to be tired, hungry, afraid, angry, heartbroken, and overwhelmed. He tasted many of our most urgent and anxious human experiences. The darkness did not extinguish or overcome His light, but at times, it was difficult to see.

When we face our darkness and our dark times, we can remember that Jesus, the light of the world, has already been there. Sometimes, the darkness seems even harder to pierce when we have just stepped out of the light. One of the effects of the light we have been given is that much of the surrounding darkness looks darker still. But we know that the light of the world has been here, and the darkness is that much thinner for the lingering of that light. We no longer need to be afraid of the dark because when following Jesus, we have light.

Jesus might even have been referencing that favorite psalm, drawing out the power of light to overcome the deepest darkness: "Even though I walk through the darkest valley, I will fear no evil, for you are with me" (Psalm 23:4).

Jesus did not promise that we would avoid dark times or would be able to bypass all the dark valleys. The darkness is real, often painfully so, but we need not be afraid. We can make it through, never completely lost in the darkness, never completely alone, when we walk with His light. He is the light of the world; He wants to be the light of our lives.

August 29

CONFRONTING JESUS

"Very truly I tell you," Jesus answered, "before Abraham was born, I am!"

—John 8:58

Of course, it was a ridiculous claim to make. The Jewish leaders, who were on the other side of this running argument, could not help but point out that Jesus was only a few decades old, yet He claimed to have known Abraham. To which Jesus replied, "Of course—I'm God!" His claim was so offensive that "they picked up stones to stone him, but Jesus hid himself, slipping away from the temple grounds" (John 8:59).

Jesus had been in disagreement with these leaders for some time, but this was a step too far. They were prepared to stone Him on the spot, and they had the rocks ready to do it. His really was an absurd claim—unless, of course, it was true. As unlikely as the things Jesus was saying seemed—and might seem to us as readers—they made sense to many people in the temple courts that day. "Even as he spoke, many believed in him" (John 8:30). There was something about Jesus that they dared to believe.

Jesus confronts us. If we begin to understand Him and consider Him honestly, we must be confronted and challenged. If our reading of the Gospels, particularly what Jesus taught and claimed, has lost that power, we need to find ways to get past our assumed familiarity with Him. Many people find comfort and reassurance in the well-known stories and sayings of the Gospels, but the real opportunity is in finding something about Jesus that challenges us, yet we might dare to believe.

In Jesus' day, it seemed unlikely that Jesus was God and almost impossible that we would still be retelling the stories about Him 2,000 years later. But across the centuries, there have been countless people who have found something in Jesus that they have dared to believe. So, those stories are worth our serious attention and consideration, as confronting as they might be.

August 30

THE SHEPHERD AND HIS SHEEP

"I am the good shepherd. The good shepherd lays down his life for the sheep."

—John 10:11

The Bible's use of shepherd imagery to portray God's care for His people is both gentle and fierce, tending to their needs and defending them from attack. We also see both facets of shepherding in the way Jesus used the metaphor. Of course, they would have been familiar images to those who first heard His descriptions and parables. Even today, shepherds are commonly seen around the seemingly barren Judean hills.

But Jesus went further with His use of this model of care. He described the close relationship that He has with His sheep. "He calls his own sheep by name . . . and his sheep follow him because they know his voice" (John 10:3, 4). He also urged that His flock was welcoming to other sheep who would hear His voice and choose to follow. "I have other sheep that are not of this sheep pen. I must bring them also" (John 10:16).

The most significant and perhaps unexpected aspect of this imagery was the way in which Jesus declared His willingness to die for His sheep. He contrasted His commitment with that of hired shepherds, who would be more likely to run in the face of danger, leaving the sheep to defend themselves. He also warned about those who would seek to climb over the wall of the sheep pen to steal and attack the flock. "The thief comes only to steal and kill and destroy; I have come that they may have life, and have it to the full" (John 10:10).

While talking about shepherding, Jesus was talking about His sacrifice for the lives of those who would follow Him. This was something He would do voluntarily and was able to do because of His authority and that of His Father (see John 10:18). It was Jesus' ultimate claim to be "the good shepherd": "My Father, who has given them to me, is greater than all; no one can snatch them out of my Father's hand" (John 10:29).

COMPASSION OVER FEAR

"A Samaritan, as he traveled, came where the man was; and when he saw him, he took pity on him."

—Luke 10:33

In one of His most famous parables, Jesus told the story of a man who was robbed and beaten up, then left half dead on the side of the road to Jericho, a rugged and barren road through the Judean wilderness. A couple of "respectable" folks passed by without wanting to risk getting involved, staying at a safe distance. Then came the unlikely hero of Jesus' story—a "despised Samaritan" traveler who noticed the injured man and "felt compassion for him" (Luke 10:33, NLT).

While the priest and the Levite would have risked their ceremonial purity to stop to help the beaten man, anyone stopping on that roadside would have been taking a risk that the robbers were still in the area. But motivated by compassion, the Samaritan stopped and set about tending to the man's wounds. He then went even further, committing to pay the costs of the man's ongoing care and recovery at the closest inn (see Luke 10:35). In Jesus' story, the Samaritan risked himself, risked getting involved, risked inconvenience and cost—because he had compassion.

Jesus told this story in response to a leading question from a lawyer about who was the "neighbor" that the law required him to love. Jesus did not quibble. His summary answer was, "Go and do likewise" (Luke 10:37). Fear and prejudice do not discount our call to love, to serve, and to help. Compassion must be stronger than fear. As outrageous and offensive as it would have been to His original audience, Jesus was telling them to be "a good Samaritan"—before that became a cliché—and insisting that a good Samaritan was someone to keep an eye out for.

September 1

WHICH IS BETTER

"Martha, Martha," the Lord answered, "you are worried and upset about many things, but few things are needed—or indeed only one. Mary has chosen what is better, and it will not be taken away from her."

—Luke 10:41, 42

It is easy to imagine the pressure Martha was feeling. In her village home, she was hosting a large group of dusty, hungry people. There was so much to organize. And she was preparing a meal for Jesus and His disciples!

Adding to her exasperation was the glimpse of her sister just sitting, listening to Jesus. Martha probably wished she could stop to listen, but there were so many things to do. Instead, she asked Jesus to encourage Mary to do her share. "Lord, don't you care that my sister has left me to do the work by myself? Tell her to help me!" (Luke 10:40).

In response, Jesus affirmed both sisters. Martha had a valid point; it was not fair that she was doing all this work by herself. But Mary had chosen something better than the domestic worries that Martha was so worked up about. It was important that there be food for the group to share, but this was not the most important part of their time together.

Luke's Gospel does not tell us how this tension was resolved or even how all the visitors were fed and cared for that day. But later in His ministry, Jesus returned to this village in response to the sisters' message about the sickness of their brother, Lazarus. The mutual affection and respect between Jesus and Martha is notable. "Jesus loved Martha and her sister" (John 11:5). Martha was the first to meet Jesus on His arrival, making this remarkable confession amid her grief: "I have always believed you are the Messiah, the Son of God, the one who has come into the world from God" (John 11:27, NLT).

There might have been tension and worry in her earlier interaction with Jesus, but it was obvious that Martha had also chosen something better.

September 2

THE ATTITUDE OF PRAYER

"So I say to you: ask and it will be given to you; seek and you will find; knock and the door will be opened to you. For everyone who asks receives; the one who seeks finds; and to the one who knocks, the door will be opened."

—Luke 11:9, 10

Jesus' disciples had asked Him to teach them to pray (see Luke 11:1). In Luke's telling of it, this was the cue for Jesus to give them the words of the "Lord's Prayer." But Jesus followed this by teaching them the attitude they should have toward prayer. He did not explain how prayer works or why some prayers seem to produce miraculous results while others feel like they are met with silence. But through an intriguing parable and direct instruction, He urged the disciples to be audacious and persistent in prayer.

This was not so much about results, about getting what we want from God, as important as that can be. As Jesus would conclude, God is not unwilling to answer prayers and give His people what they need (see Luke 11:11–13). Rather, prayer is about boldly engaging with God in ways that will deepen our relationship with Him. "It is not a transient thought that is to be given to God. Our prayers are to be fervent and earnest, as were the petitions of the needy friend who asked for the loaves at midnight. The more you ask, the firmer will be your spiritual union. You may come into that place where you will have increased blessings because you have increased faith."*

Living as a follower of Jesus is about overcoming our fear of God and growing our trust in Him by committing all our lives—the big things and the smaller things—to Him and His care. This is the key attitude and result of prayer that Jesus taught His disciples.

* Ellen G. White, *Christ Triumphant* (Hagerstown, MD: Review and Herald®, 1999), 54.

September 3

THE CURRENCY OF WORRY

Then he said to them, "Watch out! Be on your guard against all kinds of greed; life does not consist in an abundance of possessions."
—Luke 12:15

Jesus said a lot about money. Some commentators have pointed out that money was the second most common topic in His teaching, after the kingdom of God. It seems that Jesus knew that money could get hold of us, mess with us, and would even be a rival to the way of life He was offering. "No one can serve two masters. Either you will hate the one and love the other, or you will be devoted to the one and despise the other. You cannot serve both God and Money" (Luke 16:13).

Money—and the stuff it represents—is the currency of worry. Whether getting it, keeping it, accumulating it, managing it, not having it, or losing it, we are tempted to rely on money as our key to the present and our surety for the future. Jesus' warning in Luke 12 is the introductory statement to his parable of the rich fool, a story that shows money's creeping trap.

There is no evidence that the landowner in the story had done anything wrong or exploitative in gaining his wealth. Instead, the land had produced a larger-than-expected crop, something that might have been regarded as a blessing. His foolishness was his accumulation, keeping for himself beyond what he needed, taking on the extra work and worry of building still larger barns, and expecting that this would be his ticket to "take life easy; eat, drink and be merry" for many years to come (Luke 12:19).

It might not seem like a great evil, but Jesus taught that this man—and many of us like him—was putting his faith and his hope in the wrong things. He was choosing wealth and worry over generosity and trust. This story was the launching pad for Luke's version of Jesus' "Do not worry" sermon (see Luke 12:22–34).

"For where your treasure is, there your heart will be also" (Luke 12:34).

READING THE HEADLINES

"Do you think that these Galileans were worse sinners than all the other Galileans because they suffered this way? I tell you, no! But unless you repent, you too will all perish. Or those eighteen who died when the tower in Siloam fell on them—do you think they were more guilty than all the others living in Jerusalem? I tell you, no! But unless you repent, you too will all perish."
—Luke 13:2–5

At times, we might imagine that Jesus lived and taught amid the clean storybook pictures that many of us grew up with. But Jesus was not ignorant of the headlines of His day—or unaware of the fears and urgent theological questions they raised. Like much of history, the times in which Jesus lived were dangerous and difficult. "Life was slow, hard and short."* We probably do not appreciate how much of Jesus' teaching and ministry was responding to the tragic news of that day. However, in these verses, Jesus directly addressed the questions raised by some in the crowd about recent Roman violence against Galilean worshipers—and he added another recent headline to make His point.

Like the arguments in the story of Job, the underlying questions are: Why do bad things happen to good people? Is faithfulness a guarantee of blessing and safety? Is tragedy a consequence, judgment, or merely random? Jesus rejected the formula of "Individual evil equals tragedy" and asserted the apparent senseless and random nature of much of the evil in our world. But He also urged repentance in the face of life's fragility and unpredictability.

In lives awash with news and headlines shouting one tragedy after another, we are to respond with compassion, not judgment, aware that we could be affected by the same random, commonplace, and horrific evils that happen to others. Our eternal perspective is most important, but it does not detach us from our call to empathy, service, and healing.

* Kayle de Waal, *Hearing the Way* (Warburton, Victoria, Australia: Signs Publishing, 2019), 22.

September 5

THE TAX COLLECTOR'S FEAR

"But the tax collector stood at a distance. He would not even look up to heaven, but beat his breast and said, 'God, have mercy on me, a sinner.' "
—Luke 18:13

Jesus told this story "to some who were confident of their own righteousness and looked down on everybody else" (Luke 18:9). It's a seemingly simple story of two men who went to pray in the temple.

The prayer of the first was a list of his good works—all the good things he had done "since I was a boy," to borrow the phrase of the "ruler" Jesus would encounter only a few verses later in Luke's Gospel (see Luke 18:18–23). In Jesus' parable, there is no response or outcome to the prayer of the self-righteous Pharisee. But later, when a "ruler" came to Him asking about eternal life, Jesus challenged him to give up his reliance on his good deeds and great wealth. The man "became very sad, because he was very wealthy" (Luke 18:23).

The second man who prayed in the temple was a tax collector who did not dare to come near the prominent place where the Pharisee prayed. Instead, the tax collector "stood at a distance"—like the short tax collector in Jericho who so wanted to see Jesus that he climbed a sycamore-fig tree to see over the crowd (see Luke 19:3, 4)—perhaps only a day or two later. Jesus responded to Zacchaeus' effort to see him, spent the rest of the day with him, and heard Zacchaeus's confession and determination to put things right, and Jesus said, "Today salvation has come to this house" (Luke 19:9).

The two men who prayed in the temple were reflected in the wealthy, upstanding ruler and the short, tree-climbing tax collector. They were the characters in the story that Jesus told, come to life. The ruler was proud to proclaim his own righteousness and went away sad. The outcast tax collector was afraid to come close, but his life was turned around and accepted by God. As Jesus concluded the parable, "For everyone who exalts himself will be humbled, and he who humbles himself will be exalted" (Luke 18:14).

September 6

THE CALL TO SERVE

"For even the Son of Man did not come to be served, but to serve, and to give his life as a ransom for many."
—Mark 10:45

Given how little attention Jesus gave to it, the disciples seemed quite preoccupied with jockeying for positions in the coming Messianic kingdom they imagined. Although such concerns were contradicted by much of what Jesus taught, their cultural assumptions were remarkably persistent. As Jesus' closest followers, they expected that they were the prime candidates for high positions and great responsibility. James and John had been particularly brazen in making their expectations clear, and the other disciples were upset with them. So Jesus had to be strident in His attempt to shake them free from this mindset.

In thinking this way, Jesus said, they were acting like their oppressors, the Gentile rulers over Israel (see Mark 10:42). This was the system of the world around them, particularly those who had no insight or understanding of the ways of God and His kingdom. Ironically, those most striving for positions in the kingdom of God were those least fitted for them. His was not a kingdom of striving but a kingdom of serving. Those who are most fit to lead are those who most want to serve.

And this began with Jesus Himself. He was the "suffering Servant" described by Isaiah and who would be the subject of the early Christian hymn: the one "who, being in very nature God, did not consider equality with God something to be used to his own advantage" to the extreme of "even death on a cross!" (Philippians 2:6, 8). This was Jesus' primary qualification and action as Messiah, as Savior, as King of this kingdom. So how could His followers strive for anything less—or more?

The disciples' desire for position betrayed their profound misunderstanding of Jesus and His kingdom, but they would learn. And so can we.

September 7

DRIVEN BY FEAR

The chief priests and the teachers of the law heard this and began looking for a way to kill him, for they feared him, because the whole crowd was amazed at his teaching.

—Mark 11:18

Jesus' most vocal and effective opponents were driven by fear. The Jewish leaders were afraid of Jesus, they were afraid of the people, and they were afraid of the Romans who occupied their land. They were afraid of people who were like them and afraid of people who did not live up to their expectations. They were afraid that they could never be good enough to be accepted by God and afraid that God did not fully appreciate their piety.

It was their fear of Jesus—His power and His growing popularity—that was the catalyst for their plotting to kill Him. They feared that because of the miracles He performed, "everyone will believe in him, and then the Romans will come and take away both our temple and our nation" (John 11:48). Accordingly, they reasoned that it was better that Jesus die than the whole nation be destroyed, as Caiaphas put it (see John 11:50).

The leaders also feared the people. When Jesus asked awkward questions, they flailed in search of an answer that would not implicate themselves, but that also would not offend the people who "held that John really was a prophet" (Mark 11:32). They knew what they wanted to say but did not have the courage to risk the reaction of the crowd around them.

The fear of the people and of Jesus' popularity combined to bring an end to their interactions with Jesus. Even their attempts to trick Him into a compromising answer were defeated by His careful responses, and they feared that Jesus was really making them look bad. "And from then on no one dared ask him any more questions" (Mark 12:34).

Ultimately, their fear led them to conspire with their oppressors, to plot His arrest, and to murder the Son of God!

September 8

GIVING EVERYTHING

Calling his disciples to him, Jesus said, "Truly I tell you, this poor widow has put more into the treasury than all the others. They all gave out of their wealth; but she, out of her poverty, put in everything—all she had to live on."
—Mark 12:43, 44

Given Jesus' fraught relationship with the temple and its priests, it might be surprising that He would support giving to that system. But He emphasized the kind of heart this gift represented more than the amount given or what the offering might be used for. Amid the offerings given that day—"many rich people threw in large amounts" (Mark 12:41)—the two small coins would have added little to the temple budget. The significance was in what they represented, in the widow's act of giving, and that Jesus recognized her generosity.

We know so little in this story, just the snapshot that Jesus pointed out to His disciples, but we can imagine the timidity with which the widow approached the offering box. She might well have been nervous, even hesitant, about giving "all she had to live on," but she would also likely have not wanted to attract attention, well aware that her offering was achingly small compared to the more ostentatious giving that was going on around her. Perhaps it was her timidity that drew Jesus' attention.

Whatever it was, Jesus saw her and her act of giving. He used her quiet generosity to teach a lesson to His disciples, and through them, her story has been told and retold many times since. We do not know her name or the rest of her story, but we know what she did, and her story has prompted generosity among Jesus' followers down through the centuries since. The return on investment of those two small coins has been incredible. But even that was not the point. Rather, Jesus noticed—and her courage matters to the many of us who still read her story.

September 9

REASSURANCE REJECTED

"Jerusalem, Jerusalem, you who kill the prophets and stone those sent to you, how often I have longed to gather your children together, as a hen gathers her chicks under her wings, but you were not willing."
—Matthew 23:37

We would struggle to find an image more comforting than that of a mother hen nestling her chicks under her. It is a picture filled with warmth, care, and commitment. It is a less common image of our relationship with God, but one that Jesus employed in lamenting the resistance of the people of Jerusalem to the ways and care of God. Jesus portrayed the relationship between God and His people as characterized by God's care for them in contrast with the people's stubborn rejection of that care.

This lament is similar to the scene described in the Gospel of Luke, where Jesus paused in the midst of His triumphal entry into the city (see Luke 19:41–44). The story is memorialized today in a small church about halfway down the western slope of the Mount of Olives. The church—named *Dominus Flevit,* meaning "the Lord wept"—was built in the 1950s in the shape of a teardrop. When one is seated inside the church, the arched window at the front of the church is frosted glass except for a wide "letterbox" panel that offers a panoramic view over the Old City of Jerusalem, with its high stone walls, steeples, spires, and domes.

That church is a poignant place to reflect on those moments of care, rejection, lament, and judgment in the ministry of Jesus, and His demonstration of God's continuing love and care for the city and its people both by His presence and in His words of lament. But Jesus was also warning the people that their continuing rejection of God's care and His messengers would leave them exposed to oppressors and conquerors. Jesus' warnings were delivered with tears, with a mothering heart that was breaking for the children of that city.

DON'T PANIC!

"You will hear of wars and rumors of wars, but see to it that you are not alarmed. Such things must happen, but the end is still to come."
—Matthew 24:6

Spend time on any newsfeed or broadcast, flick through the headlines of the day, or reflect on some of the larger issues that confront our world—and it is not hard to feel overwhelmed with all the trouble around the globe. There are two reasons. First, there are many grim, tragic, and frightening things that happen each day and many serious threats that confront us individually and collectively in our world. Second, the phenomenon that we call *news* collects all these things in one feed, stream, or channel and constantly bombards us with the next alarming, heartbreaking headline. The next story breaks before we can get our heads and hearts around the previous tragedy, disaster, or outrage. We do not hear the resolution to many of the stories, and little time is given to understanding why or what matters most.

When we are confronted with such a torrent of wars and rumors of war, famines, earthquakes, and all kinds of falsity, it is easy to become overwhelmed, anxious, and afraid. Indeed, this is probably a healthy response to an unhealthy amount of exposure to death and disaster. Our world is broken in many ways, and our media feeds make it all too obvious and accessible every day.

In response to the chaos surrounding us, Jesus said, "See to it that you are not alarmed"—or simply "Don't panic!" (Matthew 24:6, NLT). But "see to it" carries a sense of intentionality. Be intentional about trusting God, but perhaps also be intentional about how much we choose to expose ourselves to the weight of tragedy and suffering portrayed in the news. We ought to be alert, aware, and compassionate in responding to the world around us and particularly to those most in need, but "don't panic"—and don't allow ourselves to be panicked or overwhelmed by the constant exposure to news.

September 11

FUTURE FEARS

"See, I have told you ahead of time."

—Matthew 24:25

The future is a fear-filled place—or at least our perception of it usually is. Not only do we hear repeatedly about the many threats that lurk in the future, either near or far, but we also have our own mortality to reckon with, as well as that of everyone we care about. On the whole, the future is not a safe place for us to be, yet we keep progressing toward it at a steady and relentless pace.

Jesus did warn His followers about disasters, deceptions, persecution, and disappointment in their future and ours. But rather than reasons for alarm, these would become reminders of Jesus' foreknowledge, not to be celebrated in themselves—they are tragedies, after all—but to be noticed as signposts that God already knows the road. He has seen and heard our fears in the future as surely as He has seen and heard the present suffering and injustice endured by His people.

The point of Bible prophecy is not so much predicting the future but recognizing God at work in our present and past, thus growing our confidence in His presence with us as we step into an uncertain future. When we recognize the patterns and fulfilments of the prophetic sayings of Jesus and other biblical prophets, we are reassured about other aspects of what they said and taught. Bible prophecy is also about how we live in the present, illuminated and shaped by our beliefs and hope for the future.

Many aspects of our future can be fearful and fear-filled, but God is there with us. We are not to be fixated on the future, certainly not focused on imaginings that feed our fears and stoke those of others. Instead, we entrust our futures to God and, with Him, turn back to the needs around us in the world today, which is the most faithful way of waiting for the hope He has promised.

September 12

FEAR OR HOPE?

"When these things begin to take place, stand up and lift up your heads, because your redemption is drawing near."
—Luke 21:28

Jesus' teaching did not ignore the realities in the world around Him—or in the world around us. He warned His followers that the world was damaged and that war, disasters, and tragedy would be an ongoing part of our collective human experience. As part of this world, His followers should not expect their lives to be smooth. Rather, at times, their lives will be more difficult precisely because they follow Him (see Luke 21:12).

The history of our world throughout the 2,000 years since this sermon has proved Jesus' insight and the reality that He brought to His teaching. Jesus taught His followers that they had two choices as to how they would respond to the fearful and frightening things in their lives and experiences. As difficult as it might be, it is simply a matter of choosing to live in fear or in hope.

Jesus warned that, whether by choice or habit, some people's thinking would come to be dominated by fear. He warned that fearfulness would become more prevalent as His return drew nearer. "People will faint from terror, apprehensive of what is coming on the world" (Luke 21:26). Indeed, pervasive fear would be a sign of the age in its own right.

But other people—and Jesus pressed this for His followers—would choose to live with hope, even when it might seem their world was falling apart. As difficult as these various circumstances might be and as fragile as human life so often seems, rather than seeing them as a cause for alarm or panic, followers of Jesus were urged toward assurance and even a sense of eager anticipation. We are not to revel in the misery of the world as some grim vindication, but we are to lift our eyes to the Source of our hope and trust His presence and promises for resilience, rescue, and restoration.

September 13

READY OR WORRIED?

"Be careful, or your hearts will be weighed down with carousing, drunkenness and the anxieties of life, and that day will close on you suddenly like a trap."

—Luke 21:34

Life does not stop. It keeps coming at us with its busyness, noise, weariness, and distractions. We worry about getting by and keeping up, fitting in and standing out. It is easy enough for our hearts to be weighed down with the good things of life—and too many of them. Even more, we can be weighed down with anxieties, entertainment, procrastination, and temptations. The world tends to grind us down and wear us out. The life that does not stop is a trap that locks us in and uses us up.

Life does not stop—until it does. An end—and *the* end—"will come upon all those who live on the face of the whole earth" (Luke 21:35). Jesus warned that an awareness of the end—whether for us individually or for our world as a whole—should perpetually reprioritize our concerns and anxieties. Some things that seem so urgent, important, or attractive are simply not so when considered in the context of our mortality. And we should be looking to invest our lives, our time, our resources in things that matter.

Living ready—for death, for the end, for Jesus' return, for eternity—is about living well. It is not about grim survival through difficult times, although we all have those times. It is about living in the way Jesus laid out, with the assurance of His presence in all our circumstances and in all our times. This frees us from the traps of our many anxieties and trivialities, meaning we can live with greater freedom and joy, even amid trials, challenges, and disappointments.

A FOOT-WASHING GOD

Jesus knew that the Father had put all things under his power, and that he had come from God and was returning to God; so he got up from the meal, took off his outer clothing, and wrapped a towel around his waist."
—John 13:3, 4

There are many superlatives in this short description, setting the scene for Jesus to wash the dusty feet of His disciples: "Now he showed them the full extent of his love" (John 13:2, NLT, note); "all things under His power;" He "had come from God and was returning to God." Something momentous was about to take place. So He took off His cloak, wrapped a towel around His waist "and began to wash his disciples' feet, drying them with the towel that was wrapped around him" (John 13:5). The language of these verses tells us something significant—that He washed their feet *because* of who He was, b*ecause* He had all the power in the world, *because* He had come from God, and *because* of the fullness of His love.

The other Gospels describe the lead-up to this meal—how the disciples were arguing among themselves about who was or would be the greatest in Jesus' kingdom. With these arguments echoing in their minds, it was Peter, as the spokesperson in this story, who recognized the offensive nature of what Jesus was doing—and protested. In a sense, he was protesting about the nature of the kingdom Jesus kept insisting upon. He feared—but he also knew—that if their Lord and Teacher acted in this way, this would be the example they would be expected to emulate. And this is exactly what Jesus said: "I have set you an example that you should do as I have done for you" (John 13:15).

This humble but powerful act took place *because* Jesus was who He said He was. His disciples should not be afraid to follow His example because Jesus was God, and He called them to be like Him.

September 15

OVERWHELMED BY HOPE

*"Do not let your hearts be troubled.
You believe in God; believe also in me."*

—John 14:1

Jesus' final sermon in John's Gospel begins with this significant "Do not be afraid." It was part of His earnest conversation with His disciples between their last meal together and His arrest, perhaps sometime past midnight. This context alone would render it an important discourse—but it is also the longest in all of the Gospels, stretching over four chapters in John's Gospel, with the final chapter being a prayer with and for the disciples.

Jesus' focus was on the future, from the immediate context of His imminent arrest to the completion of His kingdom, the many rooms available in His Father's house, and His promise to "come back and take you to be with me that you also may be where I am" (John 14:3). At times, Jesus was blunt about the challenges and trials His disciples would face, but He was even more adamant that the disciples need not be afraid and that He would send a Comforter who would be ever with them. With the disciples about to witness His arrest and crucifixion, Jesus wanted to give them hope that would be larger than their fears, sorrow, and doubts that would threaten to overwhelm them.

It seemed that Jesus well understood that we cannot merely decide to feel less fear. "Quite the contrary, our overwhelming fears need, themselves, to be overwhelmed by bigger and better things, by a sense of adventure and fullness of life that comes from locating our fears and vulnerabilities within a larger story that is ultimately hopeful and not tragic."* This was the invitation to continue to live with the indwelling presence of Jesus—by His Spirit, even after Jesus' departure—in the fullness of life He offered and in the hope of His return.

---

* Scott Bader-Saye, *Following Jesus in a Culture of Fear* (Grand Rapids, MI: Brazos Press, 2007), 60.

September 16

WITH YOU FOREVER

"I will not leave you as orphans;
I will come to you."

—John 14:18

Jesus was preparing His disciples for one of the most difficult experiences of their lives. They would have been aware of the threats and animosity toward Jesus, but they seemed to have missed His warning and could not have imagined how these would play out so dramatically and suddenly over the following twenty-four hours. The thing Jesus wanted them to know was that this would not be the end of their story with Him. Even when everything seemed to be going wrong, and all their hopes about Jesus had turned to tragedy, with real fear about whether they might be next, they would not be left alone.

There were two important ways that Jesus promised that He would still be with them. "If you love me, keep my commands. And I will ask the Father, and he will give you another advocate to help you and be with you forever—the Spirit of truth" (John 14:15–17).

First, His teaching would continue to resonate and unfold in the way they would live. When they followed His teachings, they would continue to walk with Him as an expression of their love and faithfulness. He had taught them enough for His presence to continue to shape them and the world around them by their presence and work.

Second, the Father would send His Spirit to dwell within them as an abiding and eternal presence. The Spirit would be the guiding voice of help, comfort, and instruction in the disciples' lives. What this would mean would become clearer after Jesus' resurrection and would be manifested fully at Pentecost, but they were given this promise while Jesus was still with them. As fearful as the next hours would be, they did not have to feel like orphans, abandoned by their Teacher and Lord. Even as He prepared for His own ordeal, He was thinking first about them.

September 17

PEACE

"Peace I leave with you; my peace I give you. I do not give to you as the world gives. Do not let your hearts be troubled and do not be afraid."
—John 14:27

Peace is one of those words that has come to mean so many different things that it often seems to mean little of anything. But it is one of those words that we need to reclaim and renew, particularly when we have heard it uttered by Jesus. He insisted that He was not talking about peace as the world around Him might have understood it or offered it. His peace is a gift—a gift worth holding onto.

In Jesus' understanding, experiencing peace is the opposite of being afraid, the opposite of troubled hearts. As Jesus would make clear in the rest of this discourse, such peace was not dependent on external circumstances. At least as often as the world around us offers or proclaims peace, the world also takes it away. When it comes, peace almost always feels like a temporary lull rather than an ongoing reality. But the peace that Jesus gives has substance and will remain even amid fear and persecution, disappointment and grief.

Again, we must remember that Jesus was saying this within hours of His urgent prayers in the Garden of Gethsemane, His betrayal and arrest, the mocking trials, and ultimately His cruel crucifixion. It was hardly the context for "Do not let your hearts be troubled" and "Do not be afraid"—except that those words were exactly what was needed—for His troubled heart and for His disciples' hearts that were about to be also greatly troubled.

As Jesus and His disciples left the upper room and headed out into the night (see John 14:31), Jesus gave them the promise and possibilities of peace to prepare them for the troubles and fears they were about to confront.

MUCH MORE TO SAY

"I have much more to say to you, more than you can now bear. But when he, the Spirit of truth, comes, he will guide you into all the truth. He will not speak on his own; he will speak only what he hears, and he will tell you what is yet to come."
—John 16:12, 13

Many readers have suggested that verse 12—Jesus' statement that He had much more to tell the disciples—foreshadowed John's visions that would comprise the book of Revelation. According to this interpretation, these are the difficult truths, more difficult than they could bear immediately before Jesus' death and resurrection.

What is recorded in Revelation was likely a partial fulfillment of this statement of Jesus, included in the description of the Spirit's role to "tell you what is yet to come." But Jesus' promise also seems to be a broader description of the ongoing work of the Holy Spirit in the disciples' lives. It was not that Jesus did not want to share more or that He was reserving special information for a more select group. Rather, this was an acknowledgment of the limited capacity that the disciples had—that all of us have—to grasp new ideas, particularly in relation to our understanding of the ways and purposes of God.

The Spirit was to guide the disciples as they grew in their understanding of Jesus and their experiences in following Him. They were about to endure a dark and difficult experience as Jesus would be taken from them. They would witness His brutal death and experience their own fears and doubts before being astounded but also further troubled by the reports of Jesus' resurrection. It would take time for them to fully appreciate what they were witnesses of, but Jesus promised them a guide and a comforter—and that they would come to accept and celebrate what they were now part of. "I tell you the truth, you will weep and mourn while the world rejoices. You will grieve, but your grief will turn to joy" (John 16:20).

September 19

"YOU WILL HAVE TROUBLE"

"I have told you these things, so that in me you may have peace. In this world you will have trouble. But take heart! I have overcome the world."
—John 16:33

Jesus did not want His disciples taken by surprise by the trouble in the world around them or even by direct threats and attacks aimed at them. He was referring to His arrest and the fact that they would soon be scattered, but He was also describing life in a broken and troubled world, particularly for those who would choose to live as His followers. They should not expect that following Jesus would smooth their path, clear all obstacles out of their way, and guarantee trouble-free lives. Instead, trouble would be a recurring experience.

That Jesus was able to warn them about some of what they would face was one way in which He offered assurance. When experiencing trouble, they need not be afraid that He had abandoned them or that somehow God's plan had been defeated. Instead, they could have peace in the knowledge that Jesus knew and understood, that He had seen and heard their troubles. Jesus knew their world, and He knew them.

But Jesus took His assurance a step further in urging that He had, and would, overcome all the trouble in the world. When we begin with Jesus, whatever we encounter in our lives and in our world has already been overcome. The worst of suffering, grief, isolation, and fear are already defeated in Jesus. And He was already working out the plan for the full and final defeat of all that is evil, with the promise of a full reunion with His Father.

Jesus' disciples could have the confidence that Jesus had as He approached His arrest, trials, and crucifixion with the knowledge that His Father was with Him (see John 16:32). And ultimately, in His resurrection, His followers could have the confidence that Jesus had truly overcome the worst that our world could offer.

September 20

IN THE WORLD

"My prayer is not that you take them out of the world but that you protect them from the evil one."

—John 17:15

One of the tendencies of people of faith across the generations has been to withdraw from the world around them. In Jesus' time, there were sects, such as the Essenes, who believed that the way of faithfulness was to establish their own communities away from the surrounding society and devote themselves to studying and practicing purity. But this was not the way Jesus set out for His followers.

He acknowledged the tensions and trouble that would be part of His disciples' relationship with the world around them, but Jesus was explicitly *not* asking that they be taken out of the world. Instead, He commissioned them to step boldly into the world in His name. "As you sent me into the world, I have sent them into the world" (John 17:18).

By virtue of being human, we are not only *in* the world; we are *of* this world—it was good enough for the incarnated Jesus; it must be enough for us. In a sense, we do not belong to the world as it is (see John 17:14), yet in a larger sense, this world rightfully belongs to God and to His people, so we are engaged with our world and its people.

Again acknowledging the troubles in this world, Jesus prayed for the protection of His disciples from the evil one. Throughout His ministry, Jesus had confronted evil in various forms, including direct temptations by Satan and various evil spirits who were causing great damage in individual lives. Jesus acknowledged the realities of those powers but demonstrated that they should not hold us in their sway or in fear. They, too, were overcome and would be defeated. Jesus' prayer was for our resistance and resilience against their attacks and temptations.

Jesus seemed to be saying that the disciples did not need to be rescued and removed as much as they needed to be reassured and resourced. That's what He prayed for.

JESUS PRAYED FOR YOU

"My prayer is not for them alone. I pray also for those who will believe in me through their message, that all of them may be one, Father, just as you are in me and I am in you. May they also be in us so that the world may believe that you have sent me."

—John 17:20, 21

One of the strongest evidences for Christianity about 2,000 years after its beginnings is Christianity itself. That Christianity has grown from its mustard-seed-like beginning in a backwater of the Roman Empire with a few frightened disciples and the story of someone executed as a criminal but somehow returned to life is a remarkable testimony.

For every follower of Jesus today, there is a chain of sharing—parents to children, colleagues to friends, believers to neighbors, preachers to hearers, and strangers to strangers—that stretches all the way back to the disciples who first heard Jesus pray this prayer. We are privileged to have benefited and received from such a long line of witnesses across the centuries. And we carry the responsibility of continuing the unfinished task that Jesus gave to His disciples, and which has now been handed on to us.

As recipients of this story, this testimony, and this task, we are encouraged to know that Jesus prayed for us in His prayers for His followers. "Those who will believe in me through their message"—as Jesus phrased it—includes you and me. He prayed that we would be united in our connection with God and that through us and our witness, still more people today will believe in Jesus and believe that He is who He claimed to be.

Pause and reflect on this: Jesus prayed for you and for the opportunities you have to share the story of His love. As we faithfully play our roles as witnesses to His story, Jesus prayed that the world and the people around us will know who He is and how much God loves them (see John 17:23).

OUR SUFFERING SAVIOR

Then he said to them, "My soul is overwhelmed with sorrow to the point of death. Stay here and keep watch with me."
—Matthew 26:38

As we near the end of the Gospel stories, it can be painful to watch Jesus' sufferings. The One who healed the sick, calmed the storms, fed the crowds, and taught so wonderfully seems suddenly reduced to a human being, peculiarly vulnerable and painfully aware of His burdens of sorrow, anxiety, and fear. And His ordeal seems all the more intense for His understanding of what He was about to endure, that it would ultimately destroy Him, and that He seemed so alone as it loomed over Him.

In the Garden of Gethsemane, Jesus had two requests. The first was that His select group of disciples would "keep watch" with Him, adding their presence and their prayers to His. But they fell asleep and left Him alone with His earnest and urgent prayers. The second was that somehow God would find for Him a way out of His predicament, a way other than the suffering before Him. "My Father, if it is possible, may this cup be taken from me" (Matthew 26:39). He paused, hoping for a response from the heavens and perhaps some support from His disciples, but He heard only silence, perhaps punctuated by snoring, before He continued His prayer. "If it is not possible for this cup to be taken away unless I drink it, may your will be done" (Matthew 26:42).

Jesus knew what it was to suffer, to be overwhelmed by fear and dread, but He also knew what it was to be let down by His friends and to feel like He was receiving no answer from God despite His most desperate prayers. Even in our most frantic and distressed experiences, we are assured in this account that Jesus has been there with us, and somehow, we are less alone.

September 23

DENYING FEAR

Then he began to call down curses on himself and he swore to them, "I don't know the man!"

Immediately a rooster crowed.

—Matthew 26:74

We have seen it before in the Bible's stories, but fear can make us do strange things, things we would never do in a normal state of mind. Only a few hours earlier, Peter had been adamant in his response to Jesus' prediction that before the rooster crowed—before the morning came—that Peter would deny knowing Him three times. "Even if I have to die with you, I will never disown you," Peter insisted (Matthew 26:35).

But what he asserted in the relative safety of the upper room was a long way from struggling to stay awake in the garden, seeing Jesus arrested, then lurking in the shadows of the courtyard of the high priest in the early hours of the morning as Jesus was put on trial. While many of the other disciples had disappeared into the night, Peter had been trying to stick with Jesus, albeit from a safe distance, but the queries from a couple of servant girls provoked his fierce denials.

The circumstances and surroundings were different, but the primary difference was fear. The bold fisherman from Galilee who had followed Jesus for a couple of years and then to the nation's capital was suddenly trying to suppress his northern accent and distance himself as far as possible from the accused. As the curses of the third denial stunned the crowd around him, the crowing of the rooster sparked Peter's memory of Jesus' warning. "And he went outside and wept bitterly" (Matthew 26:75).

But this was not the end of Peter's story. After Jesus' resurrection, special mention was made that Peter was to receive the news that Jesus was alive (see Mark 16:7), and, in John's Gospel, Jesus gave Peter three opportunities to affirm his love for Him (see John 21:15–19). Fear had undone Peter, but Jesus loved him still, and that love gave him new courage and a larger mission.

September 24

NOTHING LEFT TO FEAR

Jesus answered him, "I tell you the truth, today you will be with me in paradise."

—Luke 23:43

We should not underestimate the horror of crucifixion. It was a tool of terror and oppression, including public shame and physical torture. Crosses would line the main roads outside the cities of Roman-occupied nations as a grim warning to anyone who contemplated revolt or rebellion. This was the exclamation point that punctuated Paul's description of Jesus' trajectory of humility and descent. "And being found in appearance as a man, he humbled himself and became obedient to death—even death on a cross!" (Philippians 2:8).

With a storyteller's symmetry—crucified between two criminals, "one on his right, the other on his left" (Luke 23:33)—Jesus "was numbered with the transgressors" (Luke 22:37, quoting Isaiah 53:12). And these two hardened criminals, despite, or because of, their common suffering and shame, chose two alternative responses to Jesus' presence with them. Bizarrely, the first joined in with those who were insulting Jesus. But his mocking suggestion that Jesus save Himself—"and us!"—from the cross brought a rebuke from the one on the other side of Jesus.

"Don't you fear God," said the second criminal, "since you are under the same sentence?" (Luke 23:40). We do not know what previous interactions they might have had with Jesus, whether through His public ministry or just on the day of their crucifixion. Perhaps the one had simply been observing the way in which Jesus suffered, but he recognized something different in Jesus. Somehow, in Jesus, he saw a peace and hope that transcended even the horror and hopelessness of crucifixion.

Imagine how this must have encouraged Jesus as He neared the end of His ordeal and His mission. In contrast to the mocking of the first criminal, this second man made an unlikely but heartfelt confession: "Jesus, remember me when you come into your kingdom" (Luke 23:42). And Jesus heard and acknowledged his prayer as they suffered and died together.

September 25

THE FORSAKEN GOD

About three in the afternoon Jesus cried out in a loud voice, "Eli, Eli, lema sabachthani?" (which means "My God, my God, why have you forsaken me?")
—Matthew 27:46

It is unnerving to hear Jesus proclaim His forsakenness as He did from the darkness and agony of the cross. While we have the human fear that comes from God walking toward us in the garden—the sound from which Adam and Eve first hid—we have another, perhaps deeper existential fear that God is *not* walking toward us in the garden, that He might not exist at all, that God is an idea we have made up in our own minds and fooled ourselves into believing. And this fear can become urgent when we so desperately want to hear from God, yet the silence seems so loud.

In Jesus, God was there with us. It is one of the unique elements of the Bible story. "They will find only one divinity who ever uttered their isolation; only one religion in which God seemed for an instant to be an atheist."* In Jesus, God experienced a broken relationship with God! He experienced how His seeming silence in the face of our suffering and despair makes suffering all the more intense. Remarkably, God knows what it is like to feel forsaken by God!

The irony is that Jesus likely experienced it more intensely as a result of the close relationship He had maintained with His Father. Rather than having some kind of divine advantage, He simultaneously submitted Himself to being murdered by human beings He had created and was cut off from the presence of God, the community in which He had created. We can understand only those elements of this forsakenness that feel human, with the divine dynamic so far beyond our understanding or imagination. Perhaps our discomfort at hearing these anguished words of Jesus is never unnerving enough.

---

* G. K. Chesterton, *Orthodoxy* (London: Hodder & Stoughton, 1996), 206.

September 26

GOD WAS HERE!

When the centurion and those with him who were guarding Jesus saw the earthquake and all that had happened, they were terrified, and exclaimed, "Surely he was the Son of God!"

—Matthew 27:54

Perspective is important. Only a few verses after Jesus' anguished cry of forsakenness, the Roman centurion—a pagan military oppressor—was acknowledging Him as the Son of God in those moments of death, upheaval, and terror. He and his fellow soldiers guarding Jesus had been witnesses to the whole crucifixion story, perhaps including mocking Him in Pilate's courtyard (see Matthew 27:27–31). Jesus had experienced only darkness, suffering, and silence, but this centurion—who had likely overseen many crucifixions—saw something unique and profound, something divine. In that moment of fear, the centurion and his men asked deeper questions and found a meaningful answer.

This is an enigmatic story. We were not told why the centurion and his men arrived at this conclusion or their understanding when describing this executed criminal as "the Son of God." Given so few details, we can imagine that this centurion might have been known to the first readers of the Gospels; perhaps he became a member of one of the earliest groups of believers after Jesus' resurrection and ascension. Or perhaps he and his men were simply overwhelmed by the strange events of this particular crucifixion, and the Gospel writer used this unlikely voice to remind us at this point in the story just who Jesus is and how significant His death was in almost every imaginable way.

Sometimes, fear reveals truth. It can jolt us to authentic, unscripted, and otherwise unlikely conclusions, even if we do not fully understand or grasp what we are saying. But as the feeling of fear passes, so too can our moment of clarity and honesty. We tend to revert quickly. That doesn't diminish the truth we might have stumbled upon, but it means we have to choose what we do with that insight, whether we shrug and move on or whether we allow it to settle more deeply into our lives.

September 27

A TIME FOR BOLD ACTION

Joseph of Arimathea, a prominent member of the Council,
who was himself waiting for the kingdom of God,
went boldly to Pilate and asked for Jesus' body.

—Mark 15:43

While many of the Jewish leaders were plotting against Jesus, there are hints throughout the gospel stories that some among the leaders were curious about Jesus and quietly supportive of Him.

We have already noted that Nicodemus was "a member of the Jewish ruling council" who met with Jesus under cover of darkness (see John 3:1, 2). He later spoke up carefully in a meeting of the leading priests and Pharisees and was accused of being a Galilean (see John 7:50–52), but he did not reveal his allegiance to Jesus until His burial (see John 19:39).

John's Gospel hints that amid the ongoing conflicts and plots of the priests and leaders concerning Jesus, there were more leaders who may have been covert followers of Jesus. "Yet at the same time many even among the leaders believed in him. But because of the Pharisees they would not openly acknowledge their faith for fear they would be put out of the synagogue; for they loved human praise more than praise from God" (John 12:42, 43).

Among this group of leaders was Joseph of Arimathea, the first to step out, boldly asking the Roman governor for permission to bury Jesus and providing his own nearby tomb for the burial. Perhaps prompted by the miscarriage of justice that he had seen in the council, he risked his reputation and place in society to demonstrate his allegiance to Jesus. Remarkably, he expressed his support at exactly the moment when Jesus seemed most defeated. Whether it was regret that he had not spoken up sooner or hope that this was not the end of Jesus' story, Joseph overcame his fear and provided for Jesus in a way that none of His other followers were able to.

September 28

"HE HAS RISEN!"

The angel said to the women, "Do not be afraid, for I know that you are looking for Jesus, who was crucified. He is not here; he has risen, just as he said. Come and see the place where he lay."
—Matthew 28:5, 6

As with the announcements of Jesus' birth, an angel appeared to deliver incredible news to unlikely recipients. And again, it was an unexpected appearance from this strange being. This was not what the women were expecting to find at the tomb where Jesus had been buried. The description of the angel's appearance—"His appearance was like lightning, and his clothes were white as snow" (Matthew 28:3)—and the terrifying effect it had on the Roman soldiers who had been guarding the tomb (see Matthew 28:4) underline the alarming nature of this encounter.

But there was also the surprising content of the angel's message. It was difficult to understand and accept; it would test their faith; it would be a dangerous message for them to proclaim, and it was profoundly world-changing. It also marked another important step forward in repairing the broken relationship between God and humanity. Thus, "Do not be afraid" was a far-reaching and necessary introduction to the angel's message to Mary and "the other Mary."

As overwhelming as his appearance and message were, the angel also showed them the evidence, demonstrating the emptiness of the tomb in which they had seen Jesus buried on Friday afternoon. And then he charged them with the task of going to tell the rest of the disciples.

Heading back to the awakening city as bearers of this astounding news, the women were simultaneously "afraid yet filled with joy" (Matthew 28:8). They could hardly bring themselves to believe it at the same time as they set out to share it. Their lives, the city, and all our world would be transformed by the terrifying and wonderful news that only they yet knew.

September 29

THE END OF THE STORY?

Trembling and bewildered, the women went out and fled from the tomb. They said nothing to anyone, because they were afraid.

—Mark 16:8

Most Bible translations show the variations in the ending of Mark's Gospel in the various manuscripts that have been found. The older translations use the longer ending that stretches to verse 16, but the older manuscripts—discovered more recently than the older translations—have a shorter ending. As the footnote in the New Living Translation puts it: "The most reliable early manuscripts of the Gospel of Mark end at verse 8."

It is tempting to conclude that some readers of the earliest versions of Mark's Gospel were uncomfortable with having the story end with the trembling and bewildered women fleeing from the empty tomb in fear. So, the later readers might have added a more complete and comforting ending, which then became part of the traditional text.

We can understand the desire for a more satisfactory resolution, but we should not hurry too quickly past the startling disruption that the Resurrection was—to Jesus' first disciples, to the city of Jerusalem, to the history of our world, and even to us. It seems Mark "knew how the women felt as they picked up their skirts and made a dash for it anyway. Wonderful and terrible things were happening, and more were still to come. He knew what fear was all about—the scalp cold, the mouth dry, the midnight knock at the door—but he also knew that fear was not the last thing. It was the next to last thing. The last thing was hope. . . . So Mark stopped there."*

That we are reading the Gospel story proves that there was more to the story, more chapters to be written, but it is always worthwhile to pause at the wonder and the terror of the moment of discovering Jesus' resurrection.

* Frederick Buechner, *Peculiar Treasures: A Biblical Who's Who* (New York: Harper and Row, 1979), 112, 113.

September 30

IN THEIR FRIGHT . . .

While they were wondering about this, suddenly two men in clothes that gleamed like lightning stood beside them. In their fright the women bowed down with their faces to the ground, but the men said to them, "Why do you look for the living among the dead? He is not here; he has risen!"

—Luke 24:4–6

Each of the Gospels tells the story of the resurrection of Jesus with different emphases and variations. Different people who visited the empty tomb that Sunday morning had different memories. There were different variations of the interactions with the angel or angels who announced the news, and some of the conversations were reported with differing details.

This kind of variation would be expected from the retold reports across a group of people who had experienced different aspects of the most startling and surprising, terrifying and wonderful thing they could imagine. But the most important details are in agreement across all the different reports: After Jesus had died and was buried the previous Friday afternoon, the tomb was empty by the time the first women got there early on Sunday morning. A number of the male and female disciples of Jesus were witnesses of this and interacted with the angels who were part of the Resurrection scene. Then, quite a few of them actually met and talked with the resurrected, fully alive, fully human Jesus, even on that first Sunday. Despite their sorrow, surprise, fear, resistance to the news, and initial doubts, many knew that Jesus really was alive.

Since that early Sunday morning, many have regarded the Resurrection of Jesus as a mystery to be solved. This was Peter's experience when he went to the tomb and looked over the scene. "He went away, wondering to himself what had happened" (Luke 24:12). But putting all the evidence together, multitudes across the centuries since have concluded that, as impossible as it might seem, the best explanation is that Jesus actually rose from the dead—and that changed everything.

October 1

JESUS HIMSELF

Then Jesus said to them, "Do not be afraid. Go and tell my brothers to go to Galilee; there they will see me."
—Matthew 28:10

As the women hurried from the tomb, perhaps filled with equal parts fear and joy at the incredible news they had to share, Jesus interrupted them. Their unprompted response was to worship, but Jesus seemed to sense their lingering fear and uncertainty. He repeated the angel's "Do not be afraid" with a particular focus on the message they were to deliver, as He repeated the specific message the angel had given them to deliver to the rest of the disciples.

It was one thing for an angel to say to the women, "Do not be afraid," as incredible and world-shaking as that was. But their moment with the resurrected Jesus, still early on that Sunday morning, was on another order of magnitude. And the core of His simple statement to them was this: "Do not be afraid." Do not be afraid of this new and disrupting reality that His resurrection signified. Do not be afraid of their own fears and doubts as they try to make sense of this remarkable thing to which they were now witnesses. Do not be afraid to deliver the message that the angel and Jesus had entrusted to them. Do not be afraid of those who would doubt and scoff in response to that message. Do not be afraid of death because it is now defeated. Do not be afraid of God, who was continuing to work out His plan for relationships, restoration, and re-creation in the world.

As startling and disruptive as His appearances were in themselves, the "Do not be afraid" messages after His resurrection were so much more powerful. The world was changed; the stakes were higher, and the reassurance was all the more certain. Jesus truly was now "the resurrection and the life" (John 11:25). His resurrection changes everything—so do not be afraid.

October 2

ON THE ROAD

"In addition, some of our women amazed us. They went to the tomb early this morning but didn't find his body. They came and told us that they had seen a vision of angels, who said he was alive."
—Luke 24:22, 23

It seems sometimes that faith is more important than revelation. Two disconsolate and confused disciples were heading home, away from Jerusalem. And Jesus took the opportunity to teach them about who He really was and how His death and resurrection actually made sense of everything. "Beginning with Moses and all the Prophets, he explained to them what was said in all the Scriptures concerning himself" (Luke 24:27)—all while they did not know that they were actually walking and talking with Jesus Himself.

They must have been walking slowly when Jesus caught up to them and overheard their conversation, "but they were kept from recognizing him" (Luke 24:16). Feigning ignorance of the events that weighed so heavily upon them and that were the topic of almost every conversation in Jerusalem that weekend, Jesus asked them the questions that led to His walking Bible study.

In response, "they stopped short, sadness written across their faces" (Luke 24:17, NLT). They explained their confusion about the report of the empty tomb, which they obviously did not believe. If they had, why would they have been heading home? They also expressed their shattered hopes in Jesus: "We had hoped that he was the one who was going to redeem Israel" (Luke 24:21). Significantly, they were talking about Jesus in the past tense while Jesus was right there with them.

The Bible study was important, building their understanding of Scripture and the revelation that was yet to come. But it was the simple act of eating together, prompted by these disciples' hospitality, that showed them Jesus (see Luke 24:30, 31). Suddenly, their confusion and fears were gone, their hopes were vindicated, and their faith was all the stronger as they hurried back to Jerusalem to share this incredible news.

October 3

"PEACE BE WITH YOU"

While they were still talking about this, Jesus himself stood among them and said to them, "Peace be with you."

They were startled and frightened, thinking they saw a ghost. He said to them, "Why are you troubled, and why do doubts rise in your minds?"

—Luke 24:36–38

After Jesus disappeared, the two disciples hurried back to Jerusalem to tell the other disciples that they had seen Jesus. As they shared their news, Jesus suddenly was there among them. He gave them a greeting of peace—which initially brought them anything but peace. Still not convinced that Jesus really was alive, they instinctively reacted with fear.

Jesus chided them gently, both with His rhetorical question and also with the assurance that everything had gone exactly as had been planned. At the time when the disciples had been most convinced that their hopes in Jesus had come to nothing and most afraid that a knock on the door would mean that they were about to be arrested, the divine plans were finally accomplished, and the person entering the room was the resurrected Jesus.

They were still not sure what to make of Jesus, so He asked for something to eat and began a Bible study similar to the one He had shared with the two disciples on the road. He concluded with a commission: "You are witnesses of these things" (Luke 24:48). Their role would now be to testify to the story of His resurrection.

Significantly, their fears and doubts would be part of their testimony. They, too, struggled to believe at first. But their fears were replaced with peace, and their doubts faded as they spent time with the resurrected Jesus. He explained to them how "everything must be fulfilled that is written about me in the Law of Moses, the Prophets and the Psalms" (Luke 24:44). Their lives were turned around by the reality of the risen Jesus that they experienced and witnessed. In turn, their story and testimony would begin changing the world.

SOME DOUBTED

When they saw him, they worshiped him; but some doubted.
—Matthew 28:17

It is likely that this took place on top of Mount Arbel, the tallest hill on the western shore of the Sea of Galilee, with a commanding view of the region and across the lake to the "foreign" peoples beyond. This meeting was in response to Jesus' resurrection-morning instruction to His disciples to meet Him at "the mountain where Jesus had told them to go" (Matthew 28:16). So it is notable that Matthew included both responses to Jesus—they worshiped, but some doubted.

The resurrected Jesus was standing in front of them. Many of them would have witnessed His death, so it is hardly surprising that some of them would have questions and much that they did not understand. But this did not exclude them from the story, the invitation, or the commission.

Some doubted—yet we are told about them. The Gospel writer did not need to include this troubling detail in the climactic announcement and conclusion of his story of Jesus. But he did. He understood that it was an important reality to note that faith and doubt are not always incompatible or so far apart.

Some doubted—yet they were invited, and they were there. Neither Matthew nor Jesus felt that the doubts of some members of this crowd of disciples should exclude them from being invited. But it is also interesting that these doubting followers of Jesus did not see this as a reason *not* to be there. They did not know or understand everything about Him—but they showed up anyway.

Some doubted—yet they were commissioned. Again, neither Matthew nor Jesus argued that those who doubted should be excluded or excused from the call to mission that was to come (see Matthew 28:18–20). These followers of Jesus did not need to have all the answers before they could step out and speak up to share what they *did* know about Him.

October 5

EVER PRESENT

"Surely I am with you always, to the very end of the age."
—Matthew 28:20

Jesus gave His disciples a daunting task. He had spent as long as three years with some of them, teaching and training them in the ways of His kingdom, with the ministry and service that were entailed. He had sent them out on practice mission trips (see Matthew 10:5–16). He had assured them that the good news about Him would ultimately be preached to the entire world (see Matthew 24:14). Now He was sending them to all the nations of the world to continue His ministry, to share the good news about Him, and to teach the things He had taught them.

Still coming to terms with His death and resurrection, they now had to consider ministry and mission without Jesus, even venturing into the pagan territories they could see on the other side of the lake from their mountaintop vantage point. This was a big commission, but it also came with big promises.

Jesus bookended this commission with two assurances. First: "All authority in heaven and on earth has been given to me" (Matthew 28:18). The resurrected Jesus rightly claimed all power for Himself. Then He concluded with, "I am with you always, to the very end of the age" (Matthew 28:20). All power, everywhere; all presence, always—to the ends of the earth and to the end of the age. Wherever and whenever you are reading this—this promise includes you.

We are recipients of these promises, of this power, and of His presence. As the story has been told and retold across the centuries and generations and from nation to nation, tribe to tribe, language to language, it has arrived at us. Whether we grew up with these stories as children or are reading them for the first time on this page, these words speak to us. They give us hope and courage, and invite us to share them again in our time and place.

October 6

THINGS WE DON'T KNOW

He said to them: "It is not for you to know the times or dates the Father has set by his own authority."

—Acts 1:7

The disciples were anxious over whether the time had finally come for Jesus to set up His kingdom—or to restore *their* kingdom, as their question really suggested—as have been many generations of His followers since that time. Despite this very clear statement from Jesus, even our Adventist history is punctuated by attempts to know the dates on which specific events in God's plans and promises would take place, beginning with the Great Disappointment. It has been a source of anxiety for those who have wanted to get it right and for so many of those who have gotten it wrong.

Such date-setting has also been used by some preachers to urge people to get ready and get right. Fear can be a powerful motivator, but its effect is often short-lived and requires increasingly larger doses to maintain the impact. Some people will progress beyond fear to a deeper engagement with faith; many more will respond but then move on to the next idea, next story, or next thrill. Some preachers are drawn into a cycle of sensationalism as they seek the next story or prediction that will catch and hold their listeners' attention for as long as possible. It is an unhealthy cycle and a poor tool for the task Jesus gave to His disciples.

Jesus' statement is a way to break the hold and attraction of fear. When Jesus said that we do not know, that it is not ours to know, it lifted the burden from the disciples. Yes, Jesus had given them signs that would act as way markers (see Matthew 24), but more importantly, He had given them a blueprint for living and waiting well (see Matthew 25). Now, He also gave them a specific task—a growing mission to be His witnesses in the world around them—and the power of the Spirit as a healthy guide and motivator.

October 7

TO THE ENDS OF THE EARTH

"But you will receive power when the Holy Spirit comes on you; and you will be my witnesses in Jerusalem, and in all Judea and Samaria, and to the ends of the earth."

—Acts 1:8

It would be fascinating to know what the disciples imagined when they heard Jesus describe their witness as extending "to the ends of the earth." In the Gospel accounts, there were occasional excursions into the neighboring regions to the north and east of Galilee, but even the journey to Jerusalem was a long way for the disciples, who had spent most of their lives around the lake. It is another way in which the disciples' time with Jesus transformed their lives in remarkable ways.

As Jesus had done previously, He walked the disciples through their assignment. It would begin where they were, then include regions in which they had already traveled with Him, and then would ripple out to the next closest places. But He was adamant that their witness would ultimately reach everywhere in the world.

At that time, when they were still preoccupied with the restoration of the kingdom of Israel, it is unlikely that the disciples could have imagined where this task would take them. But later historical tradition has it that, in their lifetimes, some of these disciples traveled as far as Rome, Spain, and even India. And, of course, the mission would grow much further beyond their individual travels and encompass the whole world.

This must have seemed overwhelming, except for the foundational promise and motivation that Jesus gave in the same breath. The Holy Spirit would come upon them and go with them as His witnesses. They need not be daunted or afraid—though it was beyond anything they knew—because they were not and never would be alone. By the Holy Spirit, Jesus would be with them to the end of the age and to the ends of the earth, whenever and wherever they would go.

THEY HAD BEEN WITH JESUS

When they saw the courage of Peter and John and realized that they were unschooled, ordinary men, they were astonished and they took note that these men had been with Jesus.

—Acts 4:13

It is something that all followers of Jesus should aspire to—that other people, perhaps particularly our critics or accusers, should recognize the difference in our lives because we have "been with Jesus." The obvious change in the disciples' lives—including the courage with which they proclaimed the story of Jesus—was an important element of their witness in Jerusalem.

Peter and John had been arrested and spent the night in prison before being called to answer to a council of Jewish leaders. It was an august assembly of "the rulers, elders and teachers of the law" (Acts 4:5), as well as the High Priest and various members of his family. As the disciples took up Jesus' ministry of preaching and healing—including healing a lame man at the temple the previous day—these rulers had a simple question for them: "Who gave you permission to do these things?" (see Acts 4:7).

Always ready to give an answer to such a question and a reason for the hope he had (see 1 Peter 3:15), Peter recapped the story of Jesus and the salvation that He had brought to the world. As individuals who had followed Jesus over the previous few years, the disciples would have been known to many of the Jewish leaders. They knew that Peter and John were Galilean fishermen with little formal education, but they could now also see the boldness with which they addressed the council. Something had changed, and the Jewish leaders recognized that it was the influence of Jesus.

From frightened, up-country fishermen to courageous apostles for Jesus, even in front of the most powerful and learned men in Jerusalem, their transformed lives were their ultimate witness. It was Jesus who had made the difference for Peter and John, and they were ready to tell anyone who would listen.

October 9

A SHIFT OF POWER

Then they called them in again and commanded them not to speak or teach at all in the name of Jesus. But Peter and John replied, "Which is right in God's eyes: to listen to you, or to him? You be the judges! As for us, we cannot help speaking about what we have seen and heard."

—Acts 4:18–20

The esteemed members of the council had a simple yet complex question to answer: "What are we going to do with these men?" (Acts 4:16). They knew they could neither explain nor deny what Peter and John had done in healing the lame man at the temple gate. All of Jerusalem knew about this miracle, and the Jewish leaders were afraid of public backlash if they dealt with the disciples too harshly. As powerful as this group of men was, in light of the reality of Jesus' power and the witness of the disciples, all they could do was ask them to stop, albeit with various threats.

With a courage that undermined the assumed power imbalance between the council and the disciples, Peter and John said no: "We cannot help speaking about what we have seen and heard." Their answer demonstrated the reality that the real power was now in favor of the disciples. The council could warn, threaten, and even begin to persecute the apostles and their new converts, as they soon would, but this new movement was not going to be stopped.

As witnesses of Jesus, the disciples were beginning to fulfill the commission He had given them, and the community of disciples was growing strongly in Jerusalem. This was not a carefully formulated strategy for evangelism but an organic movement that combined the courageous witness of the disciples with the presence and power of the Holy Spirit. This combination was far greater than the power of the Jewish council. Peter and John had made the correct decision about which power to obey, and their enthusiasm for sharing the story of Jesus carried them on.

A PRAYER FOR COURAGE

"Now, Lord, consider their threats and enable your servants to speak your word with great boldness."
—Acts 4:29

Many of us spend much of our prayer lives asking God for protection and safety for ourselves and our families. This is valuable, and it's good that we can entrust ourselves and those we care about to God's care and provision. But a smooth and untroubled journey through life is not guaranteed, and, in Jesus' teaching and the experiences of the early church, we can observe that following Jesus can often be a narrow and rough road (see Matthew 7:14).

It is also interesting to note that safety was not at the top of the prayer list for the early believers in the aftermath of this first arrest of Peter and John. These disciples reported their appearance before the council to the rest of the church, and the gathering became a prayer meeting. But instead of praying for safety and protection, they prayed for courage that despite the warnings and threats from the Jewish leaders, they would be able to continue to preach and teach "with great boldness." Rather than praying for their circumstances to change, they followed Jesus' model (see John 17:15) and prayed for courage and endurance in whatever those circumstances might be.

This was a prayer that God responded to immediately and that the people themselves helped to answer. "After they prayed, the place where they were meeting was shaken. And they were all filled with the Holy Spirit and spoke the word of God boldly" (Acts 4:31).

It is not wrong to pray for God's protection and care. In their prayer, these first disciples did entrust the threats from the Jewish leaders to God. But we should also pray for courage to live and love well, to face our inevitable trials and challenges, and to share the story and power of Jesus in our families, communities, and the wider world.

October 11

AFRAID OF HYPOCRISY

Great fear seized the whole church and all who heard about these events.

—Acts 5:11

We like to idealize the picture of the early Christian church, a community that worshiped God and proclaimed Jesus boldly, cared for one another, shared their possessions, ate together regularly, and grew rapidly (see Acts 4:32–35). So, we are not sure what to do with the story of Ananias and Sapphira, a couple who wanted to appear generous but who succumbed to the temptation to keep some of their intended generosity for themselves. In short, "Ananias and Sapphira practiced fraud in their dealing with God; they lied to the Holy Spirit, and their sin was visited with swift and terrible judgment."*

Despite the surrounding threats and looming persecution, great fear *within* the church seems a jarring contrast to the idyllic picture of the church that we like to assume. Could the Spirit, who had so recently emboldened the believers in their proclamation of Jesus, now be responsible for this couple's sudden deaths? The story does not fully explain why Ananias and Sapphira died, or who or what caused their deaths.

This was the kind of religiosity that Jesus warned against so many times (see, for example, Matthew 6:1–6, Matthew 23:1–36, or Luke 18:9–14). Yet it seems that God's hatred of hypocrisy was still underestimated. God did not want the believers or the surrounding people to be afraid of Him or the Holy Spirit. Rather, they should be afraid of the evil of hypocrisy and how such lies would destroy the church community and everything He wanted the church to become. The witness of these early Christians would be damaged and diminished if their commitment to the community was devalued and undermined. Like Israel before it, the church was to be a new kind of community, and the attitudes and actions that Ananias and Sapphira chose were a threat to this movement right at its beginning.

---

* Ellen G. White, *The Acts of the Apostles* (Mountain View, CA: Pacific Press®, 1911), 72.

REJOICING IN SUFFERING

Peter and the other apostles replied:
"We must obey God rather than human beings!"
—Acts 5:29

Peter and the other apostles were arrested again. It was almost a repeat of the story in the previous chapter—healing and preaching, imprisonment and interrogation by the Jewish council, the Jewish leaders' fear of the people, the responses by the apostles, and the warnings not to continue preaching—but, this time, all the stakes were raised.

On this second occasion, the apostles were miraculously released from prison, then re-arrested the next morning as they were already back, teaching in the temple courts. The anger of the Jewish leaders was clearly rising, but it also seems that the believers' prayers for courage had been answered. Peter explained in simple terms why the apostles could not comply with the council's orders: "We must obey God rather than human beings!"

This time, the apostles were flogged in addition to being ordered not to continue preaching. Tensions were rising, and the responses from the Jewish leaders were becoming more violent, showing the first suggestion of martyrdom. It seems that it was only Gamaliel's wise and careful counsel that staved off more violent persecution for a while longer and allowed the apostles' work and witness to continue to grow. "Day after day, in the temple courts and from house to house, they never stopped teaching and proclaiming the good news that Jesus is the Messiah" (Acts 5:42).

The continuing progress of the gospel was remarkable, but the disciples' immediate response to their warning and beating was perhaps more remarkable. "The apostles left the Sanhedrin, rejoicing because they had been counted worthy of suffering disgrace for the Name" (Acts 5:41). It was a literal fulfillment of what Jesus had taught in Matthew 5:11—"Blessed are you when people insult you, persecute you . . . because of me." Their prayer for courage and boldness was answered in this most immediate way. God was with them and would continue to be with them amid the growing reality of persecution.

October 13

CROSSING THE LINE

While Peter was still thinking about the vision, the Spirit said to him, "Simon, three men are looking for you. So get up and go downstairs. Do not hesitate to go with them, for I have sent them."

—Acts 10:19, 20

In a small back street of Old Jaffa, just to the south of modern Tel Aviv, is a small house that is sign-posted as the traditional site of the home of Simon the Tanner. The rooftop looks out over the Mediterranean Sea and seems an ideal location to get some sun and fresh air and to pray while waiting for a midday meal. This site is a significant marker of the church's growth beyond its Jewish roots.

In the minds of the Jewish people, the line between themselves and the Gentiles was deeply demarcated and should be strongly defended. Even when Jesus first sent out the disciples, He told them not to go to the Gentiles (see Matthew 10:5). But after His resurrection, Jesus told them that they needed to begin to broaden their expectations of who would be included in His kingdom. He told them that after the Holy Spirit came, they would witness for Him beginning in Jerusalem, then Samaria, and beyond. Now, that time had come.

Such was Peter's reluctance that He was given the same vision three times before the men arrived who would invite him to the home of Cornelius, the Roman centurion who was devout in seeking and serving God (see Acts 10:1, 2). As Peter tried to make sense of what he had seen—a sheet from heaven filled with all kinds of animals, reptiles, and birds, including those that were considered "unclean"—the Spirit made it plain: "Get up, go downstairs, and go with them without hesitation. Don't worry, for I have sent them" (Acts 10:20, NLT).

As a first step, "Peter invited the men into the house to be his guests" (Acts 10:23), and the next day, they set out together to nearby Caesarea—and into the future of the church.

FROM EVERY NATION

Then Peter began to speak: "I now realize how true it is that God does not show favoritism but accepts from every nation the one who fears him and does what is right."
—Acts 10:34, 35

Peter had taken some convincing to encourage him to accept the invitation to Cornelius' home. Thankfully, the Holy Spirit had already done the work before the men sent by Cornelius arrived, and Peter was prepared to go with them. But a greater revelation came when he arrived at Cornelius' home and encountered his entire household, as well as extended family and friends.

They shared their stories. Cornelius told Peter his story, including the appearance of the angel three days earlier. Peter responded by again telling the story of the time he had spent with Jesus: "We are witnesses of everything he did in the country of the Jews and in Jerusalem" (Acts 10:39).

While this was a significant experience for Cornelius, and the story recounts how the Holy Spirit then came upon him and his family and that they were then baptized, Peter and his traveling companions were also having a kind of conversion experience of their own. "The circumcised believers who had come with Peter were astonished that the gift of the Holy Spirit had been poured out even on the Gentiles" (Acts 10:45).

Peter recognized that what he was now witnessing was important. This experience of the faithfulness of Cornelius and the work of the Holy Spirit among the Gentiles was stretching the theology that Peter and his companions had grown up with. It was consistent with what Jesus had taught and told them, but this was the first time they had seen the Spirit act in this way. Peter recognized that this was not only about Cornelius and his household but about God's acceptance of those from every nation who would seek Him. Peter's worldview, theology, and understanding of the mission that God had given him was growing rapidly.

October 15

ANSWERING THE CRITICS

"So if God gave them the same gift as he gave us, who believed in the Lord Jesus Christ, who was I to think that I could oppose God?"

—Acts 11:17

After witnessing the Holy Spirit manifested among Cornelius and his household, Peter said, "Surely no one can stand in the way of their being baptized with water" (Acts 10:47). He assumed it was a simple matter. But after spending a few days with them, Peter returned to face criticism from the "circumcised believers" in Jerusalem: "You went into the house of uncircumcised men and ate with them" (Acts 11:3). They were right; Peter had done what they accused him of, and he had to work hard to allay their fears.

Peter did this by recounting his story—from his vision on the rooftop in Joppa to the Holy Spirit's presence among the people. The experience had been challenging for Peter, but it was even more difficult to explain and justify to his critics who were not there. Imagine the deflation that Peter would have felt. He had gone from buzzing about the experience at Caesarea to feeling that he had to defend and explain his actions. We can imagine him praying silently but urgently as he retold his story.

He concluded with the question, "Who was I to think that I could stand in God's way?" The implicit challenge he put to the Jerusalem believers was: "Who are *you* to think *you* can stand in God's way?" They were wrong to criticize what Peter had done, but he probably held his breath as he waited for their response.

"When they heard this, they had no further objections and praised God, saying, 'So then, God has granted even the Gentiles repentance unto life' " (Acts 11:18). It was an important moment for the growing church. Not only had Peter witnessed the Holy Spirit anointing the first Gentile believers, but he was also able to answer his critics in such a way that they all could celebrate this new movement of God together.

THE FIRST PASSOVER AFTER

So Peter was kept in prison, but the church was earnestly praying to God for him.

—Acts 12:5

It seems this might have been an important anniversary for the early church. It was Passover time, possibly the first Passover after the crucifixion of Jesus. Whatever was happening, it would have been a time of memories and reflection. But their remembering was not allowed much time amid the urgency of persecution.

King Herod Agrippa—grandson of the King Herod at the time of Jesus' birth—had a new plan for popularity: arresting and killing Jesus' followers. His first victim was James, the brother of John. Then, just before the Passover celebrations, Peter was arrested and put in prison, giving Herod the opportunity to plan a public trial after the religious festival. Likely remembering Peter's previous escape from prison, the captain of Herod's guards put extra security precautions in place. But the church was praying earnestly.

The night before he was to be brought to trial, Peter was asleep, even though he was chained between two guards and would have been justified in worrying about his trial looming the next morning. An angel appeared in Peter's cell and escorted him out into the street, leaving him to find his way to Mary's house, where members of the church were praying. They were so surprised to see him at the door that he was left there, even as they began to celebrate his release.

We do not know why James was executed but Peter was miraculously rescued. Both were prayed for by the same group of people and just as earnestly. But we do know that even after James was killed, the believers continued to pray for Peter.

One of the first Passovers after Jesus' crucifixion saw the execution of James—and the rescue of Peter. The believers trusted that God was with them in both circumstances.

October 17

TURNING TO THE GENTILES

Then Paul and Barnabas answered them boldly: "We had to speak the word of God to you first. Since you reject it and do not consider yourselves worthy of eternal life, we now turn to the Gentiles."

—Acts 13:46

As Paul and Barnabas set out on their first missionary journey, they were met and resisted by members of the Jewish community in almost every city and town. The apostles went out of their way to include their own people in their proclamation of the story of Jesus, usually beginning in the local synagogue and usually being expelled from the synagogue as the groups of Christian believers grew. It must have been especially difficult for them to face the opposition their message generated among their own people in these foreign cities, as well as risking the threats, abuse, and violence that often resulted from the jealousy of the Jewish leaders.

Despite the resistance, Paul and Barnabas spoke with courage in responding to the recurring rejections. The message they had been entrusted with was important enough to face those risks, and at the same time, the message itself gave them courage. The power of the message was also the reason they would turn their attention to the rest of the city after the Jewish leaders had made their rejection clear. In turn, this would often be a catalyst for the Jewish leaders to increase their efforts to create trouble for Paul and Barnabas.

In Pisidian Antioch, the pattern was repeated. As "the word of the Lord spread through the whole region," the Jewish leaders worked with prominent citizens who "stirred up persecution against Paul and Barnabas, and expelled them from their region" (Acts 13:49, 50). But the conclusion to this story was notable. Rather than being discouraged, frustrated, or afraid as they began walking to the next city, "the disciples were filled with joy and with the Holy Spirit" (Acts 13:52).

THROUGH MANY HARDSHIPS

They preached the gospel in that city and won a large number of disciples. Then they returned to Lystra, Iconium and Antioch, strengthening the disciples and encouraging them to remain true to the faith. "We must go through many hardships to enter the kingdom of God," they said.
—Acts 14:21, 22

It does not sound like the most encouraging message—that the way of the kingdom of God would encounter many hardships—but Paul and Barnabas could not be accused of sugarcoating the experience of following Jesus. They had only just escaped Lystra, where the crowd turned on them, and Paul had been stoned, dragged outside the city, and left for dead. He would have still been nursing those wounds when they arrived in Derbe, "where they preached the gospel . . . and won a large number of disciples." Then they turned around and went right back to Lystra!—and Antioch and Iconium as well, the home towns of the Jewish leaders who had caused them such trouble!

While the message that they were preaching was important, the fact that Paul and Barnabas returned to these cities would have encouraged the new disciples in these places. Their mere presence in each of these places was a demonstration and an example of courage. They did not leave these new converts alone to face the attacks from these same persecutors, and, in risking being there with them, their encouragement to faithfulness was more than words.

Paul and Barnabas also took the opportunity on these return visits to strengthen the church organizationally by appointing local leaders and, "with prayer and fasting, committed them to the Lord, in whom they had put their trust" (Acts 14:23). Seeing the treatment of Paul and Barnabas, these new leaders must have been people of courage, who would continue to encourage their communities of new disciples by their own trust in God and His presence with them. Courage is contagious, particularly when intentionally fostered and founded on the power and promises of God.

October 19

WRESTLING WITH CHANGE

"It is my judgment, therefore, that we should not make it difficult for the Gentiles who are turning to God."

—Acts 15:19

The early success of the apostles' mission—beginning in Jerusalem, then extending throughout Judea and Samaria, and beyond—created theological challenges for the Jewish followers of Jesus. While they had celebrated Peter's encounter with Cornelius and his Gentile household, the reports coming back from Paul and Barnabas clashed with the preaching of some of the Jerusalem-based believers that anyone who wanted to be a true follower of Jesus must first become a Jew.

For many of the disciples who had grown up with the Jewish laws and regulations, imagining a faithful believer apart from these requirements and practices was challenging, perhaps even alarming. God had given these laws to His people centuries earlier as defining elements of their lives and faith, but now it seemed that Peter, Paul, and Barnabas, among others, were ignoring them.

Setting the standard for church councils and committees for centuries to come, the Jerusalem council brought these parties together to seek God's leadership on this church-defining question. From the discussion summarized by James—a leader in the Jerusalem church—it was clear that they had heard the stories from Samaria, Caesarea, and Asia Minor where the work of the Holy Spirit had been seen. But they also studied the Scriptures for insight into what the new direction would mean.

The council concluded that while there were important principles for the new Gentile believers to live by, it was not the place of the apostles or church leaders to get in the way of what God was doing or to discourage these new believers by making it more difficult for them to follow Jesus. The council wrote an open letter to the new Gentile believers and sent it with messengers to these new communities of faith. "The people read it and were glad for its encouraging message" (Acts 15:31).

October 20

SINGING AT MIDNIGHT

About midnight Paul and Silas were praying and singing hymns to God, and the other prisoners were listening to them.

—Acts 16:25

It takes a certain kind of courage to sing hymns at midnight in prison. Paul and Silas had been dragged through the city by a mob, arrested and beaten by the authorities, then imprisoned and placed in stocks, likely designed for maximum discomfort—yet they were singing at midnight. Their faith, joy, and courage were not dependent on their circumstances.

It is significant that Paul and Silas were not merely singing; they were specifically "praying and singing hymns to God." Their focus was on God, not on themselves, not on their circumstances, not on those who might be overhearing. In the poetry of the book of Job, God is described as the one "who gives songs in the night" (Job 35:10). It is God who inspires us with the ability to respond with joy and courage in the midst of difficult circumstances.

We might also observe that other people noticed. The narrative makes it clear that "the other prisoners were listening to them," but so too was the jailer and his family. After an earthquake shook Paul and Silas free, they were able to rescue the jailer from his fear and share the story of Jesus with him and his family. The earthquake would have caught the jailer's attention, but it must have seemed to him that it was a response to the prayer and praise of Paul and Silas.

The next morning, Paul and Silas were released by the embarrassed city officials, but the apostles stopped by Lydia's house on their way out of the city. The encouragement that Paul and Silas left with this small church community would have mattered all the more as they heard the story of how Paul and Silas had responded to their beating and imprisonment, and how God used that circumstance to connect the jailer and his family with the joy that Jesus brings.

October 21

TO THE UNKNOWN GOD

"God did this so that they would seek him and perhaps reach out for him and find him, though he is not far from any one of us."
—Acts 17:27

Even at the height of the Roman Empire, the Greek city of Athens continued to be a significant center of learning, philosophy, and knowledge. "All the Athenians and the foreigners who lived there spent their time doing nothing but talking about and listening to the latest ideas" (Acts 17:21). Indeed, Paul noted that the people of Athens were so religious that they even had an altar to the God they did not yet know (see Acts 17:23).

As Paul appealed to these impulses, he tried to present the dynamic nature of the relationship between the God who had created the world and marked out history and nations but who seemed distant from human beings. This was the broken relationship between God and humanity, adapted to the metaphysical language of the Athenian scholars and philosophers. Paul urged them to believe that their "Unknown God" was not so distant from them and that He could be found in the unlikely story of a teacher from Nazareth whom God had raised to life after He had been unjustly and cruelly executed. Seeking Him would be more productive than developing their "big ideas."

But it was a tough crowd to move beyond their intellectual curiosity and cultural religiosity. "There comes a moment when people who have been dabbling in religion ('Man's search for God!') suddenly draw back. Supposing we really found Him? We never meant it to come to *that*! Worse still, supposing He had found us?"*

Only a few in Athens believed. Some of them sneered at the idea of resurrection; others thought it a good topic for further discussion another day. This was another group of "Adams" who were afraid and hid in the bushes when they heard the sound of His footsteps.

---

* C. S. Lewis, *Miracles* (London: Fount, 1974), 98.

"I AM WITH YOU"

One night the Lord spoke to Paul in a vision: "Do not be afraid; keep on speaking, do not be silent. For I am with you, and no one is going to attack and harm you, because I have many people in this city."
—Acts 18:9, 10

We are tempted to imagine the people in our Bible stories as unwavering in their faith and purpose, always courageous, always joyful—except when they weren't. Paul had his list of trials—stonings and beatings, imprisonment and shipwrecks, robbers and weather (which he told the Corinthians believers about in 2 Corinthians 11:23–27), as well as the burden of almost constant opposition wherever he went sharing the good news about Jesus. As he moved into Corinth for a posting that would last about eighteen months, he had been traveling for some time and found himself immediately under threat again.

So God spoke to Paul in a vision with a simple message: "Do not be afraid." God pointed out that Paul was not alone. God was with him, and despite the initial opposition, there were many people in the city who would welcome his message.

It was one of the recurring reminders and encouragements throughout the Bible to messengers of God in trying circumstances—Moses trying to take on the power of Egypt by himself, Gideon assembling an army, Elijah as he ran for his life into the desert, Elisha's servant seeing the armies that surrounded Dothan, and so many more. One of the assumptions the Bible should lead us to is that there are more people of God than we may see. God is at work beyond our field of vision, and there are always more on our side than against us.

We do not know exactly why God chose to give Paul this special message of encouragement, but we can hear it for ourselves today: "Do not be afraid. I am with you, and there are more people with you than you might think."

October 23

MOTIVATING FEAR

When this became known to the Jews and Greeks living in Ephesus, they were all seized with fear, and the name of the Lord Jesus was held in high honor.

—Acts 19:17

Fear can be an effective motivation for people to make changes in their lives. As such, it has been used by politicians, preachers, and peddlers throughout history. The easiest way to move a crowd or population is to unite them against a common enemy or threat. Fear is never the best motivation, but it can sometimes get people to think in different ways and lead to positive results. We should not be trying to create, stoke, or exploit fear, but when people are fearful, we should be willing to offer comfort and reassurance as we are able.

Paul ministered for about three years in the city of Ephesus. As was his practice, he began at the synagogue, then moved to another location when the opposition grew. He was also doing extraordinary miracles, which seemed to fit with some of the religious expectations in that city.

Noting the success and attention Paul was receiving, others tried to copy his miracle-working exploits and found themselves quickly beaten up by a demon-possessed man. This encounter with spiritual powers caused fear across the community. The people recognized the serious nature of what Paul was talking about and turned to the power of Jesus all the more. "Many of those who believed now came and openly confessed their evil deeds" (Acts 19:18). A group of these new believers brought their books of sorcery and destroyed them, recognizing that they did not want this power in their homes and lives any longer.

This was a breakthrough moment for the message Paul was preaching as it "spread widely and grew in power" (Acts 19:20). Paul had not caused this fear among the community, but by the power he was preaching and demonstrating, he was ready to point the people to Jesus as a source of greater power in their lives.

October 24

LIVING ENCOURAGEMENT

Paul went down, threw himself on the young man and put his arms around him. "Don't be alarmed," he said. "He's alive!"
—Acts 20:10

As Paul embarked on what he expected would be his last journey to Jerusalem, there was a greater urgency to his already keen sense of mission. He revisited many of the churches he had helped establish, encouraging the believers, praying with them, and saying goodbye. In one sense, it must have been gratifying for him to reflect on the progress of the message of Jesus in these cities and across these regions, but it also seems that Paul always had a sense that there was more to do and more to say.

This was his experience on his last night in Troas. Paul had much to say. He talked until midnight, and all that interrupted him was young Eutychus falling asleep and falling to his death from a third-story window. A night that was already emotional had now become a tragedy as the group rushed down the stairs to the street below. Clearing a way through the horrified crowd, Paul took Eutychus in his arms, and returned him alive to his family and church family. It was a "Do not be afraid" message they would never forget.

Paul could have stopped talking at that point. What more was there to say after he had demonstrated the power of resurrection? On the other hand, he had their refocused attention, and he talked until daybreak when he had to leave.

It seems unlikely that Paul would have planned it this way, and we do not know why this death was undone when others in the early church were not. But the effect must have been powerful. "The people took the young man home alive and were greatly comforted" (Acts 20:12). Imagine as they met together each week and Eutychus arrived as a living reminder of the power of God and of the last time they saw Paul and the encouragement he had given them.

October 25

A LAST SERMON

"However, I consider my life worth nothing to me; my only aim is to finish the race and complete the task the Lord Jesus has given me—the task of testifying to the good news of God's grace."

—Acts 20:24

As Paul continued his journey, he had a deadline he was trying to meet in Jerusalem, so he sent a message asking the church leaders in Ephesus to meet him at Miletus, the nearby seaport where Paul's ship was docking. He admitted his uncertainty regarding what he was about to face, but he understood that there were trials ahead. "I only know," he said, "that in every city the Holy Spirit warns me that prison and hardships are facing me" (Acts 20:23). But he expressed his commitment to the mission he had been given, the work he had done, and his determination to be bold with the opportunities that still lay ahead. "I have not hesitated to proclaim to you the whole will of God" (Acts 20:27).

Paul had words of warning and encouragement for the Ephesian believers. Like him, they would experience attacks from without and challenges even from among their own group of believers. But Paul used himself and his ministry as an example, including the courage and commitment he had demonstrated during the three years he had spent in their city when many of those leaders had first become believers.

But their real assurance—both Paul's and what he offered to the Ephesian believers—was not *their* work or courage; rather, it was the grace and goodness of the God he had taught them to serve. "Now I commit you to God and to the word of his grace, which can build you up and give you an inheritance among all those who are sanctified" (Acts 20:32).

As Paul prayed for those leaders, they wept and embraced. It was a scene of tenderness and courage, of gospel comradeship and common humanity, of shared history and an uncertain future, of grief and hope.

October 26

A SPECIAL MESSAGE OF COURAGE

The following night the Lord stood near Paul and said, "Take courage! As you have testified about me in Jerusalem, so you must also testify in Rome."
—Acts 23:11

After Paul was arrested in Jerusalem, he embarked on a series of defenses—or sermons—to a succession of councils, courts, governors, and kings that would take him all the way to the court of Caesar in Rome. But he began with the Sanhedrin in Jerusalem, a group that likely still included members who had trained with Paul when he was a zealous young Pharisee by the name of Saul.

Though he probably followed Jesus' advice, "not to worry beforehand how you will defend yourselves" (Luke 21:14), Paul also drew on his years of education and his understanding of the various groups that made up this council. With a few well-chosen words, he reduced this esteemed council to confusion, dispute, and violent uproar. Those who were applauding Paul's provocation argued for more than they knew when they suggested in his defense, "What if a spirit or an angel has spoken to him?" (Acts 23:9).

In contrast to the confusion of the day, that night, Paul received a message of assurance that set out his path and urged him to have courage for the testimony he would have the opportunity to give before rulers and courts from Caesarea to Rome. This would be a unique phase of his ministry—testifying to the story of Jesus in a variety of unusual and powerful contexts, as well as writing many of his letters to the churches and people he had worked with in his earlier journeys.

But the messenger was not merely a spirit or an angel; Jesus Himself delivered this encouragement to Paul. The same Jesus he had met on the road to Damascus now directed him on his final journey to Rome. As had Paul's journeys to date, this next journey would require courage, but he had the assurance that Jesus would be with him all the way.

October 27

INCONVENIENT TRUTH

As Paul talked about righteousness, self-control and the judgment to come, Felix was afraid and said, "That's enough for now! You may leave. When I find it convenient, I will send for you."
—Acts 24:25

Sometimes, fear will prompt people to re-examine their lives and turn to God. This happened in Ephesus after dangerous encounters with evil spirits (see Acts 19:11–20). But sometimes fear causes people to pull back and avoid the gospel invitation. Such was Felix's response to Paul's testimony.

Felix was procurator of Judea for most of the decade of the 50s A.D. Historians of his time regarded him as a cruel and ruthless ruler. Perhaps this is why Paul "talked about righteousness, self-control and the judgment to come"—and why these topics caused Felix such discomfort, prompting him to put off Paul's appeal to a more "convenient" time. Felix's fear was the working of his conscience and his opportunity to repent, to choose a different ending to his story.

However, Felix was a successor to Pilate as procurator of Judea, and he seems to have shared his predecessor's hesitation (read, fear) to make a courageous decision, even though they each recognized the baseless nature of the respective cases against Jesus and Paul. Throughout his involvement with Paul's case, Felix tried to keep everyone happy. He seemed to want to befriend Paul—talking with him frequently and hoping for a bribe to secure his release (see Acts 24:26)—and to pander to his Jewish accusers at the same time, particularly by leaving Paul in prison when he himself was recalled to Rome.

Fear wrote Felix out of history, with nothing more known about him after he left Paul in prison in Caesarea. But more importantly, it left him unchanged, afraid of who he was, afraid to choose differently, and perpetually putting off the inconvenience of the gospel.

October 28

EXCEPT FOR THESE CHAINS

Paul replied, "Short time or long—I pray to God that not only you but all who are listening to me today may become what I am, except for these chains."

—Acts 26:29

Festus' courtroom had been set up for King Agrippa and Bernice, who arrived "with great pomp and entered the audience room with the high-ranking military officers and the prominent men of the city" (Acts 25:23). Agrippa was another Herodian king, great-grandson of Herod the Great. Like his predecessors, he was appointed and supported by the Roman authorities because of his loyalty to them. But what he lacked in real power, he made up for with pomp and pretension.

Amid all these important people, Paul was brought out as a prisoner in chains but proceeded to hold the attention of the room as he retold the story of Jesus and of his own encounter with Him on the road to Damascus. Festus was looking for advice from Agrippa about how to explain Paul's case to Caesar. But Paul focused on the king and his knowledge of Jesus and the movement that had grown after His resurrection. Paul said, "The king is familiar with these things, and I can speak freely to him. I am convinced that none of this has escaped his notice, because it was not done in a corner" (Acts 26:26).

Despite the apparent power dynamics, Festus and Agrippa broke first; their discomfort led them to ridicule Paul and his assertions. Agrippa rejected Paul's appeal to his Jewish understanding, expressing doubt that Paul could persuade him so easily.

Belying the important people, pomp, and power surrounding him, Paul shifted the dynamic in the room. He insisted that except for the chains he was required to wear, he would prefer to be the prisoner with a story of Jesus than to be any of the rich and powerful people who did not have such a story. It was a powerful testimony—one that sent the powerful people scurrying from the room.

October 29

AMID THE STORM

"Last night an angel of the God to whom I belong and whom I serve stood beside me and said, "Do not be afraid, Paul. You must stand trial before Caesar; and God has graciously given you the lives of all who sail with you."

—Acts 27:23, 24

Amid the storm, a seemingly unnecessary additional peril on Paul's journey to Rome as a prisoner destined to appear in the court of Caesar, an angel not only spoke to Paul but "stood beside" him. God gave Paul a "Do not be afraid" that he could share with the rest of the passengers and crew on that stricken ship, which had been at the mercy of the wind and waves for days by that time. "So keep up your courage, men, for I have faith in God that it will happen just as he told me" (Acts 27:25).

Paul told them that the ship would be lost but that they would all survive, particularly if they stayed together. With that reassurance from God, Paul became a leader of the ship, advising the captain and coaching everyone on board through their ordeal. His was a voice of comfort and courage, as well as a voice of experience. In 2 Corinthians 11:25, he reported that he had been shipwrecked on at least two other occasions. As he stood in front of the passengers and crew of this ship, he had stories to tell about how God had been with him in similar situations in the past. The risk and rescue that were part of his mission experiences were a source of hope for those traveling with him.

For Paul, this was also a reminder that after the storm had passed and they were rescued from the shipwreck, the angel who stood beside him would also be standing beside him when they arrived in Rome, when he spoke at his trial before Caesar, and when he faced whatever would result from that. God was with him—and all who sailed with Him.

October 30

WITH ALL BOLDNESS

For two whole years Paul stayed there in his own rented house and welcomed all who came to see him. He proclaimed the kingdom of God and taught about the Lord Jesus Christ—with all boldness and without hindrance!"

—Acts 28:30, 31

To some readers, the book of Acts might seem to have an anticlimactic ending. We have a single picture of Paul under house arrest in Rome but continuing to preach and write and "boldly proclaiming the Kingdom of God and teaching about the Lord Jesus Christ. And no one tried to stop him" (Acts 28:31, NLT). And then the picture simply fades to black. Yet this picture represented the gospel going "to the ends of the earth"—as Jesus had predicted (Acts 1:8). This was Paul in the capital of the then-known world. And the good news about Jesus was continuing to spread without hindrance.

This picture also presents believers and churches continuing to boldly proclaim the kingdom in Jerusalem and Samaria, in Antioch and Cyprus, in Philippi, Corinth, and Ephesus, and in places as far away as Ethiopia, Iran, and India. The good news of the kingdom of God truly had spread to the ends of the earth within the first generation of the church.

However, in another sense, the story remains incomplete even today. The ending of the book of Acts begs for another chapter—and another and still another until we reach today, until the gospel of the kingdom reaches your nation, your city, town or village, your family, until it reaches you and your encounter with the resurrected Jesus, who transformed the disciples and Paul and countless others throughout the Christian story.

There was a boldness and courage in Paul's continuing proclamation of the good news about Jesus, even as he drew near the end of his life. That boldness has continued wherever and whenever the story has been proclaimed since. There is boldness and courage when we share it today.

October 31

THE MINISTRY OF ENCOURAGEMENT

"I long to see you so that I may impart to you some spiritual gift to make you strong—that is, that you and I may be mutually encouraged by each other's faith."

—Romans 1:11, 12

Wherever you were across the Roman Empire at the time of Paul's ministry, it took courage to be a follower of Jesus. Throughout the history of the Christian faith, it has taken courage to follow Jesus, just as it does today. But such courage does not come by locking ourselves away to muster moments of courage from our own limited emotional and spiritual resources. Rather, one of the key reasons for participating in a community of faith is to create and share a collective courage, acknowledging our many fears and uncertainties while borrowing from the faith, hope, experience, and wisdom of fellow believers.

As the body of Christ, the church should be a community of courage. Paul regularly urged the early Christians to encourage—literally, "to inspire with courage"—one another. Encouragement was a recurring theme of his ministry and his many letters. Perhaps it would be more accurate to say that, second only to the proclamation of the story of Jesus, encouragement was the reason for his ministry and letters.

But courage is not based merely on a collective resource of courage. Our true courage is built on God and His goodness. This was the core message that Paul wanted to share with the believers he was concerned about. In relationship with and knowledge of this God, we find courage to live with our fears and doubts, to confront the wrong around us, and to live with thoughtfulness and love, whatever our circumstances. After all, He is the God who is almost always cued onto the stage of history, our lives, and our world with a "Don't be afraid" directed to His people. This was the same God that Paul preached, who had now become part of our human history in the person and presence of Jesus.

November 1

A NEW AND RECONCILED RELATIONSHIP

"Therefore, since we have been justified through faith, we have peace with God through our Lord Jesus Christ . . .

Not only is this so, but we also boast in God through our Lord Jesus Christ, through whom we have now received reconciliation."

—Romans 5:1, 11

At times, Paul's theology is dense. Before he was a pioneering missionary, he was a theological scholar trained by some of the best rabbis of his day. So his theological earnestness was more than zeal; he was also deeply informed. Between his conversion and the missionary journeys that make up much of the story of Acts, he spent time—perhaps about twelve years, including time spent in the Arabian desert and in his hometown of Tarsus—studying into the story of Jesus and how He fulfilled the expectations of the Hebrew scriptures as well as the deepest human needs. We see the results of that study in his letters to the churches, which tend to have a more scholarly tone than the sermons recorded in Acts.

One of the key themes of Paul's writing was the relationship between God and humanity. Paul believed that God was working, through Jesus, to restore the relationship that had been broken by sin, stretching all the way back to the Garden of Eden. Paul uses the language of peacemaking and reconciliation, recognizing both the fear and distance that had been introduced into humanity's relationship with our Creator and the work of renewal that was underway.

This was the experience that Paul was so passionate about inviting everyone to enter. The life, death, and resurrection of Jesus offered a fresh start for humanity, whether Jew or Gentile—particularly in their relationship with God. "So now we can rejoice in our wonderful new relationship with God because our Lord Jesus Christ has made us friends of God" (Romans 5:11, NLT). This was something to be studied, celebrated, and shared.

November 2

WHAT GOD DID

Therefore, there is now no condemnation for those who are in Christ Jesus, because through Christ Jesus the law of the Spirit who gives life has set you free from the law of sin and death.

—Romans 8:1, 2

As Jesus explained to Nicodemus, His was a mission of salvation, not condemnation (see John 3:17). This was a theme that Paul expanded on in his letters. The concepts and language can seem complicated, but the key is to remember that Paul was always talking about what "God did by sending his own Son" (Romans 8:3).

While Paul's arguments were about making sense of what God had done in Jesus, his case was built on the experiences with Jesus that he and his fellow apostles were testifying to. "Knowledge of revelation does not always begin with clarity. . . . But under all circumstances, it begins with certitude. Either God has spoken or He has not spoken. If He has spoken, He has done so in such a manner that it is impossible not to heed Him. . . . Doubt and despair, human unbelief, and even a sea of uncertainties on our behalf will not be able to change the certitude of His presence."*

If Jesus was who He claimed to be and who the apostles believed Him to be, we can then believe what He said about God's love for us and our world, the new relationship we can have with God, and our freedom from sin and death as the ultimate powers in our lives. Our relationship with God is no longer one of fear, and our common human experiences of fear, doubt, and uncertainty do not reflect or affect this new relational reality. This was the certitude with which Paul lived and that he wanted to share with the new believers to whom he was writing.

---

* Karl Barth, *God in Action* (Eugene, OR: Wipf & Stock Publishing, 2005), 8.

November 3

WHAT THIS VERSE DOESN'T SAY

We know that in all things God works for the good of those who love him, who have been called according to his purpose.
—Romans 8:28

Romans 8:28 is a longtime favorite memory verse—but one that has often been mistranslated, misread, and misused.

This verse does not promise that everything goes smoothly for followers of Jesus. The tragic experiences of most of the apostles and many faithful believers should demonstrate this clearly. This verse does not promise that God works out everything for the best, even if things might seem a little difficult for a while. This verse does not say that God causes or sends suffering for our good or for purposes that only He understands, so we have to just trust grimly.

This verse does not say that tragedy, sorrow, and disappointments do not matter or that true believers can merely shrug their shoulders at suffering. This verse does not argue that tragedies and suffering make sense somehow or that multiple evils somehow add up to a greater good in our lives. This verse does not promise—or demand—that we will never be afraid of the bad things that will happen to all of us and those we love over the course of our lives.

What Romans 8:28 does say is that even on the worst day of our life, God is with us. Even amid troubles, trials, and tragedies, God is always with us by His Spirit. While all the circumstances around us, and even within us, might be pushing us the other way, God is working with us and for our good. And in His love, grace, and power, He can salvage and redeem something even from our most difficult experiences—something that we may be able to look back on as a blessing from some future vantage point. Despite its various misreadings, Romans 8:28 remains a remarkable promise and a worthwhile memory verse.

November 4

WHAT GOD HAS PROVIDED

What, then, shall we say in response to these things? If God is for us, who can be against us? He who did not spare his own Son, but gave him up for us all—how will he not also, along with him, graciously give us all things?
—Romans 8:31, 32

Many of us tend to divide our lives into different segments. It might be sacred and secular, church and community, our spiritual lives and our physical lives, or our faith and work. Jesus, Paul, and other Bible writers argued against this way of thinking. In their understanding of life and faith, God's provision for our salvation is not disconnected from His provision for all that pertains to life. As Paul put it, if God has given us Jesus, what won't He also graciously give us?

In a sense, Paul was echoing what Jesus taught: "Seek first his kingdom and his righteousness, and all these things will be given to you as well" (Matthew 6:33). But Paul expanded on our understanding of God's graciousness. In Paul's understanding and experience, God's provision is always at God's initiative. "God demonstrates his own love for us in this: While we were still sinners, Christ died for us" (Romans 5:8). And that same abundance applies to all aspects of our lives.

For Paul, salvation was not mere theory or theology. God's power and presence had transformed all of his life. Yes, he had experienced a dramatic conversion, and he had found salvation and forgiveness in Jesus, but he had also learned to trust God in all things. This was the experience and trust that he wanted for the believers to whom he was writing. Life and salvation are not segmented. When following Jesus means risking your life or otherwise radically transforming life and all its priorities, this is not a distinction that believers can afford. Salvation in Jesus must be life, life-giving, and life-sustaining.

November 5

THE REACH OF GOD'S LOVE

For I am convinced that neither death nor life, neither angels nor demons, neither the present nor the future, nor any powers, neither height nor depth, nor anything else in all creation, will be able to separate us from the love of God that is in Christ Jesus our Lord.
—Romans 8:38, 39

Paul began with rhetorical questions: "Who shall separate us from the love of Christ? Shall trouble or hardship or persecution or famine or nakedness or danger or sword?" (Romans 8:35). He could have added another: Shall any of those things that make us afraid—or even fear itself—separate us from God's love?

No matter how we might rephrase or recast these questions to reflect our particular circumstances, challenges, troubles, or fears, the answer will always be the same.—No! Nothing will ever separate us from God's love. In Jesus, who was, and always is, God with us, the answer is always no; nothing can separate us from His love.

This was one of my father's favorite Bible verses and one of his favorite sermons to preach as a long-serving pastor. It is now inscribed on his grave marker. Whenever we visit there—or whenever anyone else passes by and notices—it reminds us that even in the seeming finality, separation, and silence of death, my father is still not beyond God's love. It also reminds us that we, in our grief and amid the challenges of our ongoing lives, are also never beyond the reach of that same love.

Placing this verse on my father's grave was an act of faith and hope, a statement that we trust in the truth of Paul's assertion and the promises God has given us. It was also an act of witness—perhaps someone mourning their loved one might see this brief reminder of God's love and be encouraged, or perhaps curious. It is the one thing my father, Paul, and God would want them to know: nothing can separate them from His love.

November 6

THINK DIFFERENTLY

"Do not conform any longer to the pattern of this world, but be transformed by the renewing of your mind. Then you will be able to test and approve what God's will is—his good, pleasing and perfect will."
—Romans 12:2

Many voices in our world urge us to prioritize self-interest and self-preservation—or greed and fear—as our primary ways of thinking and responding to the world around us. These are the core appeals of most advertising and much of the entertainment offerings. Some elements of these are found in almost all political campaigns and even in some church evangelism and media. These motivations do not need much fostering, as they are embedded in us by instinct and reinforced by the assumptions and insistence of the cultures around us.

It is hardly surprising that one of the repeated messages of the Bible challenges these human instincts and cultural values—"Think differently." The power that these influences have on us is such that we need to practice this counsel, meaning that we need to do it repeatedly for the purpose of getting better at it. We must invite the Holy Spirit to change our hearts and minds, but we also must train ourselves by intentionally choosing to think differently, even when that is not our initial response to a fear or challenge that we confront.

One important component of this intentionality is spending time with the Bible, learning the words, ways, and will of God, and embedding them in our minds. For so many believers throughout history, this has been a transformative practice of faith, a source of comfort and reassurance in whatever circumstances they face. "If God's word were studied as it should be, men [and women] would have a breadth of mind, a nobility of character, and a stability of purpose rarely seen in these times."*

Thinking differently, faithfully, and courageously does not happen accidentally. So, let's begin practicing today, renewing our minds and seeking God's will.

---

* Ellen G. White, *Steps to Christ* (Mountain View, CA: Pacific Press®, 1892), 90.

November 7

GROWING TOGETHER

We have different gifts, according to the grace given to each of us. If your gift is prophesying, then prophesy in accordance with your faith; if it is serving, then serve; if it is teaching, then teach; if it is to encourage, then give encouragement; if it is giving, then give generously; if it is to lead, do it diligently; if it is to show mercy, do it cheerfully.

—Romans 12:6–8

One of the keys to reading Paul's letters is to remember that most of them were written not to individuals but to churches. Most of his uses of the word, *you,* were plural, meaning that his instructions, admonitions, greetings, and blessings were directed to groups of believers. (This is more apparent in the Greek language in which Paul wrote than it is in English.) A number of times in his letters, Paul gave extended descriptions of the church as the body of Christ with different parts that work together and complement each other's unique roles. "Just as each of us has one body with many members, and these members do not all have the same function, so in Christ we, though many, form one body, and each member belongs to all the others" (Romans 12:4, 5).

Such an extensive and diverse list of gifts should remind us that no one member has to do it all. We all have a role to play, but we do not have to play all the roles—or assume that we should. We should not be afraid to serve according to the gifts and opportunities we are given, but neither should we be afraid to avoid being overburdened.

One of the gifts that Paul included on this list is encouragement. It could be argued that all the other gifts are ways in which we can encourage each other, but encouragement was also recognized as a role in itself and one of the vital ways in which we practice our faith together.

So, if your gift is to encourage, then give encouragement.

November 8

MAKING PEACE

If it is possible, as far as it depends on you,
live at peace with everyone.

—Romans 12:18

Not only is the relationship between God and humanity broken, but many of our relationships with each other—between people and people groups—are also broken or damaged. We have a deep-seated fear and suspicion of people who seem different. There are even those who seek to emphasize or exacerbate those fears as a way of building a particular group identity, often for political advantage. But our relationships within our families and in our communities are also not always as they should be. Instead, they often cause suffering and fear. The faithful response to this human reality is to seek to build better relationships in all aspects of our lives, families, communities, and the wider world.

At its most intentional, we would talk about this as the call to peacemaking. Jesus taught His disciples, "Blessed are the peacemakers, for they will be called children of God" (Matthew 5:9). We are to be agents of healing in the broken relationships around us. In some instances, this requires specialized skills and training, but ordinarily, this is something that each of us can contribute to in our personal interactions, committing to using our attention, time, influence, and resources to listen, learn, and understand.

Jesus also said that different responses to Him and His message would cause division (see, for example, Luke 12:51–53), and Paul pointed out that we do not choose how other people react to us. He added provisos to his instruction about living at peace with everyone—"if it is possible" and "as far as it depends on you." We cannot force people into living peaceably, but we can work for peace nonetheless. We begin by being first to disarm, surrendering our instincts of fear and revenge, seeking to forgive, and "overcome evil with good" (Romans 12:21).

OVERFLOWING WITH HOPE

May the God of hope fill you with all joy and peace as you trust in him, so that you may overflow with hope by the power of the Holy Spirit.
—Romans 15:13

Hope is one of those words that needs a better, stronger definition. Too often, the way we think and talk about hope feels like wishful thinking or perhaps a remote possibility, as desirable as it might be. But hope is so much more than that. Hope is not feeling vaguely positive about the future; instead, the practice of hope is the present reality of living in the light of what we believe matters most and what we know will endure into God's future, whatever our present circumstances might be.

As such, hope is a Christian imperative: "It has been well said that a true Christian should have but one fear—lest he [or she] should not hope enough."* In fact, Paul went so far as to suggest that followers of Jesus should "overflow with hope."

For Paul, God was the "God of hope" who fills us with joy and peace as we put our trust in Him. Such confidence in God comes with the power and presence of the Holy Spirit. It was a remarkable message for the Christians in Rome, a place in which being a believer would have felt particularly precarious with the ever-looming threat of persecution.

As people who follow a God of hope, we have good reason for hope. But we can also have hope amid the circumstances and in contradiction of the evidence around us when we might not see or feel the possibilities for hope. At those times, practicing hope is how we trust. And that is the source of all joy and peace.

* Walter Elliot, *The Spiritual Life*, 2nd ed. (New York: The Paulist Press, 1918), 144.

November 10

WHAT WE DON'T KNOW

Those who think they know something do not yet know as they ought to know.

—1 Corinthians 8:2

The humility to admit that we do not know it all, that we do not have all the answers, requires a certain kind of courage. "While knowledge may make us feel important," Paul wrote, "it is love that really builds up the church. Anyone who claims to know all the answers doesn't really know very much" (1 Corinthians 8:1, 2, NLT).

To some, this might seem a denial of certainty and hope. But even Paul, for all his learning and insight, admitted his limitations—and his hope. "For now we see only a reflection as in a mirror; then we shall see face to face" (1 Corinthians 13:12).

To be able to admit, "I don't know"—or, at least, "I don't know it all"—means we do not have to force our limited knowledge and understandings to answer questions much larger than those for which they are fitted. It is an expression of intellectual, faith-filled honesty and humility that opens us to fresh possibilities of learning and living.

As Paul suggested, the more we learn, the more we discover we don't know. But this should not be grounds for loss of faith, or discouragement or despair. The awesome vastness and wonder of the word, world, and ways of God are our greatest evidence of who we believe Him to be. A God merely like us, understandable by us, managed by us, is ultimately of little use to us. Instead of roadblocks to faith, the challenges of explaining God and His ways are the starting points for wonder, worship, and further exploration.

So, do not be afraid to not know it all, urged Paul. "Now I know in part; then I shall know fully, even as I am fully known" (1 Corinthians 13:12).

TRUE LOVE

Love does not delight in evil but rejoices with the truth. It always protects, always trusts, always hopes, always perseveres.
—1 Corinthians 13:6, 7

It seems everyone believes in love; we are just not quite sure what it means. Love is one of those good ideas that is often treated as fragile and ephemeral in much of how it is talked about or described. But this is not the understanding of love described by Paul in 1 Corinthians 13, renowned as the Bible's great chapter on love. Partly because such love is not so much an idea but an attitude, an action, and an intentional choice, this love is bold and enduring. "Love never gives up, never loses faith, is always hopeful, and endures through every circumstance" (1 Corinthians 13:7, NLT).

The love that Paul described is the bridge that crosses the broken relationships that mar our humanity and begins to heal those wounds. While based firmly on the love of God, it is larger than any and all of our religiosity (see 1 Corinthians 13:1–3) and is not dependent on our contexts or circumstances. Of course, our human love will not be perfect or complete, but it will bring out the best that we are able to be. It is our "most excellent way" (1 Corinthians 12:31).

True love is courageous. In reclaiming the word *love* and seeking to give it a stronger meaning, we might try to live in a way that refuses to give up on or lose faith in those we love, that practices hope, and seeks the good of those we love no matter the circumstances. Such love has no room for fear because "love never fails" (1 Corinthians 13:8).

When some people feel let down or disappointed by love, their hurt proves that what they call love is only imperfect love or something less. It could not be love because "love never fails." When founded on the extravagant love of God, there is nothing stronger or safer than love.

November 12

DARING TRUTH

If Christ has not been raised, our preaching is useless and so is your faith.

—1 Corinthians 15:14

Paul seems to be raising the stakes. He sums up the faith of Jesus' followers as hanging on a single historical event. All our preaching and faith is useless, he urged, if Jesus has not been raised from the dead. And if Jesus has not been raised from the dead, nothing matters beyond this life. "If only for this life we have hope in Christ, we are of all people most to be pitied" (1 Corinthians 15:19). To put all the emphasis on this single claim feels daring.

But Paul was not arguing that our preaching and faith are useless, nor that followers of Jesus are the most pitiful people in the world. He had already presented the remarkable evidence for the truth of the resurrection of Jesus. After His resurrection, Jesus was seen by progressively larger groups of disciples, including appearing "to more than five hundred of the brothers and sisters at the same time, most of whom are still living" at the time of writing (1 Corinthians 15:6).

The point that Paul was making in these bold and dramatic statements was that the resurrection of Jesus was the single most important fact of their faith. He made this argument after presenting his list of witnesses, many of whom his first readers might have met or could track down. It was not an obscure theory but something that had happened in the real-life experience of a significant number of the earliest believers in Jesus.

So, the stakes had already been raised. The hundreds of witnesses to Jesus and His resurrection gave ample evidence that the scenarios Paul was detailing were not a cause for fear but a cause for celebration. Because Jesus has been raised from the dead, our preaching and our faith change everything. And because our faith gives us hope in this resurrected Christ, we are blessed beyond all imagining.

THE LAST ENEMY

The last enemy to be destroyed is death.
—1 Corinthians 15:26

Fear of death is one of the most common of human fears. While some try to argue that death is just a natural part of life, there is something in us that innately recoils from death. When it takes our loved ones from us, when it threatens us in some way, death is again revealed as unnatural, something that should not be part of our human experience.

Here is the Bible's understanding of death. Death is evil in itself, as well as being the result of evil. It is an enemy to be resisted. But it is also already an enemy that has been defeated. Paul's extended reflection on death was introduced by the assurance of its defeat. Because Jesus was raised from the dead, death would no longer be all-powerful. As fearsome as it remained, it was no longer a reality to be surrendered to with a "Let us eat and drink, for tomorrow we die" attitude (1 Corinthians 15:32). Nor was it be feared in quite the same way it might have been in the past.

Of course, death still hurts terribly when it strikes those close to us. And the prospect of our own death is daunting. But by faith and with courage, we are able to look forward to when Jesus' victory over death will be made complete, and we can truly sing, "Where, O death, is your victory? Where, O death, is your sting?" (1 Corinthians 15:55).

Death is the source of so much of our human fears and frailty, but Jesus' defeat of death transforms our attitude to life and the choices we live by. We need not be afraid for our lives because we can trust Him with them, even beyond the tragic but temporary reality of death. When death can be undone, its power, and its power to make us afraid, are already diminished and doomed to final defeat.

November 14

RESURRECTION CHANGES EVERYTHING

Therefore, my dear brothers and sisters, stand firm. Let nothing move you. Always give yourselves fully to the work of the Lord, because you know that your labor in the Lord is not in vain.

—1 Corinthians 15:58

First Corinthians 15 is one of the Bible's great theological passages, and it is bookended with history, experience, and life. As we have seen, Paul began the chapter with a catalog of the groups of people, most of them still alive and contactable at the time of writing, who were witnesses to the resurrected reality of Jesus. They had talked with Him, eaten with Him, and listened to Him talk after His death and resurrection. They knew the story was true and were prepared to testify to it, even at the risk of their lives.

Then Paul concluded his argument with a surprisingly practical real-world application. Because of the defeat of death and its promised eradication, followers of Jesus—including those who were witnesses to His resurrection—will be people who resist the fear of death and its effects on the world around us. They will celebrate life and all that affirms and adds to its goodness—and they will be determined and steadfast in doing so.

The followers of Jesus today will insist that fear and death are never the most powerful things we confront or the most important factors to be taken into account. But this is not only a theological assertion; it is a way of living with hope and confidence that actually changes things in the world around us. "Always work enthusiastically for the Lord, for you know that nothing you do for the Lord is ever useless" (1 Corinthians 15:58, NLT).

Because of Jesus' resurrection, everything matters. What we do to serve Him and others is part of a much larger rejection of death and fear and will have the final say in the story of our world, so it should have a greater influence on the realities of our lives today.

November 15

SIGNING OFF

Be on your guard; stand firm in the faith;
be courageous; be strong. Do everything in love.
—1 Corinthians 16:13, 14

The last chapters of many of Paul's letters are interesting reading. They often include lists of people and individual greetings for believers in various households and church groups. In this way, they give us insights into the personal relationships that Paul had with the leaders and members of these diverse church groups. He would often set out his plans for further travel and give details of who was with him, as well as brief reports and reminiscences.

But Paul's closing remarks, blessings, and greetings also included some of his pithiest instructions, reflecting his desire for the believers he was addressing to live and love well. The combination of commands at the end of his first letter to the Corinthians is a good example of his seemingly hurried enthusiasm to get in just a few more words of encouragement as he prepared to sign off this letter.

It feels like Paul was trying to drive home a point, like the repeated blows of a hammer, saying almost the same thing in a variety of punchy statements. He could have been reciting his own motto for life and mission: "Be on your guard; stand firm in the faith; be courageous; be strong." In Paul's experience, faith was a call to action, a blueprint for bold living and loud proclamation. This was what he wanted for those he had brought to faith, and it was what he knew they needed in order to be able to sustain their faith amid the culture and context in which they lived.

But this bold and fearless faith was not to be cold or unfeeling. Their faithfulness was to be both motivated and transformed by love. As Paul described it in chapter 13 of this letter, love has strength and endurance, but there is also a necessary tempering that comes with doing "everything in love."

November 16

TRANSFORMING HOPE

Therefore, since we have such a hope, we are very bold.
—2 Corinthians 3:12

Paul's life and mission were transformed by his confrontation with Jesus on the road to Damascus. His story was narrated by Luke in Acts chapter 9, then re-told twice more in Acts as Paul shared his testimony with courts and rulers. Snippets of his story also appeared from time to time in his letters.

But his experience with Jesus was more than that one-off encounter. He had been committed beyond the point of violence to defending the faith as he had understood it. He had been driven by fear of this strange story of Jesus and the threat it posed to his faith and his nation. Perhaps he also claimed that he was seeking to correct those who had been deceived and bring them back to the true faith. After his dramatic conversion, he spent years re-studying the Hebrew scriptures, finding and fitting Jesus into the Pharisee's training that had been such a part of his former life.

Beyond the glory Moses had encountered and even reflected at the beginnings of the Israelite nation, Paul had now discovered a greater glory. While the glory reflected in Moses was temporary and even then had to be veiled to avoid alarming the people he was leading, Paul showed that a greater revelation of God's glory had been unveiled in Jesus. He argued, "Whenever anyone turns to the Lord, the veil is taken away" (2 Corinthians 3:16).

For Paul—and for all believers in Jesus—this is transformative. We "are being transformed into his likeness with ever-increasing glory" (2 Corinthians 3:17). And this transformational experience is the foundation for hope, which is, in turn, the foundation for boldness. Paul's encounter with Jesus changed the way he believed, thought, and lived in the world. And because of that, it also changed the world around him and everyone he met.

AN ETERNAL PERSPECTIVE

Therefore we are always confident and know that as long as we are at home in the body we are away from the Lord. We live by faith, not by sight.
—2 Corinthians 5:6, 7

What gave Paul such confidence? What motivated him to live such a life of risk, discomfort, and danger? What allowed him to speak boldly before angry mobs, skeptical rulers, and foreign scholars? What allowed him to be so certain of what he could not see?

Paul believed in God's plan, which he could see working out in the life of Jesus and His resurrection, in the testimony and growth of the church, and in the progress of the gospel across the world as he knew it. He saw lives changed by this message, not least of which was his own. And he believed in the promises of God, "who has given us the Spirit as a deposit, guaranteeing what is to come" (2 Corinthians 5:5). By His presence, the Spirit infused a present reality of the coming kingdom into the lives of believers—and, Paul urged, was his foundation for being "always confident."

This is not to say that Paul never had moments of uncertainty, fear, or doubt. From his dramatic conversion to his earliest ministry, from travels across Asia Minor, and his final journey to Rome, Paul seemed perpetually at risk. "I have faced danger from my own people, the Jews, as well as from the Gentiles. I have faced danger in the cities, in the deserts, and on the seas" (2 Corinthians 11:26, NLT). But these were not the determining or driving experiences of his life. His life always demonstrated a larger confidence.

Such was the dominance of his confidence and the realities on which it had grown that he literally and figuratively staked his life on it. Less about Paul himself, his confidence was primarily a testimony to the reality of the God he served and the Jesus he preached.

November 18

AMBASSADORS OF RECONCILIATION

We are therefore Christ's ambassadors, as though God were making his appeal through us. We implore you on Christ's behalf: Be reconciled to God.

—2 Corinthians 5:20

As we have seen, the big story of the Bible is God's plan to restore and redeem the relationship between Himself and humanity. It is the story of a grand project of reconciliation. "God was in Christ, reconciling the world to himself, no longer counting people's sins against them" (2 Corinthians 5:19). This was about our forgiveness and healing, something that each and every one of us needs.

The more we recognize our need and accept the reconciliation God offers us, the more we discover that we are participants in God's greatest project. "And he has committed to us the message of reconciliation" (2 Corinthians 5:19). We become ambassadors of God's reconciliation, sharing the story and message of Jesus and inviting others into this same story.

The hope and healing we find in Jesus are precious, but they are never only about us or for us. Whenever we accept these into our lives and allow them to change our story, we become an operational part of God's project of reconciliation. We are Christ's ambassadors, and through our lives, witness, and influence, we share His invitation and healing with those around us and with the wider world. Through His people, God's appeal can reach other people who might not otherwise be able to hear His voice.

As a former enemy of Christ and persecutor of His followers, Paul knew the power of forgiveness and reconciliation in his own life. And this was the core of the message he had to share with anyone who would listen across as much of the world—and as much of history since—as his voice and his letters could reach: "We implore you on Christ's behalf: Be reconciled to God" (2 Corinthians 5:20).

November 19

THE GOD WHO COMFORTS THE DOWNCAST

When we came into Macedonia, we had no rest, but we were harassed at every turn—conflicts on the outside, fears within. But God, who comforts the downcast, comforted us by the coming of Titus.
—2 Corinthians 7:5, 6

Looking at all of Paul's apparent certainty, bold words of faith and encouragement, and the courage with which he confronted those who opposed him, as well as the dangers of travel and mission, we can be tempted to forget that he was human. He admitted it in a theological sense, as he described wrestling with sin and weakness (see, for example, Romans 7:8–24). But there is less evidence in his letters of such all-too-human experiences as fatigue, fear, or discouragement, which is why the personal insights in a comment such as this are an important reminder of Paul's common humanity.

Beset by conflict and fear, Paul and his traveling companions were tired and downcast. But Paul recognized God's provision and comfort in Titus' arrival and the news he brought from the believers in Corinth. That the Corinthians had encouraged Titus was also encouraging for Paul (see 2 Corinthians 7:6, 7).

They were not alone. God, too, had noticed their discouragement, which was a source of comfort in itself. Titus and his report of the Corinthian believers' "ardent concern" for Paul meant that his "joy was greater than ever" (2 Corinthians 7:7). He admitted that he had been downcast, but he now had fresh energy.

That Paul sometimes needed encouragement does not undermine the powerful things, the words of courage and encouragement, that he wrote in his letters to the churches. Instead, his discouragement makes his faith, hope, and courage shine all the brighter. This experience also reminds us of the importance of believing and working together with others with whom we can share encouragement. Most importantly, Paul's fears point us to Jesus, the One who can give us courage when we are afraid, new hope when we are weary, and His presence when we are threatened and troubled.

November 20

A COMMUNITY OF GOD

Finally, brothers and sisters, rejoice! Strive for full restoration, encourage one another, be of one mind, live in peace. And the God of love and peace will be with you.

—2 Corinthians 13:11

Paul spent about eighteen months working and witnessing in Corinth around 51 A.D. It is believed he wrote his first letter to "the church of God in Corinth" in 56 A.D. (see 1 Corinthians 1:2), while he was based in Ephesus. Then he briefly revisited Corinth (see 2 Corinthians 13:1) and wrote another—now lost—letter "out of great distress and anguish of heart and with many tears" (2 Corinthians 2:4) around the time of that visit. About a year later, what we know as 2 Corinthians was written to follow up on his previous letter, and Paul proposed a third visit to the city. This was an ongoing ministry for Paul and one that also gave him great joy when he heard the Corinthians believers were doing well.

So, the closing thoughts of 2 Corinthians are the last known words of Paul to those believers after growing and nourishing the church in Corinth for most of a decade. Given the tension there had been in Paul's relationship with them, he was now pleased with their progress. It was a moment to reflect and celebrate their progress. But he admonished them to continue to grow to maturity. With the history of tensions among the believers in the city, he also urged them that this maturing faith would be demonstrated by mutual encouragement, unity, and peace between them.

What they were maturing into with Paul's ongoing encouragement and care would increasingly reflect God's character. God was a God of love and peace, Paul reminded them, so this would be the nature of the community that carried God's name. God was with them, and His nature would be more obviously manifested among them as they grew together in courage, love, and peace.

DISAGREEMENT AND FEAR

When Cephas came to Antioch, I opposed him to his face, because he stood condemned. For before certain men came from James, he used to eat with the Gentiles. But when they arrived, he began to draw back and separate himself from the Gentiles because he was afraid of those who belonged to the circumcision group.
—Galatians 2:11, 12

It is generally believed that the church council in Jerusalem, described in Acts 15, took place in 49 A.D., and it seems that the letter to the Galatians was written in the lead-up to that meeting. In a sense, Paul was describing the core disagreement that was to be addressed and resolved by the Jerusalem meeting: How Jewish did Gentile believers in Jesus need to become in order to be welcomed and accepted into the church? This question was made all the more urgent by the evangelistic and church-planting success that Paul and Barnabas reported from their first missionary journey through Asia Minor, which included the region of Galatia.

Paul's report of his rebuke of Peter (*Cephas* is the Syriac version of the name given to him by Jesus; see John 1:42) demonstrated the personal dynamics that are often included in that kind of disagreement. We can imagine what the in-person argument was like as two strong-willed, outspoken, and sincere apostles expressed their points of view. At the same time, Paul and Barnabas were also arguing with "the circumcision group" who had arrived in Antioch:"This brought Paul and Barnabas into sharp dispute and debate with them" (Acts 15:2).

But Paul particularly called out Peter's fear of standing up for the Gentile believers, pointing out that he had been eating with Gentiles until those critics arrived in the city. It was a strong challenge, but it seemed to have an effect. When the council met in Jerusalem, Peter spoke boldly for the inclusion and welcome of Gentiles into the church community: "[God] made no distinction between us and them, for he purified their hearts by faith" (Acts 15:9).

November 22

TAKE YOUR STAND

Finally, be strong in the Lord and in his mighty power. Put on the full armor of God, so that you can take your stand against the devil's schemes.
—Ephesians 6:10, 11

By the time Paul wrote to the believers in Ephesus, he was living under house arrest in Rome. This letter was a follow-up to the tearful farewell with the leaders from Ephesus as Paul had passed by on his final trip to Jerusalem almost five years earlier. As a final summary of his ministry to them, he urged them to stand strong in God and in His power.

Of course, this also recognized that there would be attacks. There would be things that would threaten them and make them afraid, but Paul assured them that they had everything they needed to withstand the devil's schemes. Despite all the physical dangers they faced, he insisted that the greater threat was the spiritual battle in which they were engaged (see Ephesians 6:12).

Perhaps describing the armor of the Roman soldier standing at his door (see Acts 28:16), Paul highlighted truth, righteousness, and the gospel of peace, as well as faith, salvation, and the word of God as the believers' tools of defense and protection. And he urged them to put these things on, to cover themselves with them, filling their lives with what God had provided in the truth about Jesus and His plan for salvation and reconciliation, healing and hope.

The final glimpses that the Bible gives us of the Ephesus church are in the letter to the churches at the beginning of the book of Revelation, probably written about thirty years after Paul's letter to the Ephesians. Revelation 2:4 is a call to Ephesus to repent and return to "the love you had at first." It describes a falling away, but also includes an invitation to return and a promise to those who, as Paul put it, would remain strong. "To the one who is victorious, I will give the right to eat from the tree of life" (Revelation 2:7).

November 23

. . . AND PRAY

Pray also for me, that whenever I speak, words may be given me so that I will fearlessly make known the mystery of the gospel, for which I am an ambassador in chains. Pray that I may declare it fearlessly, as I should.
—Ephesians 6:19, 20

The final instruction Paul gave to the Ephesian believers was to pray. "Pray in the Spirit on all occasions with all kinds of prayers and requests. With this in mind, be alert and always keep on praying for all the Lord's people" (Ephesians 6:18). Prayer of all kinds and for all things was prescribed as the all-over covering—the final piece—of the armor God had given to His people.

Not only were they to pray for individual Christians, but prayer was a way in which they could add to the strength and courage of "all the Lord's people." Even if we do not fully understand how it works, Paul insisted that prayer matters and that we can make an important contribution to the lives and faith of others by praying for them.

And this was the request he made of the Ephesian believers. As with the first disciples in the book of Acts (see Acts 4:29), prayer was not so much for protection and safety but for courage to meet the challenges, stand up to the threats, and be able to continue to share the message of Jesus boldly. It seems likely that Paul had his potential court date before Caesar on his mind. He asked the Ephesian believers to pray for the words that he would speak, but also that he would "declare it fearlessly."

Neither history nor the Bible reports the confrontation between Paul and Nero, who was Caesar at the time Paul was in Rome. But we can expect that the Ephesians' prayers for Paul's fearlessness would have been answered—as the mystery of the gospel was proclaimed by one of its most courageous ambassadors in the world's most powerful court within a generation of Jesus' crucifixion on the fringe of the empire.

November 24

REJOICING IN ROME

And because of my chains, most of the brothers and sisters have become confident in the Lord and dare all the more to proclaim the gospel without fear.

—Philippians 1:14

Paul had written to the believers in Rome three or four years before he arrived there and had expressed his hope that he would be able to visit them as part of his ongoing missionary journeys (see Romans 1:15; 15:24). When he finally got to Rome, it was not in the circumstances he had imagined, but the manner of his arrival—a high-profile prisoner under the watch of the palace guards—brought greater attention to his presence there.

"What has happened to me has actually served to advance the gospel," Paul reported to the Philippians (Philippians 1:12). He described how he had been recognized as a different kind of prisoner than the political prisoners and criminals with whom the palace guards would have been much more familiar. What Paul wanted everyone to know about him was that he was "in chains for Christ" (Philippians 1:13).

But Paul was also excited to note that his presence in the city and the unconventional connection he had with the palace was an opportunity for the believers in Rome to share their faith. Paul was in the news—or at least the gossip—across the city, and he was glad to see and hear many of the believers growing in daring to proclaim the gospel in the capital city of the empire. It was a daunting place to live and witness as a Christian, but the attention brought by Paul's arrival and ongoing witness in the city gave the believers a new sense of courage.

These were the people he would work and worship with during his last few years in Rome. Despite his imprisonment and the ongoing threats he faced, seeing the newly emboldened Christians in Rome sharing the good news about Jesus was a reason for Paul to rejoice. "Christ is preached. And because of this I rejoice" (Philippians 1:18).

November 25

SUFFICIENT COURAGE

I eagerly expect and hope that I will in no way be ashamed, but will have sufficient courage so that now as always Christ will be exalted in my body, whether by life or by death.

—Philippians 1:20

Paul was well aware of the dangers he faced and the likely end that he was approaching. These were not new situations, but his circumstances in Rome would have constantly reminded him that his life was in the hands of his Roman captors—except that he knew that his life was always and ultimately in the hands of God. He lived with both realities, and he was prepared to die in light of both realities.

What he sought through his fellow believers' prayers and God's provision of "the Spirit of Jesus Christ" (Philippians 1:19) was to have "sufficient courage" to represent God well whatever his fate might be—whether he lived and continued preaching, or he died as a martyr for the faith.

But if Christ had already been exalted "to the highest place" (Philippians 2:9), how much courage would be "sufficient" for Paul to add to such complete exaltation? Clearly, this was about Paul wanting to live up to his identity as a follower of Christ—living a life of what other translations have termed "complete boldness" or "continuing to be bold" so that Christ would be honored in places where He was not yet acknowledged.

It was the Holy Spirit as the source of Paul's courage that would add to Christ's glory. If Paul could die for his faith as courageously as he had lived for it, it would be another witness to Christ's power over death. These were not new dangers, and this was not a new task, but he sought the Philippian believers' prayers for him to continue in faithfulness as he approached what he expected would be the end of his life, which would require further courage.

November 26

COURAGE TOGETHER

Whatever happens, conduct yourselves in a manner worthy of the gospel of Christ. Then, whether I come and see you or only hear about you in my absence, I will know that you stand firm in the one Spirit, striving together as one for the faith of the gospel without being frightened in any way by those who oppose you.

—Philippians 1:27, 28

In the first section of his letter to the believers in Philippi, Paul reflected on the circumstances he was in, that of the believers in Rome he was working with, and then those of the Philippians he was writing to. All of them faced serious dangers and threats. Each of these groups required courage to live faithfully, to love each other and those beyond their community, and to continue to share the story and message of Jesus.

As he had desired for himself, Paul urged the Philippians to live in a way that was "worthy of the gospel of Christ." A life worthy of the gospel would include refusing to allow fear of their inevitable opposition to daunt their faith or dim their witness. Both Paul and the Roman believers would be the Philippians' role models for growing courage, which is what he was offering them in sharing his stories from Rome, "since you are going through the same struggle you saw I had, and now hear that I still have" (Philippians 1:30).

As they faced their fears, dangers, and uncertainties, each group would encourage one another by sharing reports of what they were able to do despite opposition and intimidation, and by praying for each other and for God's presence and intervention on their behalf. Together with the presence of the Spirit among them, they would have more courage than they would alone. They would be "striving together as one for the faith of the gospel without being frightened in any way by those who oppose you."

TRANSCENDENT PEACE

And the peace of God, which transcends all understanding, will guard your hearts and your minds in Christ Jesus.
—Philippians 4:7

I have a hazy memory of a song we sang at church when I was growing up—or it might have been how this verse was quoted from an older translation by a longtime church member who knew it so well. It talked about the "peace of God which passeth all understanding" (KJV), and I remember trying to work out how peace could pass—or give—understanding to us. It was a language puzzle for my young mind.

Only when I read it for myself and in a more contemporary translation did the meaning of the older language click into place. Paul was not talking about ordinary peace, but peace that comes from God and *surpasses* our understanding, or "which exceeds anything we can understand" (Philippians 4:7, NLT).

In one sense, Paul was actually describing peace that we would be unable to understand, peace that would make no sense if we were to look only at our context or circumstances. For Paul, writing from imprisonment in Rome, God was the source of peace to whom he could commit his worries, to whom he could pray, and in whom he could rejoice (see Philippians 4:6). And this was what he hoped for the Philippian believers to whom he was writing.

But, in another sense, perhaps my youthful misunderstanding was not so wrong. Paul explained to his readers that this peace of God would guard their hearts and minds in Jesus. Rather than being overwhelmed by the worries and fears that would be pushed at them from life and the world around them, the peace of God would allow them to think and understand, love and serve with strength and courage. God's peace will allow us to live without being afraid, overwhelmed, or anxious; it will help us make sense of our lives in new ways.

November 28

DARING TO TELL

We had previously suffered and been treated outrageously in Philippi, as you know, but with the help of our God we dared to tell you his gospel in the face of strong opposition.
—1 Thessalonians 2:2

Paul and Silas had been summarily beaten and imprisoned in Philippi—that occasion on which they were singing at midnight when an earthquake shook them free and led to the conversion of the jailer and his family (see Acts 16:22–40). After Paul and Silas were released from prison, they went back to Lydia's house. "There they met with the believers and encouraged them once more. Then they left town" (Acts 16:40, NLT).

As they traveled west along the Aegean coastline, their next destination was Thessalonica. However, Paul and Silas were not able to stay there long. Their early evangelistic success was met with fierce opposition as Jewish critics worked with local troublemakers to start a riot (see Acts 17:1–5). That night, the first few Thessalonian believers helped Paul and Silas escape from the city under the cover of darkness.

This was a rather inauspicious beginning for the church in Thessalonica. Writing back to those believers, Paul seemed surprised at the daring they had shown: "Yet our God gave us the courage to declare his Good News to you boldly, in spite of great opposition" (1 Thessalonians 2:2, NLT).

The circumstances in which Paul and Silas were sharing the story of Jesus had the additional function of authenticating what they were sharing. If it was a scheme for popularity or wealth, it was not working out well. If they were uncertain about the message, why would they be taking such risks? As Paul explained it: "For the appeal we make does not spring from error or impure motives, nor are we trying to trick you" (1 Thessalonians 2:3). As we see throughout Paul's letters, he was compelled by the story and reality of Jesus. That's what gave him courage, and made his message so important and worth whatever risks might come.

November 29

A MISSION OF ENCOURAGEMENT

We sent Timothy, who is our brother and co-worker in God's service in spreading the gospel of Christ, to strengthen and encourage you in your faith, so that no one would be unsettled by these trials. For you know quite well that we are destined for them.

—1 Thessalonians 3:2, 3

Paul did not need to convince the Thessalonian believers that they were destined for trials. The church there had been planted amid trials. Anyone who joined a church that was presently the target of a riotous mob would not have been under any illusions that faith was merely a positive lifestyle choice or a pathway to greater position or respectability in Thessalonian society.

So, since Paul had been able to spend only a short time in their city, compared with the extended time he had ministered in Corinth and Ephesus, Paul sent Timothy to Thessalonica to spend more time teaching the new believers. This was a mission to strengthen and encourage them in their faith. Knowing the troubles they had faced, were facing, and would continue to face, he did not want them to fall away "when trouble or persecution comes because of the word" (Matthew 13:21), as was the case with the seed that fell on rocky soil in Jesus' parable. Those hearers received the message with joy, but "when the sun came up, the plants were scorched, and they withered because they had no root" (Matthew 13:6).

Facing trials and persecution, Paul knew that encouragement must be not merely a short-term motivational speech but a process of growing deeper roots into faith. Deep encouragement takes time. This was important enough for Paul to assign one of his best co-workers to the task of strengthening these believers, and he was encouraged by their response. "Timothy has just now come to us from you and has brought good news about your faith and love. . . . Therefore, brothers and sisters, in all our distress and persecution we were encouraged about you because of your faith" (1 Thessalonians 3:6, 7).

November 30

WORDS OF ENCOURAGEMENT

Therefore encourage each other with these words.
—1 Thessalonians 4:18

I have heard this final instruction in 1 Thessalonians 4 taken seriously many times: "Encourage one another with these words." It is a go-to passage for funerals and memorial services, whether simply as a reading or as the key text for a short sermon or reflection for those who are assembled to grieve together.

This passage is one of the Bible's simplest descriptions of Jesus' Second Coming, written particularly because "we do not want you to be uninformed about those who sleep in death" (1 Thessalonians 4:13). At times, I have heard undertakers and funeral attendants comment that Adventist funerals tend to be different—and it is likely that this passage explains why. In Paul's understanding, remembering this promise is the reason believers in Jesus "do not grieve like the rest of mankind, who have no hope" (1 Thessalonians 4:13).

This passage also brings together two elements of hope that we have reflected on in earlier readings. Hope is not simply a point of light in the distance; it is a light that shines from what we believe about the future and changes our experience today, even in the depths of grief. But the Christian hope is also based on what we believe about what has happened in our history. "We believe that Jesus died and rose again, and so we believe that God will bring with Jesus those who have fallen asleep in him" (1 Thessalonians 4:14).

For some of the worst days of our lives, when we gather to mourn someone who has been dear to us, Paul gives us this simple statement to read together to help us remember the hope that is based on our history and on our future. He offers us courage that we can share with each other for our present pain of grief, and the days of mourning and missing them that lie ahead.

ENCOURAGING ONE ANOTHER

Therefore encourage one another and build each other up, just as in fact you are doing.
—1 Thessalonians 5:11

Not only was the promise of Jesus' return a cause for encouragement, but it was also a reason for the believers to encourage each other. Faced with the tragedies and disappointments of life, the believers also had the added challenges of threats and persecution directed against them because of their faith. The promise of Jesus' Second Coming was a promise to be repeated and relied on as a note of encouragement amid whatever circumstances they faced.

But being ready for the Second Coming was also a purpose for which the believers would seek to encourage each other. With an apparently uncertain future and an unknown time for this promised event, it was—and always has been—too easy for believers to become preoccupied with the busyness and distractions of life; they might even become used to the everyday threats and challenges from those around them. Even people who claimed to be living with the expectation of Jesus' return could be taken by surprise by this event, Paul warned, so the believers should encourage one another in their everyday faithfulness and alertness, living with faith and love, hope and salvation (see 1 Thessalonians 5:8).

In this way, the work of encouraging one another is a vital role of the church community. While Adventists have often talked about the importance of "being ready" for the return of Jesus, this is not a new or additional task to that of being followers of Jesus in all areas of our lives. The kind of encouragement that Paul described is something that we do together—and for one another. By retelling the story of Jesus, especially recounting the stories of His death and resurrection (see 1 Thessalonians 5:9, 10), the believers in Thessalonica were to build each other up in their faith and faithfulness, so they would be "awake and sober" (1 Thessalonians 5:6).

December 2

ESPECIALLY THE TIMID

We urge you, brothers and sisters, warn those who are idle and disruptive, encourage the disheartened, help the weak, be patient with everyone.
—1 Thessalonians 5:14

In the ministry of Jesus and the work of the church, there is always a special concern for the weakest and those most in need. It makes sense that this is particularly true in the ministry of encouragement. "Encourage those who are timid. Take tender care of those who are weak" (1 Thessalonians 5:14, NLT). Those who are most afraid are those who most need to hear "Do not be afraid"—not as a message of rebuke, but as a message of comfort and assurance.

As with most human organizations and communities, the tendency in the church is to pay the most attention to the powerful, the loud, the beautiful, and the confident. Those with apparent success—in whatever way that is measured—are often honored more. But the church must be different. Paul wrote about this principle when he described the church as the body of Christ. "Those parts of the body that seem to be weaker are indispensable, and the parts that we think are less honorable we treat with special honor" (1 Corinthians 12:22, 23).

This means that the social relationships and dynamics in the community of believers should not mirror the society and culture around it but should be different in giving preference to those who are seen as weak and who are often overlooked or marginalized. In ministry and service, we are to prioritize encouragement and care to those who most need them and who are least likely to receive them elsewhere. In turn, this will change the nature of those relationships and will bring blessings to the church body as a whole. "But God has put the body together, giving greater honor to the parts that lacked it, so that there should be no division in the body, but that its parts should have equal concern for each other" (1 Corinthians 12:24, 25).

December 3

ANTIDOTES TO FEAR

For the Spirit God gave us does not make us timid, but gives us power, love and self-discipline.

—2 Timothy 1:7

In Paul's letters to Timothy, we see glimpses of the personal relationship between the older apostle and his young assistant. Paul referenced Timothy's family and faith and urged Timothy not to be ashamed of the story of Jesus or of Paul, who was then imprisoned for sharing that story. Despite Paul's own circumstances in Rome, in his reckoning, there was much that should give Timothy courage: "For God hath not given us the spirit of fear; but of power, and of love, and of a sound mind" (1 Timothy 1:7, KJV).

To avoid being overcome by fear, Timothy was to rely on the power of God that came by His Spirit and that had previously been gifted to Timothy "through the laying on of my hands" (1 Timothy 1:6). It seems that Paul had specifically ordained—or perhaps anointed—Timothy for the work that he would continue after Paul's imprisonment, and Paul assured him that same Spirit was still with Timothy.

Timothy's faith had been first formed by the influence and love of his grandmother and mother (see 2 Timothy 1:5). But it was the love of God expressed in the life and death of Jesus that would give Timothy the greatest courage and assurance. Such love would continue to transform this young minister.

Paul also urged Timothy to live with self-discipline, characterized by a sound mind. Clear thinking would serve as an antidote to fear, allowing faithful choices to guide his life and ministry rather than responses determined by fear.

Power, love, and disciplined thinking had been markers of Paul's ministry and letters. They would also allow Timothy to stand, serve, and speak boldly for the message, unafraid and unashamed, whatever his mentor Paul might be suffering and whatever threats might be surrounding Timothy. This is a powerful antidote to fear, a recipe for living courageously.

December 4

UNAFRAID OF SUFFERING

But you, keep your head in all situations, endure hardship, do the work of an evangelist, discharge all the duties of your ministry.

—2 Timothy 4:5

It is believed that Paul converted Timothy during his visit to Lystra on his first missionary journey. By the time of Paul's second missionary journey, when he and Silas revisited Lystra, Timothy was introduced as a young disciple who was respected by the believers in that city (see Acts 16:1, 2). It was on his first visit to the city that Paul had been stoned by an angry mob, dragged out of the city, and left for dead (see Acts 14:19, 20). It seems likely that Timothy was a witness to that violence, perhaps even among the group of believers "gathered around him," suggesting that they were praying for Paul's healing.

In one of Paul's last letters, written as many as fifteen years later, perhaps both Paul and Timothy—when reading this letter—would have remembered that scene as Paul urged him, "Don't be afraid of suffering for the Lord" (2 Timothy 4:5, NLT). Obviously, Paul could not claim that sharing the story of Jesus would be easy or popular, but he could give such instruction because his life and ministry had demonstrated this kind of courage.

In turn, being unafraid of suffering was the foundation for Paul's other ministry advice. Compared with other popular teachers whom many people would follow, those—like Timothy—who could endure hardship and rejection were those who would not be swayed by the crowd, who could speak the truth and continue to share the good news about Jesus wherever they were able.

As Paul neared the end of his life and ministry, it was such courage that allowed him to reflect, "I have fought the good fight, I have finished the race, I have kept the faith" (2 Timothy 4:7). And that is what he desired for Timothy as well.

ENCOURAGING LEADERS

He must hold firmly to the trustworthy message as it has been taught, so that he can encourage others by sound doctrine and refute those who oppose it.

—Titus 1:9

Another of Paul's apprentice ministers was a young Greek man by the name of Titus. Some commentators have suggested that Titus might have been the brother of Luke, but he is not mentioned in the book of Acts, so all we know of him is from putting together various references throughout Paul's letters. It was apparent that Paul had found a kindred spirit in Titus, who walked "in the same footsteps by the same Spirit" (2 Corinthians 12:18) as Paul.

Titus had traveled with Paul to Jerusalem, spent some time with Paul in Rome, and had been sent on other journeys by Paul. At the time of Paul's letter to him, Titus was working to establish the churches in Crete. While there is evidence of a later assignment (see 2 Timothy 4:10), one historical tradition is that Titus became an established leader of the church in Crete.

Whatever the case, it is clear that Paul did not want the future of the church in that place to depend on a single person. Part of Titus' commission was to "appoint elders in every town, as I directed you" (Titus 1:5). These would be people of good character who would be equipped to "encourage others by sound doctrine."

This was a similar qualification and injunction for leaders appointed in the early days of the Israelite nation: "The same principles of piety and justice that were to guide the rulers among God's people in the time of Moses and of David, were also to be followed by those given the oversight of the newly organized church of God."* People of courage are those who will be unafraid to be faithful and do their assigned duty and who are most fit to encourage others.

---

* Ellen G. White, *The Acts of the Apostles* (Mountain View, CA: Pacific Press®, 1911), 95.

December 6

FREED FROM THE FEAR OF DEATH

Since the children have flesh and blood, he too shared in their humanity so that by his death he might break the power of him who holds the power of death—that is, the devil—and free those who all their lives were held in slavery by their fear of death.

—Hebrews 2:14, 15

As we have seen, the Bible repeatedly acknowledges our very human fear of death. Often described as one of the inevitabilities of our lives, the consciousness of our mortality is forced to the surface of our lives from time to time by life circumstances, particularly by the death of those around us or threats to our own life or health. But even on our best days, death is a background fear, uncertainty, and unease that perennially threatens our lives: "*Thoughts of his own death, / like the distant roll / of thunder at a picnic.*"*

But the Bible does not merely acknowledge this reality of our human experience. It identifies the devil as the master of the power of death. He is the one who deals in death as a major tool of his power in our world and our lives. However, in Jesus' incarnation, He took on "flesh and blood," meaning He was able to experience death. "And being found in appearance as a man, he humbled himself and became obedient to death—even death on a cross!" (Philippians 2:8). In so doing, Jesus, as God, also defeated death and broke the power of death and the devil.

The story of the Bible offers the invitation to be set free from slavery to our fear of death. Not that such fear does not continue to be part of what it means to be human, nor that somehow death does not matter, but that—after Jesus—death is already and always defeated. For followers of Jesus, death remains an enemy, but the fear of death has also "lost its sting" (see 1 Corinthians 15:55).

* W. H. Auden, "Thoughts of His Own Death" (1965).

CONFIDENCE IN JESUS

But Christ is faithful as the Son over God's house. And we are his house, if indeed we hold firmly to our confidence and the hope in which we glory.
—Hebrews 3:6

For the people of Israel—the family, cultural, and religious forebears of the Hebrews addressed in this letter—Moses was the greatest of all their leaders, standing over all the judges, prophets, priests, and kings of their history. Directed by God and regularly encountering God, Moses led the people out of slavery in Egypt, established the new nation with the laws and history of the Pentateuch, and brought them to the borders of their promised land. So, in this context, for the writer of Hebrews to describe Jesus as "worthy of greater honor than Moses, just as the builder of a house has greater honor than the house itself" (Hebrews 3:3) was to make the largest possible claim about who Jesus was.

But this was not only about who Jesus *was* but also about who Jesus *is*. The ongoing faithfulness of Jesus was presented to the believers of Hebrew background as the foundation for their ongoing confidence and hope: "Therefore, holy brothers and sisters, who share in the heavenly calling, fix your thoughts on Jesus, whom we acknowledge as our apostle and high priest" (Hebrews 3:1).

In Jesus, the community of believers was the house that God had now built, a house greater than the house in which Moses had been such a faithful leader. However, the writer of Hebrews warned that as great a leader as Moses was, there had been those who had allowed their fears and doubts to lead them into rebellion against him and his leadership (see Hebrews 3:16, 17). Thus, this letter's counsel to "fix your thoughts on Jesus" and "hold firmly" to confidence and hope in Him. A great leader inspires confidence; following the greatest Leader should provide all the confidence we need.

December 8

THE ASSURANCE THAT FAITH BRINGS

Since we have a great priest over the house of God, let us draw near to God with a sincere heart and with the full assurance that faith brings, having our hearts sprinkled to cleanse us from a guilty conscience and having our bodies washed with pure water.

—Hebrews 10:21, 22

A guilty conscience takes us all the way back to the original broken relationship between the first human beings and their Creator. Adam and Eve hid from the sound of God approaching because they felt fear and shame. Those feelings are all too familiar as symptoms of recognizing our failures and the weight of a guilty conscience. It is not difficult to imagine ourselves hiding with that frightened couple. It is a human reality, and those who do not experience such feelings from time to time are both the most dangerous and most to be pitied.

But the picture of Adam and Eve hiding in the garden is not the end of the Bible's story. It should not be our reality today. As we have seen, God continued to pursue humanity with love, grace, and reconciliation, which culminated in Jesus, including His incarnation, life, death, resurrection, and promises for a future return and restoration. The letter to the Hebrews also highlights Jesus' ongoing priestly work, having offered Himself as the means of cleansing our consciences and our lives of our brokenness and healing our woundedness.

While this task is incomplete within each of us and for our larger world, fear and shame need not continue to dominate our relationship with God. We do not need to hide from Him or recoil with fear at the sound of His approach or the hints of His presence in our lives. Of course, this fearlessness is always based on God's loving action toward us and His radical intervention in Jesus. So, because of Jesus, "let us draw near to God with a sincere heart and with the full assurance that faith brings."

December 9

LOVE, GOOD DEEDS, AND ENCOURAGEMENT

Let us consider how we may spur one another on toward love and good deeds. Let us not give up meeting together, as some are in the habit of doing, but let us encourage one another—and all the more as you see the Day approaching.

—Hebrews 10:24, 25

What church looks like and what purpose it serves are perennial discussion topics in church circles and among many church leaders and members. Too often, it comes down to the dynamics and elements of worship services or other church meetings. We have often repeated the truism that church is not a building, but we probably need to add that neither is church only a meeting or series of meetings. Hebrews 10:25 is usually used to encourage attendance and participation at worship services, but it instead describes the larger elements of a healthy community of believers.

In this description, based on "the hope we profess" (Hebrews 10:23), the role of the community of faith is to encourage and inspire each other to "love and good deeds." This will include the attitudes and activities among church members and also their attitudes toward the surrounding community and the wider world. Such a posture was described as the primary desired outcome of the interactions between believers.

With this focus, the writer urged the believers to continue to gather, so we can conclude that the purposes of meeting together were to worship and learn together and also to encourage one another. In these verses, there is a parallelism between "spurring" and "encouraging," meaning that such encouragement was also focused on the good works of love and service to each other and the world around them.

The practical outcome was positioned in the context of anticipating the day of Jesus' return. In these verses, that is what it means to wait well and to live with the expectation of the fulfillment of this hope. In this letter to the early believers, that was what church looked like and what it was for.

December 10

PRACTICING HOPE

Now faith is confidence in what we hope for and assurance about what we do not see. This is what the ancients were commended for.

—Hebrews 11:1, 2

First comes hope. Then faith is the practice of confidence in that hope and assurance of what we cannot yet see. In this definition, faith is the opposite of fear. Faith is choosing to step courageously into our uncertain world, into our fragile lives, into living as if what we hope for is truly what matters most, even when the circumstances and available evidence suggest otherwise.

As the writer of Hebrews put it—and then went on to draw out many examples from the history of the people of Israel—this is how the ancient people of faith did it. Without knowing how their choices would turn out or where those choices would lead them, and often under threat from those around them, they chose to follow what they understood of God's leading, albeit imperfectly. As such, they re-oriented their lives around the hope that God had promised them.

Their lives were not easy and were often made more difficult by choosing to follow faith and hope. It is also important to note that none of those pioneers of faith reached or saw their hope realized in their lifetimes. As this chapter comments, "All these people were still living by faith when they died. They did not receive the things promised; they only saw them and welcomed them from a distance. And they admitted that they were aliens and strangers on earth" (Hebrews 11:13).

It may have seemed that the safer option was to refuse their calling, allowing their fears and questions to keep them at home. But hope had caught their attention, sparked their imagination, and invited them to choose faith. They determined that a life of hope was always going to be larger than a life of fear. And faith was choosing to put that hope into practice.

December 11

RECOMMENDING A MEMORY VERSE

So we say with confidence,

"The Lord is my helper; I will not be afraid.
What can mere mortals do to me?"

—Hebrews 13:6

The argument that brings us to this quote is, don't be distracted by money but be content with what you have because God has promised to always be with us and will never forsake us (see Hebrews 13:5). Then the writer of Hebrews quotes Psalm 118:6, among the closing instructions of this letter to the early Christian believers.

I confess that I have questioned the way we sometimes use the Bible to make particular points, quoting a verse here and there in support of the argument we are making—even as I have done it regularly in writing and even throughout this book, highlighting the verses that fit the theme, skipping over others that do not fit quite so well. So, it is interesting to note how the writers of the New Testament sometimes used the Hebrew scriptures in the same way. Jesus often quoted verses and referenced Bible stories in His teaching, as did the New Testament's Gospel and letter writers.

This is what is happening in Hebrews 13. In quick succession, the author draws together a verse from Deuteronomy 31 and this verse from Psalm 118 to urge that God is always with the believers so they can live with confidence. In effect, the writer is recommending a couple of memory verses that will help the readers when tempted by the desire for more money and more things or with the pressing needs they might have from time to time and the fears that come in such circumstances.

While it is important to read verses in their larger contexts, the Bible itself gives us a precedent for drawing on its promises and applying those "Do not be afraid" instructions—among many others—to our own lives and circumstances. The writer of Hebrews saw the value in quoting a "Do not be afraid" from his people's past, and so we can hear it again today.

December 12

STAND FIRM!

You too, be patient and stand firm,
because the Lord's coming is near.

—James 5:8

As we have reflected thus far, what we believe about the future shapes how we live today. The promises of God, especially that of the return of Jesus, will change our choices and priorities. While this might mean we are less focused on some aspects of our lives, it will also mean that other priorities and other people will be more important to us. Ours is not a faith of detachment but of engagement. As James urged the early believers, because of the hope we have in Jesus, we can afford to be patient, like a farmer working his or her land (see James 5:7), and we can have the courage to stand and to serve because of what we believe.

The other way of considering these instructions is to look at how we are living our lives and ask what it demonstrates about what we truly believe regarding the future. We might say we believe in Jesus and His promises for our lives and future, but what would observers see in us and how we live that is different because of such belief? Are we people who live with patience, who work faithfully with God's ultimate plan in mind? Are we people who stand firm—"to be or remain steadfast in conviction despite attack, efforts to persuade, etc."*—living with courage to be different, to risk loving and serving others, to risk being misunderstood and mistreated (see James 5:10)? In short, do we look like people—however imperfect—who seek to live as followers of Jesus today, relying on His presence and promises?

This is not about judging others (see James 5:9) but an invitation for faithful reflection on our own lives, choices, and priorities. Do our patience, courage, and conviction today demonstrate the hope we have in Jesus?

---

* *Webster's New World College Dictionary*, 4th ed. (2010), s.v. "stand firm."

December 13

AN IMPERFECT EXAMPLE

Like Sarah, who obeyed Abraham and called him her lord. You are her daughters if you do what is right and do not give way to fear.
—1 Peter 3:6

As we saw when we were following their story in Genesis, the experiences of Abraham and Sarah were patchy. At times, they demonstrated great faith in God; at other times, they tried to advance what they understood of God's plans in their own messy ways. Even at the moment of God's most direct interaction with Sarah, "Sarah was afraid, so she lied" (Genesis 18:15). In her interactions with God, her treatment of Hagar and Ishmael, and her lies to foreign leaders, Sarah was not a perfect example of fearlessness.

However, perhaps she was an example *because* she was imperfect. But, along with Abraham, she chose to follow God anyway. Her experience was summarized in the book of Hebrews' survey of the faithful ancestors of Israel: "By faith even Sarah, who was past childbearing age, was enabled to bear children because she considered him faithful who had made the promise" (Hebrews 11:11). Sarah laughed—then lied about it—because she recognized the impossibility of what God was suggesting, apart from God's intervention. She was afraid because she knew she should not argue with God. The Bible's story is explicit in setting out these challenges to her call to faithfully follow God's plans, but despite her shortcomings, she did not allow her questions, doubts, and fears to impede God's plans. She had fears, but she did "not give way to fear." Her fears, uncertainties, and disappointments were not ultimately the most important factors in her life.

Daughters—and sons—of Sarah need not be fearless. Rather, they are those who admit their fear and choose to be faithful anyway, seeking to do what is right, however imperfectly. Sarah was not offered as an example because of her courage or physical capacity—she was both afraid and infertile—but because of her lived trust in God,"because she considered him faithful who had made the promise."

December 14

SUFFER FOR DOING GOOD

Who is going to harm you if you are eager to do good? But even if you should suffer for what is right, you are blessed. "Do not fear their threats; do not be frightened."

—1 Peter 3:13, 14

It is commonly believed that Peter wrote this letter to the churches in Asia Minor from Rome in the early 60s A.D. around the time of Paul's execution and as persecution was growing across the empire. It was an important reality that Peter was addressing. He quoted from the prophet Isaiah, applying his message of encouragement to the people of Judah when confronted by the approaching armies of the Assyrians to the circumstances of the first-century people of God.

However, Peter was not urging courage merely for the sake of courage or even galvanizing his readers to endure difficult times. Instead, the previous verses were a call for the believers to be compassionate and humble. They "must turn from evil and do good." They "must seek peace and pursue it" (1 Peter 3:11), again quoting from the Hebrew scriptures (see Psalm 34:14). This was an instruction to live positive lives and to work for the good of those around them, even amid the threats and challenges of persecution: "It is better, if it is God's will, to suffer for doing good than for doing evil" (1 Peter 3:17).

Peter also encouraged them to believe that if they were harassed or arrested for their faith or their good works, they should see it as an opportunity to explain their allegiance to Jesus and the hope they found in Him. "But in your hearts set apart Christ as Lord. Always be prepared to give an answer to everyone who asks you to give the reason for the hope that you have. But do this with gentleness and respect" (1 Peter 3:15).

For Peter, the harsh realities of persecution were not about passive endurance but an opportunity to demonstrate love and perhaps explain their faith. It was a response of faithfulness rather than fear.

STAND FAST IN GOD'S GRACE

With the help of Silas, whom I regard as a faithful brother, I have written to you briefly, encouraging you and testifying that this is the true grace of God. Stand fast in it.

—1 Peter 5:12

Like the other Bible writers, Peter was open about the threats and challenges posed to the people of God from time to time by many of the people and cultures around them. He also had no hesitation in identifying the work of the devil in opposing and attacking them. "Your enemy the devil prowls around like a roaring lion looking for someone to devour" (1 Peter 5:8). But this experience was not unique to the specific people to whom Peter was writing, and he encouraged them to find solidarity in the common experiences of God's people across the world and throughout history. "Resist him, standing firm in the faith, because you know that the family of believers throughout the world is undergoing the same kind of sufferings" (1 Peter 5:9).

However, Peter also pointed his readers to the glorious alternative—the goodness and grace of God as demonstrated in Jesus. This reality made all the difference: "And the God of all grace, who called you to his eternal glory in Christ, after you have suffered a little while, will himself restore you and make you strong, firm and steadfast" (1 Peter 5:10). Whatever the devil, the culture, or the people around them might throw at the believers, the reality of Jesus and His promises of restoration and hope were always more powerful and more enduring.

This is a reality that has allowed many people to stand for truth and justice throughout history. "I believe that unarmed truth and unconditional love will have the final word in reality. This is why right, temporarily defeated, is stronger than evil triumphant."* This is what it means to stand fast in the grace and promises of God, however daunting the opposition or the circumstances might seem.

---

* Martin Luther King Jr, Nobel Peace Prize acceptance speech, Oslo, Norway, 1964.

December 16

MORE THAN A GOOD STORY

For we did not follow cleverly devised stories when we told you about the coming of our Lord Jesus Christ in power, but we were eyewitnesses of his majesty.

—2 Peter 1:16

We all have moments in our life of faith when we wonder if we are following something that is merely a nice invention, a way of trying to make sense of a world that does not make much sense—or perhaps even some kind of formulation that we might have made up in our own minds. It might happen when confronted with a major life challenge when we need to consider whether our faith has an adequate response to the tragedy or disappointment we are experiencing. Or it might be in those quiet moments when we are alone with our thoughts and allow ourselves to wonder if our faith is any more real than our imagination.

Peter had his journey of questions to faith, from denial to forgiveness, from fear to boldness. But he also had his own experiences with Jesus as a person and in His power, specifically referencing the disciples' experience of the Transfiguration (see Matthew 17:1–6). No, he insisted, we are not simply making this up. As the ranks of the eyewitnesses to Jesus' earthly life were beginning to thin, Peter wanted the second-generation believers to be sure that the Jesus they had been told about was more than a good story, that His life, death, and resurrection were embedded in the history of our world, as well as in the testimony of those witnesses.

Facing real threats and active persecution, as well as their own questions and doubts, Peter urged that their testimony of Jesus also fit with the words of the prophets as a reliable guide for their lives, their perseverance, and their witness. "We also have the prophetic message as something completely reliable, and you will do well to pay attention to it, as to a light shining in a dark place, until the day dawns and the morning star rises in your hearts" (2 Peter 1:19).

December 17

WAITING WITH PATIENCE

The Lord is not slow in keeping his promise, as some understand slowness. He is patient with you, not wanting anyone to perish, but everyone to come to repentance.
—2 Peter 3:9

In our Adventist history, most of two centuries have passed while we and our grandparents and generations before them have been expecting and waiting for Jesus to return. We might not consider ourselves among the scoffers that Peter warned "will come" (2 Peter 3:3), but for many of us, there are questions and occasional doubts about how long "soon," a word that Jesus and the apostles used, might actually mean. And, as Peter expressed in 2 Peter 1:16, this can lead to those niggling fears that we might be following "cleverly devised stories."

Peter addressed these doubts in the second generation of the church, showing that this is a very human question. He reminded his readers that our finite lives work on a different timeline than God's eternal perspective (see 2 Peter 3:8). We might not understand the seeming delay that has now stretched to almost two millennia, but Peter urged that rather than seeing this as a cause for doubt, this should remind us of God's patience and grace toward humanity.

While the disappointed expectations of Jesus' return in our history should prompt us to ask important questions about how we have sometimes fueled fervency—compared with Jesus' reply to His disciples that "it is not for you to know the times or dates" (Acts 1:7)—Peter insisted that this should not be a cause for doubt or fear. Instead, he reminded his readers that believers should be prepared to be surprised (see 2 Peter 3:10), which means living faithfully, patiently, and well today—for whenever Jesus returns, "You ought to live holy and godly lives as you look forward to the day of God and speed its coming" (2 Peter 3:11, 12).

December 18

CONFIDENT AND UNASHAMED

And now, dear children, continue in him, so that when he appears we may be confident and unashamed before him at his coming.

—1 John 2:28

When Adam and Eve heard God walking in the garden, they were afraid and ashamed, and they hid. To humanity accustomed to hiding from God, drawing back at His approach in a relationship broken by fear and shame, the promise of the glorious return of Jesus, surrounded by throngs of angels, can seem daunting, perhaps threatening. It seems John's letter was reflecting on this—and offering an alternative response.

John warned believers against people who were attempting to lead them astray by diminishing their understanding of who Jesus was. "Such a person is the antichrist—denying the Father and the Son" (1 John 2:22). But John reminded them that Jesus was the grounds for their assurance. This is why those who argued for a lesser status for Jesus had the potential to do such damage. Only for those who continued in Jesus would the promise of His return sound like good news rather than cause for alarm.

The story and reality of Jesus made the difference. In Jesus, the sound of the footsteps of the approaching God was no longer a cause for fear or shame. Instead, Jesus' return in all His power and glory would be the moment when the relationship between God and humanity would be healed and restored. As such, this was now cause for joyous hope and expectation.

And if followers of Jesus could stand "full of courage and not shrink back from him in shame" (1 John 2:28, NLT), they could use that stance as a way to begin to live now. Because of the new beginning that believers were given in Jesus, they could seek to do what was right, not to earn status as God's children, but simply because of who they were born and reborn to be (see 1 John 2:29).

PUTTING OUR HEARTS AT REST

This is how we know that we belong to the truth and how we set our hearts at rest in his presence: If our hearts condemn us, we know that God is greater than our hearts, and he knows everything.
—1 John 3:19, 20

Part of our human nature is our capacity to doubt what we say we believe, even as we seek to live out our faith. No matter how many times we have studied and affirmed our faith, there are times when we struggle to feel "saved," "right with God," or however else we might try to describe what we think we ought to be feeling. It can be easy to say that "if our hearts do not condemn us, we have confidence before God" (1 John 3:21). But our hearts are not always reliable barometers of who we are—or, more importantly, of who God is.

This is the primary claim of John: God is always greater than our hearts. Our assurance and courage are to be found in who God is, not in how we might feel on any given day. The constancy of God, as well as His knowledge of all things—including each of us and our circumstances—are the always-larger answers to our inconstancy. He is the God who sees and knows.

Knowing this can be our foundation for peace, for rest in God's presence. "You have made us for Yourself and our hearts are restless until they rest in you."* While always a work in progress in our current lives, God's presence becomes the active agent for beginning to heal our feelings of uncertainty, fear, and doubt. In Jesus, this is the invitation to restore the relationship with our Creator, which will spill over into healing all our relationships and the world around us.

---

* *The Confessions of Saint Augustine* (New Kensington, PA: Whitaker House, 1996), 11.

December 20

LOVING LIKE JESUS

God is love. Whoever lives in love lives in God, and God in them. This is how love is made complete among us so that we will have confidence on the day of judgment: In this world we are like Jesus.

—1 John 4:16, 17

One of the Bible's clear teachings is that how we live in the present will be shaped by what we believe about the future. But also, how we choose to live today sets a trajectory for how we will live in the future. That is why not only our belief in God but also what we believe about God—what He is like and His intention for humanity—will have a significant influence on who we are and who we are becoming.

So, "God is love" was an important statement for John to make. He did not simply say that *God loves*—something that God does—but that *God is love*—something that God is by nature and identity. This nature was incarnated in Jesus. "God's unfailing love and faithfulness came through Jesus Christ" (John 1:17, NLT). And it is this nature in which His followers are to walk and work in the world, as Jesus did.

When we live in the light of God's love and grace, the idea of His judgment becomes less frightening: "So we will not be afraid on the day of judgment, but we can face him with confidence because we live like Jesus here in this world" (1 John 4:17, NLT). The practice of living in His love, in accord with His character, removes the threat that seems to be an element of judgment. While the infamous sermon title described us as "Sinners in the Hands of an Angry God," in John's understanding of God's love and intention for us, a better, more theologically correct title might be "Sinners in the Hands of a Loving God."

In Jesus, we need not be afraid, even in the day of judgment, because God is love.

THE ANTIDOTE TO FEAR

There is no fear in love. But perfect love drives out fear, because fear has to do with punishment. The one who fears is not made perfect in love.
—1 John 4:18

Love tends to be a word that is diminished in what it commonly means in our world today. The word often conjures images of hearts, puppies, and flowers, which seem terribly inadequate for most of the commitments and tasks to which love calls us. But John urged his readers to see that love should be treated with at least the same seriousness as fear. According to John, love is more powerful than fear.

With fear so prevalent and powerful in our human experience and in our world today, John's description of love is all the more remarkable. As dominant as fear can be, love is stronger. While fear can impede or challenge love, it must ultimately give way to love. To present love as the antidote to fear is to return love to its rightful place, strong enough to overcome and drive out fear.

While John presented God as the ultimate source of love, the love he described was not so much an abstract or theological concept but a practical way of living our lives as God's people in our time and context. Love is not about merely trying to muster nice feelings about God; instead, it is reflected toward those around us. "Anyone who loves God must also love their brother and sister" (1 John 4:21).

God's love reaching out to restore the relationships between Himself and humanity also begins to heal our relationships with each other in real and practical ways. Not all our relationships are equal, but all our relationships can be made better and set right for the types of relationships that they are by seeking the good of the people with whom we interact in the various aspects of our lives. All of this leaves no place for fear, because love is stronger and has the final say.

December 22

IT'S ABOUT JESUS

The revelation from Jesus Christ, which God gave him to show his servants what must soon take place. . . . Blessed is the one who reads aloud the words f this prophecy, and blessed are those who hear it and take to heart what is written in it, because the time is near.

—Revelation 1:1–3

Just the mention of the book of Revelation sparks fear in the hearts of many people. For some, it is a strange, perhaps even spooky book. For others, it is regarded as something people of faith have used to justify their worst actions. For some who have grown up in church, its misuse has caused anxiety and nightmares. Even for believers, it has often been used as a warning to repent, "get ready," and work harder. Speculative interpretations of Revelation have been used as a method to grow an audience, raise donations, and grow "ministry." And it has been abused to prove who is right (us) and who is wrong (them).

But fear is a poor motivation for good results. It can get a crowd and grab attention, but it is difficult to sustain. This is why those who rely on fear need to keep increasing the volume and intensity. But our faith is not based on fear; quite the opposite is true: "The shortness of time is urged as an incentive for us to seek righteousness and to make Christ our friend. This is not the great motive. It savors of selfishness. Is it necessary that the terrors of the day of God be held before us to compel us through fear to right action? This ought not to be. Jesus is attractive. He is full of love, mercy, and compassion. He proposes to be our friend, to walk with us through all the rough pathways of life. He says to you, I am the Lord thy God; walk with me, and I will fill thy path with light."* This is the Jesus the book of Revlation is intended to reveal.

* Ellen G. White, "Rest for the Weary," *Adventist Review and Sabbath Herald*, August 2, 1881.

JESUS SAYS IT AGAIN

When I saw him, I fell at his feet as though dead. Then he placed his right hand on me and said: "Do not be afraid. I am the First and the Last. I am the Living One; I was dead, and now look, I am alive for ever and ever! And I hold the keys of death and Hades."
—Revelation 1:17, 18

Do not be afraid" is not usually the first message we think of when we think of the book of Revelation. But after instructing John to write down what he is about to see (Revelation 1:11), "Do not be afraid" is the first command of this sometimes frightening book. So, if we are reading Revelation correctly, it will be the first thing we think of regarding its message.

Even though often overlooked, the "Do not be afraid" is explicit. It is not incidental or out of place. This is the larger message in the opening of the book of Revelation. "Assurance and reassurance do not let up: in the right hand placed on John; in the claim regarding the speaker's identity; in the speaker's death and resurrection, henceforth 'alive forever and ever'; in the confident declaration that the speaker has 'the keys' that ensure the reversal of death and the exposé of 'Hades.' "*

When the one telling us not to be afraid is one who has experienced overcoming death itself, there is not much we need to be afraid of. When our worst-case scenario is already taken care of, and the forces who would pursue that option are already defeated, there is little need for fear. When read this way, Revelation is the story of how Jesus gives final effect to the victory He has already won and an invitation for us to choose to be part of that victory. So, even when it seems that the battle might be running the other way, "Do not be afraid."

* Sigve K. Tonstad, *Revelation* (Grand Rapids, MI: Baker Academic, 2019), 57.

December 24

TO THE CHURCH IN SMYRNA

"Do not be afraid of what you are about to suffer. I tell you, the devil will put some of you in prison to test you, and you will suffer persecution for ten days. Be faithful, even to the point of death, and I will give you life as your victor's crown."

—Revelation 2:10

The letters to the seven churches of Revelation have an overall "Do not be afraid" theme. These churches were reminded that our God is the God who sees and knows the locations, circumstances, and unique challenges of these different groups of early Christians. Their sufferings and uncertainties are acknowledged, and they are each given customized promises detailing how their faithfulness and endurance will be rewarded. Whether we read these letters as addressing the specific churches in these ancient cities near the end of the first century or as describing groups of Christians across the centuries since, the message is the same—God sees, and God is with you, so be courageous and hold on.

To the church in Smyrna, this message was most specific. The One who had overcome death—as introduced in the first chapter of Revelation—knew their circumstances and trials. They were "about to suffer" persecution, but it would only be for a limited time. When they experienced it, they would know that God already knew about it and knew the end point of their suffering.

Their courage would ensure their faithfulness and their participation in the victory that Jesus has already won and that God will bring to fulfillment. They would be among those many people throughout history who "did not love their lives so much as to shrink from death," overcoming the devil through the saving power of God and by their faithful testimony" (Revelation 12:11).

And the promise to the courageous believers in Smyrna was addressed in the broadest possible terms, to "whoever has ears" (Revelation 2:11). The invitation given by and in Jesus to overcome our existential fear of death is made to anyone and everyone who chooses to listen.

FEAR GOD!

He said in a loud voice, "Fear God and give him glory, because the hour of his judgment has come. Worship him who made the heavens, the earth, the sea and the springs of water."
—Revelation 14:7

As we have seen, the Bible describes a world in which fear has always been common, personally and collectively—and where fear will become more dominant as the world nears its end. In such a time and place, it might seem strange to us that the first message of the three angels in Revelation 14 is "fear." Partly, this is a limitation of the language we use; "fearing" God does not have quite the same meaning as "fearing" the dentist, the dark, or death—but this is also fear put in its right place.

The reference to creation reminds us of God's original intention for our world, where all people, creatures, and the earth itself were in harmony together and with their Creator. It is a vision of the world as it ought to be, before the broken relationships of sin and the fears that resulted.

Warning of judgment is an assurance that God will work—is working—to set the world right, to undo the wrongs of our lives and our collective history, and ultimately to re-create the world as it should be. For those who long for a better world, this is good news; for those who choose to profit from evil, exploitation, and fearfulness, judgment is something to fear.

In this way, fearing God is about understanding God in His rightful place as Creator and Judge, and responding with awe and worship. This is not adding another fear to our list of fears and anxieties; this is the fear that overcomes all others. Even as the following messages to the churches call for faithfulness, patience, and perseverance amid brokenness, threats, and persecution (see Revelation 14:8–12), this first call offers God-inspired courage. "If you fear him, you need fear nothing else" (Isaiah 8:13, NLT 1996).

December 26

A WORLD OF WOE

"Woe to the earth and the sea,
because the devil has gone down to you!
He is filled with fury,
because he knows that his time is short."

—Revelation 12:12

As the name suggests, a story that has been hinted at throughout the Bible is now *revealed* as the central story in the book of Revelation. A cosmic war that invaded Earth precipitated the broken relationships between human beings and their Creator and has continued to cause destruction, disaster, and fear across human history. As retold symbolically in Revelation 12, this conflict reached its height with the incarnation of Jesus, at which time the decisive battle was won. But evil and its agents were not yet destroyed, and suffering, confusion, and fear continue to be part of the reality we live within.

This revelation gives us an important insight into the often-asked questions about a good God and terrible suffering. "The blame for human suffering does not lie at the throne of God; rather it issues from the rebellion and activity of Satan and his angels and depraved humanity."* As we saw soon after Creation, there is an evil personality that works to cause and spread pain and fear in our world, that works to destroy human relationships and God's good creation.

One further insight: the intensity of Satan's attacks, the evil and fear he can promulgate in the world, seem somewhat proportionate to the approaching end of his influence. The more he seems to be winning, the closer he is to final defeat. Among the devil's favorite tools, fear can seem so powerful, but it has already been proved futile. It is always only temporary, and it is doomed to be destroyed.

---

* Frank B. Holbrook, "The Great Controversy," in *Handbook of Seventh-day Adventist Theology*, ed. Raoul Dederen (Hagerstown, MD: Review and Herald®, 2000), 996.

THE RELATIONSHIP RESTORED

I heard a loud voice from the throne saying, "Look! God's dwelling place is now among the people, and he will dwell with them. They will be his people, and God himself will be with them and be their God."
—Revelation 21:3

Ever since that fateful afternoon in the Garden of Eden, God has been looking for us, seeking to restore His relationship with humanity and with each of us individually. He developed a relationship with the family of Abraham, Isaac, and Jacob. He invited the Israelites to make a place in which He could "dwell among them" (Exodus 25:8). After centuries of prophets and expectancy, Jesus "made his dwelling among us" (John 1:14). At Pentecost, God's Spirit was sent to dwell in His people in a new and more intimate way.

The ultimate and final move in this trajectory is God establishing His "dwelling" among His people. This is not only about geography or proximity but signifies a renewal of a personal relationship. The same God who called out with longing and sorrow that afternoon in Eden is now reconnected with the human beings whose fear caused them to hide from His presence. Many times since, God's children have withdrawn in fear and chosen to trust their doubts. But that brokenness is undone. "In Genesis, human beings became hostages to distrust, alienation, fear, and the need to keep distance. In Revelation, the reversal is complete."*

The God who seeks became the "God who sees," became "God with us," and becomes the God who dwells with us forever. The God who was their God becomes the God who is our God.

With this one existential relationship restored, healing flows to all our relationships. The curses of Genesis are undone. Living with this expectation means that those curses will begin to lose their hold on us, even as we continue to live with their effects. The reversal has already begun.

---

* Sigve K. Tonstad, *Revelation* (Grand Rapids, MI: Baker Academic, 2019), 332.

December 28

NO MORE FEAR

He will wipe every tear from their eyes. There will be no more death or mourning or crying or pain, for the old order of things has passed away.
—Revelation 21:4

It can be hard to imagine—or describe—a world without fear. So, it is not surprising that, at its conclusion, the Bible describes God's re-created world mostly by what is *not* there. All the risks, threats, and experiences of death, sorrow, suffering, and separation are the primary causes of our many fears. Now, in this description, those enemies have "passed away," together with the whole order that they represented.

There is also a tender indication of the personal relationship God is renewing. Tears will not only be gone, but *He* will wipe them away. There is a tenderness and empathy in this depiction that we should not move past too quickly.

I write this reading on the day of the death of a friend after her eighteen-month ordeal with cancer. This promise shines all the brighter for the darkness of this day. It is terribly hard to imagine a world in which death is not something we must reckon with. But it is harder still to imagine that my friend might no longer matter if our present life and its end is all there is—if this is how the world ought to be.

As hard as it can be to imagine, it makes more sense that death will pass away than that my friend has passed away. Nothing good is achieved by death. At best, it is the end of one person's suffering, but even then, it seems to negate and threaten so much of what has been and could have been good in that life. And the rest of us carry on grimly, inwardly rocked to our core, missing those we have lost, carrying an ever-accumulating burden of grief, and trusting that a world without fear and death is as possible, even as inevitable as the Bible insists.

December 29

NO MORE COWARDS!

Those who are victorious will inherit all this, and I will be their God and they will be my children. But the cowardly, the unbelieving, the vile, the murderers, the sexually immoral, those who practice magic arts, the idolaters and all liars—they will be consigned to the fiery lake of burning sulfur. This is the second death.

—Revelation 21:7, 8

Amid the joy, celebration, and restoration in the final chapters of Revelation, this is a somber, even grim reminder that the story does not end well for those who stubbornly choose a different way. Anything that involves a fiery lake of burning sulfur and "the second death" should jolt us to attention, even if we prefer to focus on the world made new with all its goodness and move on to the descriptions of the beautiful city.

But the other second look that might be needed here is the inclusion of the "cowardly" among this list of otherwise serious evils. Is fear that bad?

First, we should note that this is not a judgment on simply being afraid. As we have seen, fear is part of the human experience and often has a legitimate place in our experiences. But being cowardly is a more entrenched response to fear. If someone persistently focuses on fear, it will become an orientation of their lives and a functional mechanism in their most important decision-making. What we focus on is what we become.

It might be that being cowardly is first on this list because, often, it is the first step toward many of those other sins. When we respond with fear, we respond poorly; when that becomes a pattern of our thinking, our lives, and even our faith can be distorted in unfaithful and inhuman ways. This is why "Do not be afraid" is one of the most repeated and important commands throughout the Bible. We can't live or love well from a place of fear—and God calls us to choose differently, offering us reassurance and promises that can transform our fearful thinking.

December 30

GOD IS LOVE

On each side of the river stood the tree of life, bearing twelve crops of fruit, yielding its fruit every month. And the leaves of the tree are for the healing of the nations. No longer will there be any curse. The throne of God and of the Lamb will be in the city, and his servants will serve him. They will see his face, and his name will be on their foreheads. There will be no more night. They will not need the light of a lamp or the light of the sun, for the Lord God will give them light. And they will reign for ever and ever.

—Revelation 22:2–5

Fear is defeated and banished. Night and the dangers and threats it represents are no more. Perhaps we will come to understand some of our fears in new ways as our stories are retold and re-explained. But everything that we have feared is either removed, redeemed, or remade.

The presence and light of God is all-pervasive. The plan, character, and love of God have been vindicated. God is no longer a cause for fear. Relationships are restored. Wrongs have been made right. The work of healing—for people and nations—is underway, and the world is re-created.

A much-loved description of the scene goes like this: "One pulse of harmony and gladness beats through the vast creation. From Him who created all, flow life and light and gladness, throughout the realms of illimitable space. From the minutest atom to the greatest world, all things, animate and inanimate, in their unshadowed beauty and perfect joy, declare that God is love."*

And—somehow, as difficult as it can be to imagine today—living in the light of His love, we will never be afraid again.

---

* Ellen G. White, *The Great Controversy* (Mountain View, CA: Pacific Press®, 1911), 678.

December 31

FOR GOD'S JOY

"So don't be afraid, little flock. For it gives your Father great happiness to give you the Kingdom."
—Luke 12:32, NLT

It begins and ends with Jesus. Choosing to "not be afraid" is living in accord with His teaching, in tune with His life, and in the light of His resurrection. It does not mean that we will not experience fear from time to time but that we will not be overcome, driven, or ruled by fear. Our faith and faithfulness are not determined by our circumstances but are found in the larger reality and hope of the kingdom of God.

In parables such as the rich fool (Luke 12:13–21) and the rich man and Lazarus (Luke 16:19–31), Jesus warned that wealth and material accumulation were, at best, only a temporary buffer against the inevitable troubles of life and death. He urged that His followers should instead invest their time, attention, and resources in the kingdom of God: "The highest good is God's kingdom, not our security, but if we seek God's kingdom, then God will provide for our security."* If "it gives your Father great happiness to give you the Kingdom," as Jesus asserted, how much more will He provide for the mundane necessities of life, just as He does for the birds and the flowers of His creation? Teachings such as this highlight how Jesus' focus on the kingdom has undeniably practical implications. A disciple of Jesus will live differently, will see with different eyes, and will respond out of faith rather than fear, whatever the circumstances of our lives.

So, what is the ultimate antidote to our inevitable fears? In the teaching of Jesus, it is the joy that God finds in us—in caring for our lives and in inviting and welcoming us into the present reality and future hope of His kingdom. And it all begins and ends with Jesus.

---

* Scott Bader-Saye, *Following Jesus in a Culture of Fear* (Grand Rapids, MI: Brazos Press, 2007), 134.

MY PRAYER LIST

MY PRAYER LIST

MY PRAYER LIST

MY PRAYER LIST

MY PRAYER LIST

MY PRAYER LIST

MY PRAYER LIST

MY PRAYER LIST

MY PRAYER LIST